Origins of Modern Witchcraft

Walking the Ancient Path

Witchcraft has evolved over time, adapting to the changes of societies and cultures, finding resistance and persecution with the formation of unfriendly and unsympathetic political bodies, yet perservering nevertheless because the truths of the ancient forces are everlasting and immanent. Today, the ogham symbol "straif," *the blackthorn: strife*, that has so long been representative of the situation of the Craft and the practitioners of the Craft, is evolving to become *the whitethorn: overcoming coercion*. Political forces are now being turned around to grant legal and judicial support to the followers of this most ancient of spiritual paths.

To find our Pagan roots, we need to walk backward through time, sorting through the cultural and social changes, the political statements, the actions of protest and desperation, to find the distilled central core of the Old Religion. This is the trek of the Seeker, a lifelong path, first walked backward, in order to turn around and move forward with renewed vigor.

To find the lost heritage, identify its threads, and trace those threads back to the present, we need to go as far back in our history as we can—to our very beginnings.

—Ann Moura

About the Author

Ann Moura (Aoumiel) has been a solitary practitioner of Green Witchcraft for over thirty-five years. She derived her Craft name, Aoumiel, to reflect her personal view of the balance of the male and female aspects of the Divine. Her mother and grandmother were Craftwise Brazilians of Celtic-Iberian descent who, while operating within a general framework of Catholicism, passed along a heritage of folk magic and Craft concepts that involved spiritism, ancient Celtic deities, herbal spells, Green magic, reincarnation belief, and rules for using "The Power."

The Craft was approached casually in her childhood, being experienced or used as situations arose. With the concepts of candle spells, herbal relationships to magic, spiritism, reincarnation, Rules of Conduct, and calling upon the Elementals and the Divine already established through her mother's teachings in particular, she was ready to proceed in her own direction with the Craft by the time she was fifteen. In her practice of the Craft today, the author has moved away from the Christianized associations used by her mother and grandmother. She is focused on the basic Green level of Witchcraft and is teaching the next generation in her family. She holds both a BA and an MA degree in history. She is married, has a daughter and a son, and is a certified history teacher at the high school level.

To Write to the Author

If you wish to contact the author or would like more information about this book, please write to the author in care of Llewellyn Worldwide and we will forward your request. Both the author and publisher appreciate hearing from you and learning of your enjoyment of this book and how it has helped you. Llewellyn Worldwide cannot guarantee that every letter written to the author can be answered, but all will be forwarded. Please write to:

Ann Moura
℅ Llewellyn Worldwide
P.O. Box 64383, Dept. K648-3
St. Paul, MN 55164-0383, U.S.A.

Please enclose a self-addressed stamped envelope for reply, or $1.00 to cover costs.
If outside U.S.A., enclose international postal reply coupon.

Many of Llewellyn's authors have websites with additional information and resources. For more information, please visit our website at www.llewellyn.com.

Origins of Modern Witchcraft

The Evolution of a World Religion

ANN MOURA

2000
Llewellyn Publications
St. Paul, Minnesota 55164-0383, U.S.A.

First Edition
First Printing, 2000

Book design and editing by Connie Hill
Cover design by Lisa Novak
Cover photo © www.dinodia.com
Interior illustrations by Carrie Westfall (pp. 9, 20, 36, 37); Ernst Lehner, *Symbols, Signs & Signets,* Dover, 1950 (pp. 49, 101); *Heck's Pictorial Archive of Art and Architecture*, Dover, 1994 (pp. 29, 33, 70, 75, 79, 87, 99, 104, 116, 119, 121, 122, 137, 151, 157, 163, 179, 217, 239); tarot cards from Ellen Cannon Reed, *The Witches Tarot*, Llewellyn Publications, 1989 (pp. 54, 58, 128, 182, 220, 228, 255); Charles Leland, *Estruscan Magic & Occult Remedies*, University Books, 1963 (p. 115)
Interior photos by Ann Moura (pp. 43, 46, 51, 161, 191, 203, 217)

Library of Congress Cataloging-in-Publication Data
Moura, Ann (Aoumiel)
    Origin of modern witchcraft : the evolution of a world religion / Ann Moura
        p.   cm. —
    Includes bibliographical references (p.   ) and index.
    ISBN 1–56718–648-3 (pbk)
        1. Witchcraft—History. 2.Paganism—History I. Title.
BF1566.A56   2000
133.4'3—dc21   00-057483

Llewellyn Worldwide does not participate in, endorse, or have any authority or responsibility concerning private business transactions between our authors and the public.
    All mail addressed to the author is forwarded but the publisher cannot, unless specifically instructed by the author, give out an address or phone number.

Llewellyn Publications
A Division of Llewellyn Worldwide, Ltd.
P.O. Box 64383, Dept. K648-3
St. Paul, MN 55164-0383, U.S.A.
www.llewellyn.com

 Printed in the United States of America on recycled paper

Dedication

This book is dedicated to the Goddess and the God, and to the Elementals for their love and assistance in keeping me on track.

Other Books by Ann Moura

Dancing Shadows: The Roots of Western Religious Beliefs (1994)

Green Witchcraft: Folk Magic, Fairy Lore, and Herb Craft (1996)

Green Witchcraft II: Balancing Light and Shadow (1999)

Green Witchcraft III: The Manual (2000)

Contents

Illustrations

Acknowledgments

I offer my deepest regards and respect to those people who have had the courage to write openly about Witchcraft and Neo-Paganism, and to the historians and archaeologists who have dared to face the criticisms of vocal members of mainstream religions in the publishing of their findings which contradict orthodox beliefs. The efforts of their work will not be in vain, for over the years I have seen their information slowly permeate the consciousness of our society.

I am extremely grateful to my family for their unconditional support and to my husband in particular for his contributions in discussions and research (and for the new computer!).

My appreciation also is wholeheartedly extended to Nancy Mostad for her continuing encouragement, and to Llewellyn Publications for being there for the Pagan community. Additionally, I extend my special thanks to Connie Hill for her editing expertise, patience, and creative assistance. Thank you also to the Llewellyn Art Department for their help in bringing this work to completion with maps and illustrations.

Where Do Pagans Fit In?

Just about every ethnic and cultural group today has some form of personalized, valid history that attests to the achievements and glory of that people, to promote a special sense of ethnic, national, racial, or religious identity.

The historical origins of Paganism have long been ignored or misrepresented by western religion historians. The time is ripe for a new perspective, for an uncensored history of Paganism, an older concept of religious belief which, unlike mainstream western religions, is not dominated by an orthodoxy held in power through threat of spiritual torment or by civil law.

Origins of Modern Witchcraft sheds new light on the ancient origins of religion to give Wiccans, Witches, and Neo-Pagans a sense of where they belong in history.

Here is an evocative, readable account of how Pagan and mainstream beliefs have evolved and interacted with each other over the centuries, written by a degreed historian who has studied and researched religious history independently over the years. Included in this volume are meditations and spells, based mainly on the major arcana of the tarot, to assist the reader in searching out the historical roots of Neo-Pagan spirituality. The Christian and Judaic faiths that now dominate Western society and our perspectives on the nature of religion, social development, and cultural values are newcomers compared to the ancient spiritual heritage they banished through civil laws. But the old spirituality refuses to evaporate, and it is in the connections between the old and the new that we may find remedies to modern religious conflicts. By understanding from whence we have come, we can determine where we will go, and the path to true religious freedom is through knowledge of the past and hope for the future.

Author's Note

When I was a child, my parents gave me a party favor from a New Year's celebration. It was a pretty thing—a ball of colorful paper ribbon with gold tinfoil edgings. But it rattled. There was a secret locked away in the core of the ball which could only be revealed by unwrapping the ribbon. I could keep it as it was, a thing of beauty to my childish eyes, or open it and discover the secrets within.

I knew that once undone, it could never return to what it once was, and in many ways, religion is like that. Many famous authors, from Arnold Toynbee to Joseph Campbell, began their explorations into their faith with the best of intentions, only to discover that what they uncovered forever changed their outlook.

That is what has happened in this book. I started with a very attractive bedecked object called religion, and yet, it had a faint rattle. Many people are content to hold on to the object, ignore the rattle, and simply admire what is visible. I am not like that, however, and just as I unwrapped that party favor to triumphantly extract little tin toys and finally a tin whistle I could blow with delight, so have I chosen to peel back the layers of religious history to acquire knowledge of our spiritual beginnings. Here I have found the rootstock of human spirituality, and the core of Pagan beliefs and practices. Others have made this trek, drawing the same or similar conclusions as I, and it is always gratifying to not be the only one.

But so much of what is written is intended for the generally secluded realm of academia, whereas I wanted to share my findings with anyone who would be interested. Here, then, is the treasure from the core of my research, which I now lay before you, the reader.

Introduction

Perhaps one of the ideas that first led me to wonder about religion was the philosophical story *Allegory of the Cave*, attributed to Socrates. Essentially, the tale describes a scene with a group of people living at the bottom of a huge cavern. They see shadows dancing on the cave wall and believe these images are deities. One of their members breaks the local taboo against cave exploration and climbs to the top, only to discover there is a shelf there that leads to the outside, and on that shelf is a bonfire around which people have been parading deity animal silhouettes. It is the images of these silhouettes that the people below have been worshipping. The people on the ledge have a taboo against leaving the cave, yet the hero of the tale breaks that one too and ventures outside where he discovers more people and the living animals represented on the silhouettes. When he returns to tell the others, the folks on the ledge jeer and toss him over. When he lands and tells his own people what he has learned, they throw stones at him.

The allegory is seen here in the sense that people would rather worship the reflected images of religions than know the reality from which these images are derived. Thus education becomes taboo when it uncovers truths that undermine orthodoxy. On each level, the hero encountered people who were secure in what they perceived to be truth, but who had created taboos to ensure their truths were never shaken. In the modern context, contrary opinions are labeled as *heresy* and legislation is created in support, but the real fear is knowledge and the loss of control over who possesses it. It is past time to put away these fears.

There are various concepts that may be unfamiliar to the reader; Green Witchcraft is one. This term is used to refer to my family tradition, passed along maternal lines from the Iberian Celtic heritage of my mother's family. This is not intended as a new Tradition, but as a description of the kind of Craft I learned. *Green* is the core element of Witchcraft, and is a word drawn from various sources. It is the color used to describe the Nature worship, the four Sabbats of the Equinoxes and Solstices (the other four being called White), and herbal usage that have been practices of humanity from the earliest times. Green relates to the Lady and Lord of the Greenwood, the Primal Father and Primal Mother, the Earth Mother, and the Lord of the Wildwood. It is a color customarily related to magic and Fairies, with rules in various societies regulating the dye-making process and taboos against the wearing of it because only those attuned to Nature could dare to wear the colors of the Other People. In Scotland it is still considered an unlucky color.

The Green Craft is the foundation upon which other traditions have been built. It is the solid base of what is called the Old Religion, and it is generally used in accordance with need, one-on-one with the Divine. The Green Craft is a natural practice, in which the Witch is not a steward of the Earth, the Witch *is* the Earth. Ritual, creed, litany, tools, and dogma are not mandatory, but can be adopted and adjusted as it feels comfortable for the practitioner. Green materials used in the practice of the Craft are generally procured from Nature as needed: rocks, nuts, sticks, flowers, herbs, feathers, shells; and also from manufacturing: candles, oils, fiber cords, string, and cloths of natural fibers such as cotton, muslin, and wool.

The main theme is that the Witch and the Divine are one; the Witch and the Earth are One; the Witch and the Elementals are One. What the Earth is, the Witch is, be it part of the solar system, the galaxy, the universe, or more—the Witch is an integrated part of the All. The color for the religion of Nature is also seen in Norse/Teutonic Paganism, and represents the realm of the Lady (Freya) and The Lord (Frey), the deities of fertility, animals, crops, and life. The people who practiced this Craft were not the warriors and priesthood of a later-developing religion, but people who lived in harmony with the cycles and seasons of Nature. The names of the deities are those of the Ancient Ones, with popular names derived from various heritages and translatable into Lady and Lord, or descriptives of Divine aspects.

While the in-text references are kept to a minimum to allow for ease in reading, the bibliography offers the serious student sources for further in-depth study. A number of texts address the migration of the Celts into the northwest sector of the Iberian Peninsula (before it became Spain), and books on Spain also discuss the peculiarities of the Galician heritage with its bagpipes and characteristic Celtic dances. Scholars know that the Celts settled in Galicia, and later many migrated on to Ireland, so there is a traditional connection between the people of Galicia and the Irish.

Studies of language and word derivations in European language branches frequently wind their way back to India, and the Indo-European language families are well accepted today. There are still historians who reject the Celtic connection with India, but they must necessarily confine the scope of their studies to continue to do so. For the most part, India is regaining the interest of the western world and, in time, the obvious connections between languages and peoples must be extended to those of religion. In this book, you will be acquainted with some of these ideas and, as in the days of the labyrinth of Knossos on the Island of Crete, you will traverse the twisting trails, letting out string from a ball of yarn in your own hand to find your way to the core of religion and back again.

Note on Dating

Years ago historians began using a new dating system, one that reflected their realization that the Bible did not deal with historical events, and thus could not serve as the marker by which all history should be written. To persist in the use of B.C. (Before Christ) and A.D. (Anno Domino—"Year of Our Lord") only served to both support a particular religious group while ignoring others, and to blur the line between history and mythology. As a result, the initials B.C.E. and C.E. began to be seen in history writings in the late 1960s. The meaning varies according to the source, and may be read as Before Common Era, and Common Era, or Before Current Era, and Current Era (which I prefer). There are some who use the initials to mean Before Christian Era, and Christian Era, but this is rare and mostly discarded as unacceptable. The reader is free to choose whichever interpretation is desired as I have used B.C.E. and C.E. throughout this book.

Chapter One

The Cradle of Civilization Rocked First in India

*Great Lady, Great Lord, united in the Dance of Life, Death,
and New Life, stretch out your hands to the people of your
creation that we may put our hands into yours to be pulled up
from the depths of ignorance into the Light of Wisdom.
Look gently upon us, for we are one with you, in form and
energy, and you are found within us all, So Mote It Be.*
—Ann Moura, *Book of Shadows*

Witchcraft, the Craft, the Old Religion, Wicca, and Neo-Paganism are all familiar names for the modern revival of an ancient world-view. Its roots are sunk deep in the shamanistic and naturalistic expressions of universal interconnection found in the earliest known spiritual traditions of humankind. Over time, the Craft evolved to reflect, and deflect, changes in society, economy, politics, and the new religions that supported these innovations. Through all these alterations, the Old Religion never lost its deeper awareness of the interrelationship of all life on Earth and our place among the stars.

Awareness of the motion of universal bodies such as meteors and comets; conscious of nebulas, galaxies, black holes, and the possibility of life on other planets we look at exploring all force us to realize that we can no longer consider ourselves isolated from the rest of the universe. Our need to recognize that we are part of the greater patterns of universal life is what turns us back to the natural spirituality and practical wisdom of our ancestors, intellectually updated, and grounded in the scientific realities of our world. The Old Religion was never intended to be *irrational*, but is a *rational* expression of the universe as it was rationally and spiritually known at the time. Witchcraft and Wicca are, after all, the root words for science (German) and wisdom (Anglo-Saxon). The unification of the mind and the spirit with the body is what makes the practitioner of the Craft a *whole* being.

Witchcraft has evolved over time, adapting to the changes of societies and cultures, finding resistance and persecution with the formation of unfriendly and unsympathetic political bodies, yet persevering nevertheless because the truths of the ancient forces are everlasting and immanent. Today, the ogham symbol "straif," *the blackthorn: strife*, that has for so long been representative of the situation of the Craft and the practitioners of the Craft, is being turned around to become *the whitethorn: overcoming coercion*. Political forces are now being turned around to grant legal and judicial support to the followers of this most ancient of spiritual paths.

To find our Pagan roots, we need to walk backward through time, sorting through the cultural and social changes, the political statements, the actions of protest and desperation, to find the distilled central core of the Old Religion. This is the trek of the Seeker—a life-long path, first walked backward, in order to turn around and move forward with renewed vigor. To find the lost heritage, identify its threads, and trace those threads back to the present, we need to go as far back in our history as we currently can— to our very beginnings.

Human history is reevaluated with each generation, and often the result is colored by the political, cultural, social, and religious demands of the time period. The study of deciphering what is real and what is format is addressed in the field of historiography, and it is through this means that the threads of history might be unraveled for the Seeker. When politics and religion combine, as has been the case in western history for over a thousand years, education and knowledge suffer. The Seeker must be especially diligent in pursuit of wisdom, and look beyond the ordinary texts found in schools for mass consumption. Instead, research is the means for striking out on a new path. The recent discoveries of various archeologists and historians must be hunted down if we want to find the true origins of civilization. We are left to take up our lantern like the Hermit of the tarot cards, to seek out the path, and perhaps light the way for those who follow. This ninth card of the Major Arcana of the tarot is often portrayed with a robed aesthetic, a staff in one hand and a lantern in the other held up to light the way to a new path he creates, diverging from a more traveled one.

Hermit Card Spell

This is a spell to use as you begin your search for knowledge. You can use a table or your altar for it. Have the usual altar items handy: anointing oil, salt, incense, water, ritual knife (athame) and/or wand. Prop up a black mirror (see p. 39 for how to make one if you do not already have one, but these are easy to find in New Age/occult shops and catalogs), and place in holders on the right side a white taper candle and on the left, a black taper candle. In front of the mirror place the Hermit card from your favorite tarot deck. Behind the mirror place the High Priestess card and a purple taper. Place a card to designate yourself closer to you. This card is normally selected to match the elemental of your zodiac sign (Earth: pentacles or coins; Air: swords; Water: cups; and Fire: wands) and your age (page for younger people; knight or princess for late teens through mid-twenties; queen or king for older people). Have a small bell to one side, or you can use hand claps instead where indicated.

Cast your Circle and call the Quarters in the manner to which you are accustomed, or use the following example, which uses candles set at the Quarters (compass points) around the circle area. Then you are ready for the spell.

Lay out the Circle and altar items. A warm bath, scented perhaps with fragrant bath salts or an herbal bouquet, will help set the mood, soothing away the cares of the day and allowing the intuitional senses to come forward. Robe in something comfortable and loose, perhaps a garment you set aside only for use in ritual, so that your mind instinctively recognizes this change in the daily routine and relaxes. Sweep the Circle area with a besom (Witch's broom), herbal sprig, or leafy twig, saying:

> *I sweep away from this space all negative and discordant energies, that I may focus and raise the energy I need for my work. Let this space be made clear for my Circle.*

Light the incense and the three tapers.
Ring the bell or clap hands three times.

> *The Circle is about to be cast and I freely stand within to greet my Lady and my Lord.*

Light the purple candle and with it light each candle of the circle, moving North (green), then East (yellow), South (red), and West (blue), saying:

> (N) *I call upon Light and Earth at the North to illuminate and strengthen the Circle.*

> (E) *I call upon Light and Air at the East to illuminate and enliven the Circle.*

> (S) *I call upon Light and Fire at the South to illuminate and warm the Circle.*

> (W) *I call upon Light and Water at the West to illuminate and cleanse the Circle.*

With your ritual knife held up, pace the Circle, moving around from the North to the East to the South to the West, and to the North, saying:

> *I draw this Circle in the presence of the Goddess and the God where they may come and bless their child, (and state your given name or, if you have one, a Craft or Working Name).*

Now lower the athame at the North, and as you walk around the Circle, envision a blue light shooting out from the point and forming the Circle boundary, saying:

> *This is the boundary of the Circle. Only love shall enter and leave.*

Return to the altar and ring the bell or clap three times. Place the point of your athame in the salt:

> *Salt is life and purifying. I bless this salt to be used in this sacred Circle in the names of the Goddess and the God,* (you can add here the names you use: Shakti and Shiva, Hecate and Herne, Bendidia and Pan, Freya and Frey, Isis and Osiris are examples).

Pick up the salt bowl and use the tip of the athame to drop three portions of salt into the water bowl; set the salt bowl back in its place.

Stir three times with the athame:

> *Let the blessed salt purify this water that it may be sanctified for use in this sacred Circle. In the names of the Goddess and the God, (N and N), I consecrate and cleanse this water.*

Take the salted water bowl in hand and sprinkle water from it as you move deosil (clockwise) around the Circle (starting at N-E-S-W-N):

> *I consecrate this Circle in the names of the Goddess and the God, (N and N). The Circle is conjured a Circle of Power that is purified and sealed. So Mote It Be!*

Return the water bowl to the altar and take the incense around the Circle, then return it to the altar.

With a dab of anointing oil on your finger, make a Solar Cross (equal-armed) ringed by a circle on your forehead:

> *I, (N) am consecrated in the names of the Goddess and the God, (N and N), in this, their Circle.*

Hold up the wand with both arms upraised, at the North of the Circle (envision a powerful bull arriving):

I call upon you, Elemental Earth, to attend this rite and guard this Circle, for as I have body and strength, we are kith and kin!

Lower the wand and move to the East; raise the wand (see an owl, Fairies, or an eagle in flight):

I call upon you, Elemental Air, to attend this rite and guard this Circle, for as I breathe and think, we are kith and kin!

Lower the wand and move to the South, raise the wand (see a lion, salamander, or dragon):

I call upon you, Elemental Fire, to attend this rite and guard this Circle, for as I consume life to live, we are kith and kin!

Lower the wand and move to the West, hold the wand aloft (see an undine, a sea serpent, or a dolphin):

I call upon you, Elemental Water, to attend this rite and guard this Circle, for as I feel and my heart beats, we are kith and kin!

Return to the altar and use your wand to draw in the air above the altar, the symbol of Infinity (an 8 laying on its side), the sign of working between the worlds.

Set your wand on the altar and raise up the athame in both hands:

Hail to the Elementals at the Four Quarters! Welcome Lady and Lord to this rite! I stand between the worlds with Love and Power all around!

Ring the bell or clap three times.

Now you are ready to begin the Hermit Spell. You may want to sit for this, which is fine. Focus your attention on the black mirror, with the card of the High Priestess symbolically beyond your reach.

Envision a dark and distant past that lies beyond your reach, holding secrets to your future. Behind the mirror is the High Priestess, the Veiled Goddess of the Horned Moon. You are calling as a supplicant upon the Goddess as Lady of Occult (Hidden) Wisdom.

> *I am the Seeker, the one who lifts the light, finding my path*
> *through my inner sight. The Lady of Wisdom, hidden behind*
> *the veil, sees my struggles and knows my travail. I call upon*
> *thee Great Lady, known as Sophia, Minerva, Artemis, Isis,*
> *Hecate, Bendidia, and many other names. Guide me now as*
> *I search out the roots of my beginnings through history's*
> *remains.*

Move the card of the High Priestess to the front of the mirror to rest beside that of the Hermit.

> *Lower thy veil to this Seeker that thy wisdom be revealed. Let*
> *me now gather thy knowledge unto me as I walk this path.*
> *Show me my future through the vision of my past.*

Slide your designator card under the two cards (Step 1). Use the purple candle to light the black and white tapers at either side of the mirror, then set it back behind the mirror. Look into the mirror and see it as a dark doorway to the past, illuminated on either side by the polarity of the Divine—darkness and light—and know that these are both part of the wholeness that is the cycle of life. Move the purple candle, symbol of spiritual/psychic power and learning. Set it in front of the mirror and look through the candlelight into the mirror to see it cast a thin light into the darkness:

> *Here is the path lit through the night, here is the way I shall*
> *wander seeking the light. The source of all wisdom is in thee,*
> *Great Lady, and I seek to learn. While other paths may cross*
> *my own, may join for a time with mine, I walk in freedom*
> *with bold determination to find the roots of my heritage*
> *without encumbrance.*

Slide your designator card out from under the Hermit and High Priestess cards, and place it on top of them. With the purple candle in one hand and the cards in the other, move the candlestick and cards to behind the black mirror and prop up the cards if possible; otherwise simply lay them down again (Step 2).

> *With my Lady as my lantern, I am the Hermit Seeker,*
> *moving through the darkness in solitary study into the light*
> *of knowledge. Blessed Be the Lady who guides me, and Her*
> *blessings upon me!*

Snuff out the white and black candles, then gaze into the mirror and see what images come to you. Consider the great adventure that lies before you, the quest for your heritage. When you feel ready, snuff the purple candle. You now embark upon your journey. You can relight the purple candle as you progress in your reading, or whenever you need guidance. You may now open the Circle.

Ring the bell or clap three times.

Hold your athame level over the altar:

> *Lord and Lady, I am blessed by your sharing this time with*
> *me; watching and guarding me, and guiding me here and in*
> *all things. I came in love and I depart in love.*

Raise the athame in a salute:

> *Love is the Law and Love is the Bond. Merry did I meet,*
> *merry do I part, and merry will I meet again. Merry meet,*
> *merry part, and merry meet again! The Circle is now*
> *cleared. So Mote It Be!*

Kiss the flat of the blade and set the athame on the altar.

Take the snuffer and go to the North Quarter, and with raised arms, say:

> *Depart in peace, Elemental Earth. My blessings take*
> *with you!*

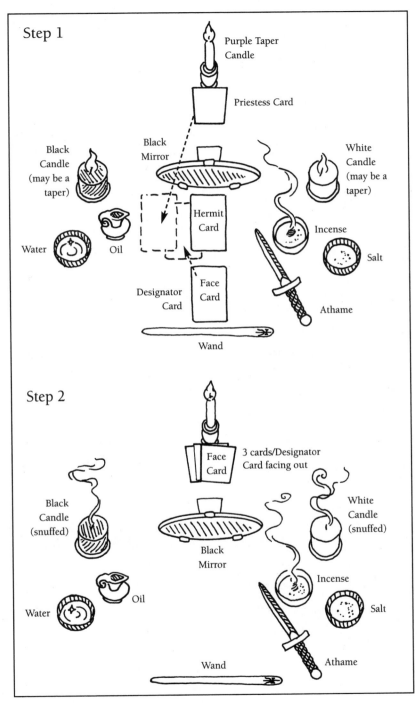

Step 1

Purple Taper Candle

Priestess Card

Black Mirror

Black Candle (may be a taper)

White Candle (may be a taper)

Hermit Card

Water

Oil

Incense

Salt

Designator Card

Face Card

Athame

Wand

Step 2

Face Card

3 cards/Designator Card facing out

Black Candle (snuffed)

White Candle (snuffed)

Black Mirror

Water

Oil

Incense

Salt

Athame

Wand

Altar arrangment for performing the Hermit Card Spell (see text, pp. 7–11).

Lower your arms and snuff out the candle; envision the Elemental Power departing.

Go to the East, raise your arms:

Depart in peace, Elemental Air. My blessings take with you!

Lower your arms and snuff the candle; envision the Elemental Power departing.

Go to the South, raise your arms:

Depart in peace, Elemental Fire. My blessings take with you!

Lower your arms and snuff the candle; envision the Elemental Power departing.

Go to the West, raise your arms:

*Depart in peace, Elemental Water. My blessings take
with you!*

Lower arms and snuff the candle; envision the Elemental Power departing.

Return to the altar; set down the snuffer, and raise your arms in benediction:

*Beings and powers of the visible and invisible, depart in
peace! You aid in my work, whisper in my mind, and bless
me from Otherworld. There will always be harmony between
us. My blessings take with you. The Circle is cleared.*

Take the athame and go to the North Quarter. Point the athame down and move widdershins (counterclockwise) around the Circle, starting at the North and ending at the North, envisioning the blue light being drawn back into the athame:

*The Circle is open, yet the Circle remains as its magical
power is drawn back into me.*

When you return to the North, having walked the Circle, touch the athame lightly to your forehead, and envision the blue light swirling around back into you.

You should now be at the altar:

> *The ritual is ended. Blessings have been given and blessings*
> *have been received. May the peace of the Goddess and the*
> *God remain in my heart. So Mote It Be!*

Set down the athame. Put away all magical tools and clear the altar. Touch the palms of your hands to the ground (floor) to drain off the excess energy, then resume a normal routine. Have a snack and beverage if it helps you to return to normal consciousness.

Searching Through History

What path takes us back to the origins of witchcraft? What are the roots of the Old Religion? And why are there so many who fear a religion based on the oneness of all beings in Nature? To understand the evolution of this spiritual path, a new perspective on history is needed. A thorough search can be initiated by reviewing the books in the bibliography and in the bibliographies of those books, but here I will present a condensed overview of these studies.

Many historians and scholars, among them John Marshall, Josef W. Hall, Jacquetta Hawkes, Will Durant (who is often disliked by educational elitists for presenting archived research sources for mass consumption), Cottie Burland, Alain Danielou, Charles Picard, and Anne Ross, discovered that the earliest-known human civilization came not from the traditionally accepted areas of Mesopotamia or Egypt, but from a place larger than either—the Indus Valley in what is called the Sind. Here is the place to look for the roots of European Paganism, witchcraft, and even modern western religions. We must turn our gaze to the wondrous and exotic land of India—an undivided subcontinent as it was before the British government forcibly divided it into warring religious factions—a land that was fabled before the development of ancient Egypt and ancient Greece.

Situated across from modern Oman at the north end of the Arabian Sea, the cities of the Indus remained forgotten by Westerners until 1925. The local inhabitants knew of these cities, removing building materials from the site throughout the centuries. Yet when archaeological digs began in earnest in the twentieth century C.E., the artifacts found clearly link the Indus as a major influence on the development of the Near East. The growth of the Indus cities and monuments were the source of inspiration for those cities developing in the Near East, and trade between these regions included not only goods, but gods. It is in the Indus Valley that we must begin our journey of discovery.

The Indus culture *predates* the Sumerian, Egyptian, and Babylonian cultures. It is known by two different names: Harappan, after the northernmost city in the valley of Punjab, built after southern Mohenjo-daro in the Sind, and Dravidic, a name so ancient no one knows where it came from. The Dravidic name is found in a present-day Indian ethnic group who are believed to date back to the original inhabitants of the Indus. It is this latter name that I prefer to use, for it provides the continuity we seek. The Dravidians become the Hermit card of our spell, holding aloft the lantern for us to follow the light into the dusty past.

The Indus civilization stretched from the Himalaya Mountains to the Arabian Sea, and historians first theorized that the vast expanse was actually two regions united by the twin capital cities of Harappa in the north and the older Mohenjo-daro in the south. But then another large city was discovered, and this, along with some seventy other settlements in the area of Sind, has led archaeologists to believe that the Indus consisted of a network of cooperative cities and towns, or city-states. To me, this is reminiscent of the city-states of Greece that used to be the indicator of the advancement of western civilization. In reality, the Greeks were simply copying an earlier pattern.

Impression seals (rather like signet rings) typical of Mohenjo-daro have been found in Sumeria, and the early Indian cobra symbols, the *Naga*, were incorporated into the seals of early Mesopotamia. Indeed, Sumerian references to a land called Melukka are believed to refer to the Indus Valley. The evidence from these two sites shows that Sumeria imported goods from the Indus, but did not export to the Valley, which is a classic colony arrangement. The Indus has a vast history as a manufacturing center, and like England exporting goods to a colonial America, the Indus is considered now to have been the parent of a colonial Sumeria.

The Mohenjo-daro of 4000 B.C.E. was experiencing a Golden Age that would compare to that of Athens under Pericles, and certainly to any town of Medieval Europe, although the sanitation of the Indus cities makes them superior to the latter. Think about what we consider the triumphs of Medieval Europe—the art, the cathedrals, the castles, the towns spreading out from the castle in jumbled cramped streets, people tossing their chamberpot contents out of upper floor windows onto the street below—and then consider for a moment what the Indus was like with its perfectly laid-out streets, sewers, public works, and civic centers, for that was what they had.

There is sufficient evidence to indicate that the most ancient Near East civilization, that of Sumeria, came from the Indus as a colony, and this would make the Indus Valley the true "cradle of civilization." The Indus has been called the oldest civilization known. I have been pleased to find that at last the Indus has made it into the average high school textbook, although reduced to a mere paragraph that amounts to: "We don't really know much about this place, but it's real old. Now let's talk about Moses and the Ten Commandments." Unfortunately, the texts are not particularly accurate in their dating of the Indus Civilization. It is too hard to explain that the Indus predates the Sumerian and the Egyptian cultures, that it is so old no one has yet discovered how old it is. The same high school textbooks that state the Indus predates Egypt of 2700 B.C.E., use an artificial estimate of 1200 B.C.E. What are students to think when a textbook contradicts itself in the same paragraph? The Indus is described as older than the pyramids, then is dated as though coming afterward.

The western world was startled by the discoveries at Mohenjo-daro, spurring the educated elite of the early twentieth century to begin intensive studies into the history, philosophy, and theologies of India. The information never filtered down from the learned journals and treatises into the school systems, primarily because India was a British colony. In England, Indians were called colored and were racially discriminated against. Liaisons between Indians and British were considered a social outrage. Instead, the British institutions of higher education instigated and supported a counter-premise, a theory of human development which has been discredited often enough to not warrant further discussion here. Funding and attention was in this way directed away from further studies in India. When the British divided the subcontinent of India and forcibly relocated Moslem and Hindu religious groups into the separate nations of West Pakistan, East Pakistan, and India, one side effect was that the Indus discoveries proceeded at a snail's pace. The Islamic lands had no incentive to encourage digs in the Indus region under their control because the revelations there would substantiate the ancientness of the native Indian culture and their deities. Yet, some excavations do continue.

The conclusions being drawn from archaelogical evidence are that Knossos on the island of Crete, the hub of Minoan Civilization, was also a colony of the Indus, Mohenjo-daro. The Indus was a place where two races of people lived and worked together in apparent harmony without any trace of class or race distinction. The people of the Punjab intermixed with the people of Sind and together they created the later city of Harappa. They were a taller race, considered to be "proto-Australoid," with long heads, low foreheads, and pronounced brow ridges, whose descendants may still be found in the jungle tribes of Central and Southern India. These aboriginal people of India are believed to be representative of humanity's most ancient race, the Kalahari Bushmen and Pygmies, who may have migrated from the Indus. Another people, who were more common in the Dravidian culture of South India, seem to have been of a Mediterranean background and were distinguished by their slighter build and higher forehead.

The excavations at Mohenjo-daro show a highly urbanized civilization with a strong social and economic foundation. The city is so ancient that no one has dug down far enough to find the *height* of this culture, much less its beginnings, for as the excavations go deeper, the city becomes *better* than what had been previously uncovered, indicating that the actual height of this culture remains undiscovered. Unfortunately, the rest of the levels of the city lie below the current water table, so both the greatest time period of this civilization and the beginnings of the city are still unknown.

Envision a peak, like a triangle. The left side rises from the ground to the pointed tip. This is the rise of the civilization from its inception to the point of its greatest achievements and grandeur. From the tip, the right side then slopes downward to the ground.

The Celtic Cernunnos figure is strikingly similar to the Indus Shiva image found on a seal in excavations of Mohenjo-Daro.

This is the side that shows the decline of the civilization to its current place or its extinction. The ground where the archaeologist starts digging is like the base of the right side of the triangle. The deeper the dig goes, the closer it comes to the peak. The site moves from the decline of a city like Mohenjo-daro, for example, to its height. The height is only identified when the recovered artifacts and building styles of a deeper level become inferior to what was previously uncovered. In the case of the Indus civilization, digging 6,000 years into the civilization has shown only improvement. This means that not only has the height *not* been found, the civilization is likely to be *at least* twice as old as what has come thus far, just to crawl down the other side of the triangle once the peak has been found. So how old does this make the Dravidic civilizations of Sind? At least 12,000 years old—and that is a *conservative* estimate. Why? Because archaeological evidence shows that the Indus Valley has been inhabited since at least 470,000 B.C.E.

It always amuses me that when I first started pointing this out, I was criticized for inventing these numbers. I was asked how I could expect anyone to take this seriously. Five years later, the popular press was finally announcing with excitement to the public the same information I already knew just from keeping current with archaeological studies—spears from 400,000 years ago were being shown off to the news media, and people were conceding that just possibly, the people who made these weapons and put them into burial sites were not the slack-jawed, bug-eyed apemen and apewomen usually depicted as our ancestors.

I am surprised, too, that it is still not popular knowledge that our ancestors of the ice ages and further into the distant past not only were skilled with sewing, they also used decorations, they had art, and they had a sense of continuance, burying their dead with red ochre—the color of birth for the obvious symbology of rebirth. Often, these burial sites show the bodies in a fetal position. Women are found buried with weapons that are clearly their own, leading any thinking person to understand that capable women were hunters along with capable men in a survival atmosphere. Why is something this apparent ignored? Because it speaks to a truth we are conditioned by mainstream, politicized religion to not accept: men and women have worked together in partnership, not in striations of superior and subordinate.

The infusion of modern religious beliefs into the government, laws, and culture has generated an atmosphere of anticipation of violence and destruction, in order to set the stage for a deity to return so that certain "believers" can escape the devastation expected to descend upon the "non-believers." I cannot help but observe that the average person on the street would not willingly want to inflict suffering on others. Surely we must expect better of the images we have for the Divine, or the title is undeserved.

Herein lies one key reason for the revival of the Old Religion. No stage need be set for a deity that is breathlessly expected to return, simply because the Goddess and God of our ancestors have never left. They are here, all around us, and within us. We have only to recognize them and call to them, and trust me, they *will* answer, and not in metaphor. The Divine is tangible, patient, loving, and quite audible, but you must shed your fear, distrust, and inhibition to hear the voices of the Goddess and the God. This is the deeper meaning of the Wiccan words, "In perfect love and perfect trust." Once you have embraced knowledge, heard the voices of the Divine, and felt the close comfort of the Divine Presence, you will know the security of connection with the All.

Although the cities of the Indus remain undated because their foundations lie beneath the water table, we do know that the region has been continuously inhabited for hundreds of thousands of years. Cave paintings discovered in 1967 at Bhimbhetka show that by 30,000 B.C.E. people were being depicted with scimitars, swords at their waists, bows and arrows, double-headed drums, and both wild and domesticated animals, whereas European cave paintings did not come into existence for another 10,000 years (20,000 B.C.E.), and those do not show swords and daggers. Indeed, 10,000 B.C.E. is typically given as the beginnings of civilization as indicated by domestication of animals and cultivation of crops, but that was before the find at Bhimbhetka.

The Bhimbhetka discovery never made it into the popular press. *National Geographic Magazine* utilized the entire year to concentrate on Biblical themes, discussing the Holy Land of Palestine "where Jesus walked," and the supposed locales of various Old and New Testament Bible stories. I do not use the word "supposed" lightly. There are in fact at least two sites offered for any number of Biblical events, as most any visitor to Israel can affirm. But many of the sites themselves are those declared holy by Saint Helena, the Christianized mother and sometime wife of the Roman Emperor Constantine, while she was on a quick tour of Palestine. Churches were immediately built over areas she designated, and "tradition holds . . ." is the usual phrase given for these sites today. Meanwhile, religious archaeology is coming to the fore in an attempt to prove the Bible as literal, but the dates, places, and events just don't come together. The hunt for the "real" Mount Sinai is still going on, with a peak in Saudi Arabia being speculated upon as a likely candidate as late as 1999. That makes three possible sites now.

Although compared once to Medieval Europe, Mohenjo-daro in the Sind and Harappa in Punjab had sewers beneath their streets—built with earthenware pipes and public drains of brick that were accessible by inspection holes (the first manholes of history); indoor bathrooms (complete with standing baths and seated toilets, unlike those of the Orient that are today still typically floor toilets that require the user to squat); public baths; houses with central courtyards; and streets that were carefully planned to be straight in a north/south and east/west pattern with crossings at right angles. This kind of city planning and authority, complete with sanitation inspectors and workers, simply did not exist in other regions. Even at its latest, less powerful phase, the Indus civilization was ahead of anything produced by Babylon, and nothing of the sort existed in Palestine.

The people of the Indus had an agricultural society based on the first known example of large scale irrigation systems, which tribes of Vedic Aryans from the steppes of the Ukraine destroyed during their invasions and then later wrote about in the Rig Veda ("Holy Scriptures" or "Holy Hymns," circa 1000–500 B.C.E.). Popular tradition holds that "Aryans" means "Noble Ones." However, others see it as a derivation for open space, nomads, or "Peasants." While amusing, this bit of word play is rather like the word "barbarian" being applied to the Germanic people simply because they did not desire to accept the rule of civilized Romans. Various tribes of Aryan peoples from the Caucasus Mountains and Ukraine swept through the regions of the Near and Far East numerous times between 2150 B.C.E. and 1000 B.C.E., until at last their populations became part of the landscape they invaded.

The Dravidians of the Indus, however, had cotton cloth when no one else did; had abundant gold which they mined and dredged from the rivers; grew wheat, barley, peas, rice, sesame, mustard, melons, and dates; domesticated numerous animals including pigs, sheep, camels, horses, elephants, cats, and dogs; made fine porcelain pottery; were excellent wood carvers; made decorative ornaments; and had the first-known minted coinage.

Examples of metal work are very rare in the digs, prompting some historians to conclude that they were not very skilled at it and turned to wheel-thrown pottery instead. This may be simplifying the matter over much, for the riches of the Indus were legendary in Mesopotamian and Chinese writings long before the Aryan invasions began in the outlaying regions of Sind circa 2150 B.C.E., reaching the great cities circa 1500–1200 B.C.E. It may be that the Aryans, who wrote in the Rig Veda of the riches they found, simply took all they could and melted down the loot. This would be a better reason for the lack of metal artifacts in the Indus, for those few metal items of the Indus culture that have been found to possess a remarkably life-like and animated quality. We must keep in mind, too, that the sites were not unknown to the local inhabitants who took building mate-

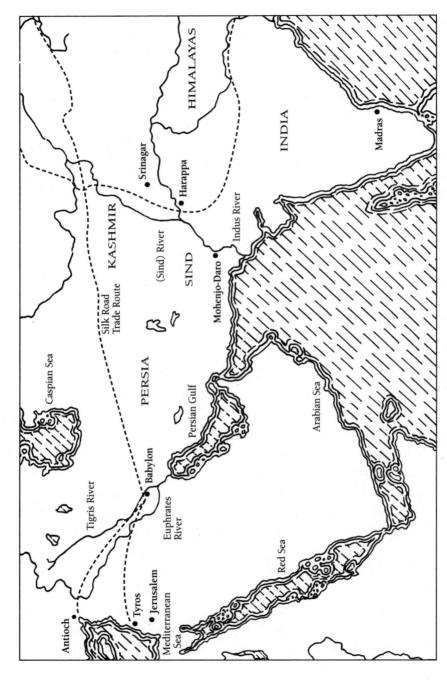

Sind and Kashmir—The Holy Lands of India—where an advanced civilization flourished as early as 30,000 B.C.E. Closely situated to the trade routes between the Orient and Europe, the culture of the Indus Valley was carried to east and west.

rials from the sites over the years. The paintings at Bhimbhetka can be seen as further evidence that metal working was not absent, and lend support to the hypothesis that the lack of metal work or weaponry at the sites of Harappa and Mohenjo-daro may have been due to the thoroughness of the Aryan conquest and subsequent picking over by the populace.

The overall picture that develops from this area prior to the invasions is one of a peaceful and cooperative community in which the rural areas and the urban centers acted in accord for mutual benefit. The grain was gathered into huge storage buildings in the cities and food was distributed from these central warehouses. Farmers used horse- or bull-drawn carts with two solid wooden wheels to take their crops to the granaries. Some crops, metal work, wood carvings, and other trade goods were shipped by boat to the Arabian Peninsula. Artifacts of the Indus have been found in Babylon as well as the more ancient Sumeria (both in modern Iraq), and the evidence shows that merchants from Sind lived in Ur and other cities of Mesopotamia.

By tracing language, it is possible to see the extent of Indus influence in western history. Alain Danielou, in *Gods of Love and Ecstacy: The Traditions of Shiva and Dionysus* (Rochester, VT: Inner Traditions, 1992), writes that the Dravidic language and culture had spread to the Mediterranean, leaving traces in the surviving cultures and languages of the Baluchistans, Transcaucasian Georgians, and Iberian Basques. The Sumerian language is seen as related to Dravidic, as are the languages of the early people of Crete, the Lydians, and the Etruscans. The Dravidic-based languages of the Pelasgians of Southern Italy were referred to by Herodotus in his *Histories* as barbarian and related to the Etruscan and Lydian languages—in other words, not like the Greek of Aryan heritage. The same appellation of barbaric is given to the language of the people of Malta in 69 C.E. by Saint Paul when he was shipwrecked there. The language of early Crete and Greece is non-Greek and was found *throughout* the southwestern part of Asia Minor before the advent of the Aryan tribes of Acheans and Dorians, but the still-spoken Dravidic language of southern India has not yet been utilized to decipher the ancient Mediterranean languages.

Objects from the Indus have been found at Troy and in Palestine, and the connection between the Indus Valley and Crete has been noted by a number of scholars. Trade goods made their way from the Indus in boats designed with high prows and a single mast, looking rather like later Viking boats. These ships are known to have been regular visitors to ancient Sumer and Akkad. By 1500 B.C.E., however, when the Vedic Aryans began their intensive assaults on the major cities of the Indus, trade slackened, then stopped altogether. Despite the waves of migrating Aryan tribes, it is clear that the cities, particularly Mohenjo-daro, continued to trade with Mesopotamia until the Vedic Aryans finally overwhelmed the Indus cities in 1200 B.C.E.

By the time the various Aryan tribes had fought their way from the outlying regions of Sind, taken the smaller towns and villages, and finally attacked the cities, citadels of fired brick on top of forty-foot high mounds of mud-brick were in existence in the center of the cities, fortified with towers and walls. The rhomboid-shaped strongholds contained massive granaries, and the indication is that the people knew that invaders were working their way across the land and they had time to prepare for a long siege.

What I find particularly revealing is that in all of the Indus cities and communities, there are no signs of any temple structure. These people were reputed to have been unusually tolerant of varying ideas, and loved to discuss conflicting concepts. They kept shrines in their homes, but apparently had no centralized clergy and no priesthood. Each person was responsible for his/her own worship, yet there is art work to suggest that the community would gather for special occasions marked by agricultural events, solstices, and moon phases. Here then are the golden threads that clearly weave through the cloth of religion, through the mists of time, and into the common characteristic of the Old Religion: witchcraft, and the modern revival of Wicca—no centralized ordained clergy; each person his/her own priest/ess; group gatherings for festivals of the Sun and Moon; agricultural celebrations; home shrines; and personalized devotion.

Sadly, the streets and houses of Mohenjo-daro also give mute testimony to the final stages of that great city. Archaeologists have unearthed the skeletal remains of those who did not flee in time from the Vedic Aryans but were cut down in that final battle for the survival of the Indus Civilization, their bodies left in the streets or huddled together in the houses where they were slain. It was for them that this amazing city was named, for Mohenjo-daro means "City of the Dead."

The Rig Veda of the Vedic Aryans recounts the tale of their hero Indra and his chariot-driving warriors conquering the contemptible but rich dark-skinned people who lived in fortified strongholds. He destroyed the forts and the irrigation canals, took the wealth of the Indus, and established the Vedic Aryan rule over what is now modern Pakistan, India, and Bangledesh. The oldest civilization of humankind fell during Egypt's Empire period and was forgotten to the western world for three thousand years, until Sir John Marshall was introduced to the remains in 1924 by his Indian aide, R. D. Banerji.

Yet this should not have come as a surprise to the western mind. Both Greek and Indian texts speak of the early westward expansion of the religion of the Indus, and Diodorus refers to the travels to India of the Egyptian Osiris. The religion of the Indus Valley covered a vast expanse, and had moved from Sind to Portugal by the sixth millennium C.E. Some historians believe the practices of the Dravidians inspired the megalithic monuments and menhirs built in Malta, Europe, and the British Isles circa 3000–2000 B.C.E. (and even these dates are being pushed further back as better dating techniques are developed). The importance, then, of the Vedic Aryan invasion of Sind cannot be stressed enough in terms of religious development in the western world, and in terms of our Pagan roots.

The Near East religious centers originally practiced the religion of Sind, and it was not until the Vedic Aryans realized that their own religion, which they had imposed on the Indus people to aid their political dominance, had become infiltrated with the religion of the Dravidians that religious orthodoxy became an issue.

The invention of *orthodoxy* has had a far-reaching effect across the past 3,000 years into the present. The immediate desire to return to a purer, non-Dravidian-influenced Aryan system resulted sequentially in the rise of Buddhism, Judaism, Christianity, and Islam, and marched directly into the horrors of the Inquisition, the World War II Holocaust, religious strife in Northern Ireland, ethnic cleansings in the Slavic lands, and battles of the Middle East and Kashmir.

The discoveries in Sind have been recounted in a number of history books, yet are barely mentioned in public school texts. This condition exists because these discoveries overturn much of what had been accepted as truth, but is now known to be mythology. Because our education system is socially directed rather than informationally directed, courses and texts that deviate from the normally accepted beliefs are regarded with suspicion. This applies to all facets of education, from the resistance to evolution—never mind the living proof of new strains of virus, visible and recorded changes in species within one or two generations, and the remains of prehistoric animals—to the denial of the cultural and religious impact of the Indus upon the western world.

The reluctance to look at the Indus Valley for the beginnings of our western civilization can be found in many writing styles. Even the popular historian Will Durant could not elude social/cultural restrictions. His statement that the earliest coins of humankind came from the Indus circa 2900 B.C.E. is only found in a footnote to a discussion on the coinage of Lydia (the area of northern Turkey today, across from Greece) between 570–546 B.C.E., a time period and location acceptable to westerners with its proximity to Greece. Then what really set the standard for coinage? Not Lydia, as stated in his main text, but the Indus, as stated in his footnote. And left unstated is that the Lydians came from the Indus Dravidians. Much of real history seems to be spoken behind the hand or under the breath lest anyone become offended, but the history remains as a silent truth, and we must let the light of our lanterns show the way to our neglected heritage.

At the time of the discovery and early excavations of Mohenjo-daro, the British archaeologists involved were stunned at what they were uncovering, but the British Empire was already in serious trouble in India. While the news of this great civilization continued to trickle into the West, it was not as important as the information of a world war and the social, political, and economic upheavals already in evidence.

A number of prominent historians, including John Romer and Neil Asher Silberman, have written about the mythic basis of the Old and New Testaments of the Bible. Many stories and anecdotes are ancient metaphors with a long history in the earlier religions and literature of other cultures (Babylonian, Assyrian, and Egyptian in particular), but even today, these myths are presented as genuine historical fact in many public school textbooks. An entire chapter in one high school world history book is devoted to the story of Moses, the Passover, and the Exodus, although modern archaeology has *proven* that these events *never took place*. Meanwhile, real history continues to languish, ignored. By bringing attention to the role of religion in society and how it affects the history writing and selection process, we can work to correct the situation and bring about needed changes to public education.

Thus far we have discovered where our journey begins. The lantern of the Hermit card has cast a glint of light into the ancient land of the Indus Valley, then swept that light across northern Turkey, northern Italy, and into the Iberian Peninsula of modern Spain and Portugal. But what about the "who" of our journey? Who are the ancestors of the Ancient Ones, the Divine as they were known in Mesopotamia, Egypt, Greece, Thrace, Lydia, Etruria, and throughout Pagan Europe?

We're all aware of the female fertility figures found throughout Paleolithic Europe and Mesopotamia. Despite the large breasts, wide hips, and often pregnant appearance of these figurines, there are still people who refuse to speculate on the reason for them, even though there are enough archaeologists and historians to state the obvious—these are the earliest images of the Divine as female—the Great Mother. The proper place to begin rediscovering the Pagan roots of religious beliefs then is by identifying the deities around whom the earliest known evidence of worship was centered. Surprisingly, the oldest recognized worshipped God and Goddess of humankind are still venerated by over 660 million people today. These two deities can be traced through the religions of Mesopotamia, Egypt, Greece, Rome, and Europe; from the ancient times of the Indus into the present, and they have made their indelible mark on religious development in one way or another.

These deities, dating back at least 30,000 years, are Shiva and Shakti, the God and the Goddess of the Dravidic Indus Valley, adopted by Vedic Hinduism. It will not be necessary to discuss the complexities of Hinduism in depth here to cover the relationship between these earliest deities and modern religions. Instead, the progression of events will be the guideposts to a nontraditional view of history and religion, one that the Seeker who embarks upon an understanding of the revival of Paganism and Wicca can turn to for glimpses of that golden thread glinting through time. Through name changes and retained mythologies, the thread links the present with the past, pointing to the singular premise of the immortality of the spirit that leads us back to the dawning of human spiritual beginnings. By any name, and they have many, the God and the Goddess are the Divine of the Old Religion. The Druidic injunction that all Gods are one God and all Goddesses are one Goddess holds the seed of truth.

By 28,000 B.C.E., the God Shiva was being depicted in cave paintings as the Lord of the Beasts, with horns on his head and animals all around him. He is seated on a low stool in what is now considered a Yoga position, with the soles of the feet touching, and he is ithyphallic (depicted with an erect penis). Here is the God familiar to the Old Religion of Europe in His earliest known portrayal; as an erotic ascetic, a god of life, fertility, wisdom, and the hunt.

But this god is not alone. His partner is literally his other half, for Shiva is also portrayed from ancient times as half male and half female. His female aspect is Shakti, the Goddess of Power compared to the God of Grace. She is Uma, by which name she was worshipped in Mesopotamia; she is the Mother Goddess, sometimes shown as pregnant or holding an infant in her arms, and she is the corn goddess. "Wheat" is the American word for the European term "corn," but historians generally use the European word, while the American word corn should more properly be called "maize." Typically, all references in history texts, and in this book, to corn mothers, corn maidens, corn dolls, and so forth, unless addressing American heritage, are speaking of wheat. Throughout ancient history, bread baking was usually part of a sacred ceremony dedicated to the corn goddess. Sometimes the Goddess is shown with sheaves of corn in her hands, and her worship spread throughout the western world in both this and the Great Mother aspect, but she is also a Goddess of Power, and this aspect also spread.

Although the Dravidians had two deities who were so close they were seen as two sides of the same being, they were not "polytheistic" in the modern misinterpretation. The multiple aspects of the Divine were (and are) understood to be only different representations of the All. The religion of the Indus is more accurately monotheistic, because even Shiva and Shakti are recognized as One Being, called Ardhanari (*Androgyne*, from the Greek andro—"man," and gyne—"woman"). Shiva Ardhanari is depicted in sculpture as divided down the center, from head to toe, exactly half male (right side) and half female (left side). The Dravidic structure can be seen in Neo-Paganism today with the usual divisions of the modern Wiccan altar setting (as the practitioner faces it) placing the Goddess on the left, the God on the right, and both at the center.

This classic androgyne, or hermaphrodite (named for two Greek deities, Hermes and Aphrodite) was evident in living human form in anyone who possessed both sexual organs or was homosexual in lifestyle. The gay male and gay female, so often condemned as immoral by modern mainstream religions, were once accepted and honored as living representations of the God of Grace and the Goddess of Power. Traditionally, shamanic power has been associated with bisexuality, and the people performing divination in ancient times were often garbed as hermaphrodites, with men dressed as women (as became traditional with Catholic priests), and women attired with a phallus attached to their girdle or otherwise strapped on.

Both dual sexuality and nonsexuality were seen as avenues to spirituality and contact with the Divine, and thus in the worship of Rhea and Attis in Greece, and Ishtar in Mesopotamia, men would castrate themselves and offer their sexual organs at the altars. Aristophanes described the first humans as androgynous and, reflecting the Aryan influence, claims that these people were split into two sexes *in order to keep them from becoming like the Gods.*

Shiva as Hermaphrodite.

This same image exists in Genesis when the female aspect of Adam is removed from him to make a separate being (the word "rib" was substituted for the more accurate "side" in later Bible translations, and thus most modern Bibles have lost this significant connection). The original Adam then, described as being in the image of God, was an androgyne appearing as the Androgyne God. From the Hindu perspective, the ultimate goal of the human species is to evolve toward bisexuality, not away from it as is taught in the Judaic-Christian-Islamic systems. The aim of evolution, according to the Hindu view, is the reuniting of the sexes. There are animal forms in existence that have this characteristic (barnacles and some tree snails, for example) and the Tantric practices are directed to this same unity and equality in humanity, for if all people are both male and female, there can be no sexual dominance.

By 5000 B.C.E., some 2,000 years before the Sumerian civilization got underway in the Near East, the Dravidians had developed a mythology that addressed the creation of the world in seven days, and had chosen names for the seven days of the week. Along with the Tree of Life, they revered the bull and the snake as sacred to the God and the Goddess as symbols of strength, life, and wisdom. The Dravidians believed that salvation came through knowledge and understanding rather than by faith or good works. They practiced ritual bathing, and baptism—in fact, there are scholars who believe that the Jesus of Christianity may well have been a student of Buddhism and Hinduism in his early years, and possibly traveling to India to study religion, as was customarily done by many of the philosophers of Greece and Rome. Buddhism, which was already underway about the time the Old Testament was being written, resulted from the Aryan attempt to restore Vedic orthodoxy to Hinduism, but Buddhism still contained Dravidic practices. The effort failed in India, with the end result that for a time, Buddhism was considered a heresy of Hinduism.

The ancient people of Sind developed mathematics; invented the zero; created algebra, astronomy, and geometry; measured the land

and divided the year; mapped the stars and knew the courses of planets and the Sun; studied animal and plant life; knew the Earth revolved around the Sun; and did not think in terms of linear time as is common with modern Western society, but instead accepted the concept of an expanding and contracting universe in which the life force alternates between a period of dreaming (expansion) and resting (contraction to a singularity)—an idea that did not take hold in Western thought until 1965 C.E. The people of Sind understood the concepts of light years and the equivalent of modern astronomy's "island universes," yet little consideration to India, is given in Western textbooks for these contributions to knowledge, much less as the cradle of civilization. The mathematical skills Westerners ascribe to the Arabs were in reality simply what Moslem invaders to the subcontinent took and transferred from India into Europe during the course of their contacts with Europeans through invasions, caravans, and the imported writings of Alberuni, a Muslim traveler who wrote much about his visit to India 1017–1030 C.E. In this way, the Indian decimal system and math symbols came to the West, where they were known as Arabic numerals. The Dravidians had calculated that the next dissolution of the universe began on what would today be written as Friday 18, 3102 B.C.E., so perhaps the Aryan invasions were anticipated as symptomatic of the beginning of the end.

The people of the Indus used a pictographic script of around 270 characters (still untranslated, but it seems to be similar to that used until recent times by the natives of Easter Island), and used ink for writing, perhaps on cloth "paper" (as is still done in China and Japan). Their tools were sophisticated, including such things as saws with teeth that allowed the sawdust to leave the cut, and they were exceptional wood carvers. Their knowledge of medical science was surprisingly advanced for the times. The dead were buried in cemeteries of barrows or stone circles, with an urn or crypt built of stone slabs with a hole on the northern or eastern side. After the Aryan invasions, cremation became the general method for disposing of the dead. Curiously, in some areas in the United States today (such as Florida), underground burial plots are required to be lined with concrete, and Orthodox Jews insist on having a hole on the north side to allow for the "dust to dust" edict to be fulfilled. This is called an "Orthodox burial" in funeral preparations, yet it is essentially a Dravidic burial.

The Vedic Aryan religion was one involving fire sacrifices and altars, but the Dravidic aspects were incorporated to form a new hybrid religion—Hinduism. The Dravidic contribution included ritual water use; reverence of trees, serpents, and bulls; veneration of stone pillars honoring the Linga (phallus) of Shiva; and ring stones honoring the Yoni (vagina) of Devi (another name for Shakti). The Linga and Yoni are the symbols of Divine creativity and the reproductive energies of Nature, with the dualistic understanding of creation and destruction as the natural rhythm of the universe. Originally, the Vedics were scornful of the Dravidic deities and religious concepts, yet they were not only unable to eliminate worship of Shiva and Shakti, the two deities endured and have become prominent in modern Hinduism. The Aryan patriarchal system was not successful in subordinating the position of women in Indian society until after the Moslem invasions, but in Southern India and in Punjab, where the populations are strongly Dravidic, matriarchies are still the norm.

By the time the earliest civilization in Mesopotamia began circa 3600 B.C.E. at Sumer, the people of Sind were engaged in trade, and one of the major exports was the Dravidic religion. The Sumerians bought many items from the Dravidians but they had nothing to exchange with them, thus creating probably the first trade imbalance in history. The Sumerians also followed the clothing style of the Dravidians. The men of the Indus Valley wore trimmed beards with no mustache, tied their long hair in a bun, and wore lightweight robes that left the right shoulder bare, The women dressed in short skirts with decorative belts at the hips, were bare-breasted, and wore numerous necklaces and large headdresses. Indus merchants had shops in the Sumerian communities and then in the Babylonian cities that followed in 2169 B.C.E., and it was not until the Aryan invaders began to lay siege to Mohenjo-daro that trade disappeared from the region.

The Old Kingdom of Egypt began around 3500 B.C.E. and lasted until 2631 B.C.E. Mohenjo-daro is known to have been a thriving urban center with foreign trade and shipping bringing vast wealth into Sind from 2900 to 1700 B.C.E. and there was still no evidence of temples or organized clergy in Sind, even when the first pyramid was being built in Egypt in 2780 B.C.E. In Egypt, the Old Kingdom came and went, the Middle Kingdom rose in 2375 B.C.E., a few years before the Sumerian Empire was destroyed by the Elamite Aryans in 2357 B.C.E. It was about 2150 B.C.E. that the Aryans began to show up in the outlaying areas of Sind, but still far from the thriving centers of commerce. A few years later Hammurabi became ruler of Babylon from 2123 to 2081 B.C.E. and created his code of laws, founded on the code of laws of the Sumerians. The religion of Babylon was not only based on that of Sumeria, but the older Sumerian language became the sacred language of the Babylonian Holy Scripture, much like Latin and Aramaic was for Christians.

By 1925 B.C.E., invading Hittite Aryans swept down between the Black Sea and Caspian Sea to strike at and conquer Babylon. In 1860 B.C.E., Stonehenge was under construction in England, while civilization was beginning to appear in Palestine around 1800 B.C.E. At this time, Egypt's Middle Kingdom period came to an end, but the Indus civilization continued to prosper. These time frames are important because they show that Aryan tribes were moving into Mesopotamia and the Indus regions, prompting the Dravidic population to flee in all directions in a series of migration waves. They may well have been the first refugees of history, for they left their mark everywhere they went.

The Egyptian Empire period lasted from 1580 to 1100 B.C.E., and the literature of this time contains the fictional stories that would much later be incorporated into the Hebrew and Christian Bible, only to be interpreted by some contemporary religious groups as actual historical people and events such as Solomon, Lazarus, and the feeding of a multitude with a few fish and loaves of bread. In 1500 B.C.E., a poem was written in Syria that would become the prototype for the Hebrew story of Daniel nearly a thousand years later.

By 1400 B.C.E. the Aryan tribes lost control of their greatest secret—the forging of iron—and the Iron Age began for the rest of human society. Between 1250 and 1200 B.C.E., the Vedic Aryans finally succeeded in capturing and destroying the great cities of the Indus, and it is during this time frame that a number of connected events transpire.

From 1200 to 700 B.C.E., the Etruscans appeared in Italy to establish their great civilization with the same structure of city-states as seen in the Indus. Although in the past historians have generally said that no one knows for certain what were the origins of the Etruscans, except to say there is some evidence that they were Lydians who migrated from Turkey, it is increasingly seen as likely that these

Serapis as the Sun—the Egyptian God created by blending the corn god Osiris with the bull god Apis.

people were Indus refugees who fled Sind at some point during the early Aryan conquests. They dwelled in what is now Turkey for a time, where they were known as Lydians, then they moved on westward into Italy when the Aryan tribes passed through Turkey. The traditions of the Etruscans were not the norm for the Greeks or the Romans, and the equality of the sexes, casual sexual attitudes, lack of inhibitions, and a theology with smiling deities strongly indicate an Indus tradition. In recent times there have been a number of scholars who have expressed this possibility.

The various Aryan tribes were very active from 1276 to 1200 B.C.E. They unified Assyria in 1276 B.C.E., and with their conquest of the Indus cities, the commercial activity that supported much of Mesopotamia collapsed. Mycenean culture disappeared in the Mediterranean, leading to the collapse of the Canaanite merchant society by 1232 B.C.E. Soon after, the Levite Aryans began organizing the populace under their rule in mountain communities, allowing for the eventual creation of the Israelites. The rest of the western world was active in warfare and expansion, with Troy falling to the Greeks in 1193 B.C.E. The Aryan conquests were completed by now, with the invaders incorporated into the societies they had overpowered, and their influence continued to be felt in the art, literature, and religion of their new subjects.

Phoenicia and Syria entered into a Golden Age from 1000 to 600 B.C.E., and during this same time the Hindu Vedas, Brahmanas, and Upanishads were completed, detailing the mythologies of the Hindu deities and setting the rules for orthodox worship that left the power in the hands of the Aryan Brahmin ruling class. The Assyrian Empire flourished from 732 to 609 B.C.E., Gautama Buddha lived eighty years, from 624 to 544 B.C.E., and finally, after all this time and all these events, writing of the first five books of the Bible, the Pentateuch, was begun in 621 B.C.E. The Roman Republic was founded in 509 B.C.E. after a series of wars against the Etruscans, whom they subdued and whose culture they attempted to obliterate (with some success), but from whom they gained invaluable information and techniques of civilization.

The Assyrian Empire ended in 609 B.C.E., a century before the founding of the Roman Republic, and the Babylonians regained prominence in the Near East until the rise of Persia in what is modern-day Iran. In 559 B.C.E., Persia entered its Empire stage, conquering Babylon in 539 B.C.E., Egypt in 525 B.C.E., and India in 518 B.C.E. It was under the rulership of these Aryan Persians that the Temple of Jerusalem was built, but it was called the Second Temple as the Bible mythology, still in the stages of rewriting by the religious leaders, stated that Solomon had built an earlier one—it simply was not in evidence. In fact, the one thing *missing* from real-time history is the Kingdom of Israel. Meanwhile, Alexander the Great invaded India in 329 B.C.E., but only stayed four years before leaving in 325 B.C.E. with a Hindu yogi as his tutor.

By 138 B.C.E., genuine Jewish history began to be written by the Maccabees, but their writings are generally left out of the Bible of Christianity as unimportant. Prior to this time, Jerusalem was under the control of the Assyrians, the Babylonians, and the Persians, and the whole of the Kingdom of Israel consisted solely of the city and the lands surrounding it.

The rest of the history of the Indus and its neighbors is fairly well known. The New Testament Gospels were written between 300 and 400 C.E. and the Roman Empire fell soon after in 476 C.E.—a traditional date based on the last of several sackings of Rome by the Germanic tribes, who were, incidentally, Christians. The gospels and rise of Christianity, then, were a byproduct of a very stressful time period for the Romans, a time when the end of the world seemed eminent.

Coincidentally, also by 400 C.E. the Great Goddess had been elevated into Hindu Vedic orthodoxy and the Tantric system was underway. India was invaded by the Huns from 455 to 500 C.E., then Sind was conquered by the Arabs in 712 C.E. The Moslem invaders pressed on throughout India from 999 to 1026 C.E., looting and destroying everything they felt offended their new religion. They killed hundreds of thousands of Hindus from time to time,

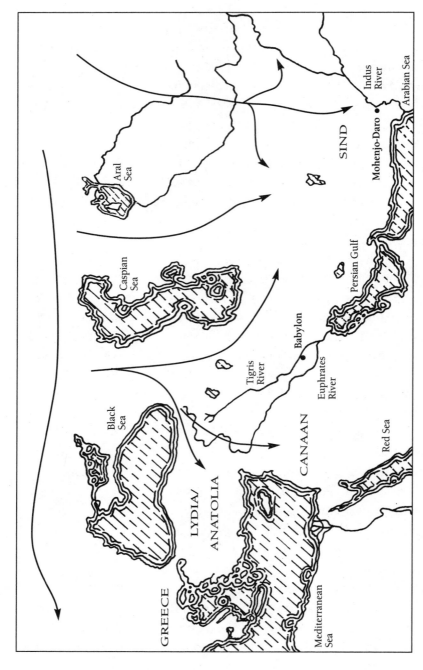

The route of Aryan Migrations took these invaders into the rich and fertile lands of long-established civilizations from India west through what is today called the Near East.

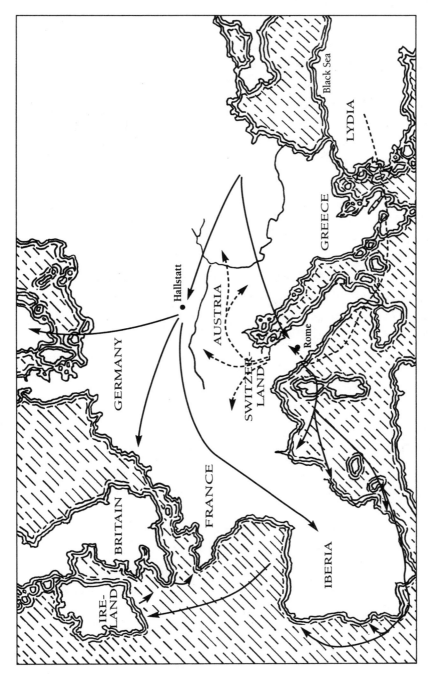

The paths of Etruscan and Celtic migrations throughout Europe and the British Isles. Their influence was widespread.

37

simply because they existed and their religion was considered an affront to the Moslem concept of deity.

It was during the Moslem atrocities, descriptions of which begin with thousands of Hindus being tossed into vats of boiling oil, that the religion of Shiva and Shakti experienced an upsurge in popularity. The worship of Shiva and Shakti began to flourish throughout South India and Kashmir, then spread into Indonesia in the wake of Moslem zealotry. Buddhism all but vanished in India by 1100 C.E., and from 1100 to 1610 C.E., Shiva was portrayed in heroic terms.

India was invaded by the Turks in 1186 C.E., and by 1236 C.E., the Moslems controlled extensive portions of India. Marco Polo visited India from 1288 to 1293 C.E., and Vasco de Gama arrived in 1498 C.E. to give Portugal a claim for a trading port, established in 1510 C.E. at Goa. After all these invasions, the wealth and grandeur of India was still legendary. The French and English fought a war in India over claims for trading rights from 1756 to 1763 C.E. The English won, and in 1765 C.E., Robert Clive was made Governor of Bengal. The British Crown took over control of India from the British East India Company in 1858 C.E., and in 1947 C.E., after numerous massacres of unarmed Hindus, massive defacing of temple art considered offensive, and general mismanagement, the British Crown granted independence to a nation it first forcibly divided into Moslem Pakistan and Hindu India. The religiously integrated society was driven apart with vast numbers of people expelled from their home to trek hundreds of miles to a region designated appropriate to their religion by a foreign and biased imperial power.

Today, the historic roots of India and Hinduism lie in the territory of a fundamentalist Islamic State. Moslem East Pakistan was nearly destroyed by invading West Pakistan, but India intervened, and East Pakistan declared its independence from West Pakistan, changed its name to Bangledesh, and the "West" was dropped from the name of the larger nation.

It was only after India had been opened for trade to the West that Dr. John Dee (1527–1608), court astrologer to Queen Elizabeth I

(1558–1603), developed the Enochian system of ceremonial magic between 1570 and 1580. Already, the Jewish kabbalah of medieval Spain had worked its way into the rest of Europe, to become incorporated into the ceremonial system of magickal practice in Europe under the guidance of Agrippa (1486–1535) and Paracelsus (1493–1541). In 1877, the Hermetic Order of the Golden Dawn was founded, and from 1875 to 1947 Aleister Crowley was a leading ceremonial magician. In 1897, Charles Leland wrote his book about Italian witchcraft, *Aradia: Gospel of the Witches,* and in 1939, Gerald Gardner was initiated into witchcraft, writing books on the subject in the 1940s and '50s. By the 1970s, popular books were available to introduce the public to modern Wicca, complete with rituals and practices that incorporated aspects and terminology from Medieval European ceremonial magic and the kabbalah. This development and the above listed dates and events are not isolated, and the importance (and irony) of these connections will become clear.

The quest for our heritage takes us on a path back through a dark doorway. Directed by the Hermit Card Spell (pp. 3–11), all we need are the tools with which to find our origins. A black mirror of your own making will assist you in casting the light of understanding on the past.

How to Make a Black Mirror

A mirror is really only a piece of glass with one side coated or painted to keep light rays from passing through. The light is then reflected back to the viewer. Take a circle of glass and wash it with spring water. Dry it and let it sit in the moonlight during a full moon and then during a dark moon. Next, paint the back of the glass with black enamel and let it dry. Cut out a piece of black felt to fit the back of the mirror and glue it into place. Another method of construction is to paint a circle of black enamel in the center of a circle of silver aluminum foil. While the paint is still tacky, but not "wet," add a clear glue to the foil rim. Lay the painted foil against the clean glass and carefully press it onto the glass. This leaves a silvery edge around the mirror. After this dries, you can then glue the black felt to the back of the mirror to avoid scratching or scraping the foil and paint. Use a tool dedication ritual to energize your mirror. You may want to set the mirror in a decorative frame or set it on a frame such as those used to display plates. Keep the mirror covered with a black cloth when it is not in use. To retain the focus of the energies, only use the mirror in your magical workings. Imbolc is a good time to cleanse and rededicate all your tools, including this one (from *Green Witchcraft II: Balancing Light and Shadow* by Ann Moura, Llewellyn Publications, 1999, used with permission of the publisher).

Chapter Two

AUM and UMA: The Foundational Deities of Pagan and Non-Pagan Religions

Great Lady and Great Lord, known by
many names, but called upon here as . . .

he ancient deities of the Indus moved through the western world under many names, but their passage can be traced by the elements of their worship that remained constant throughout these travels. The God and Goddess of the Indus can be followed in the names and variations left in the lands they visited. The idea of Deity as dualistic had entered into human consciousness by at least 28,000 B.C.E. and formed the basis of metaphysical thought. People honored a "Great He/She" deity and held in awe and reverence natural-born hermaphrodites as visible expressions of the Deity, while homosexuality was understood and accepted as a manifestation of the dual aspect of Deity in human terms. The Indus civilization has been shown to be the first to emerge in the world, and the He/She deity found expression there in the union of AUM and UMA, commonly known today as Shiva and Shakti. These latter two names come down to modern peoples from the time of conquest by various Aryan tribes, and the later Vedic writings of 1000 B.C.E. referring to events of 1500 B.C.E., so that while those names were definitely used around 1000 B.C.E., it is possible, but not certain, that they go back to the beginning of the Indus Civilization.

The current Dravidic peoples of India are acknowledged as the descendants of the original inhabitants of Sind who fled to the south of India during the Vedic invasions, taking their beliefs with them. They have basically preserved the emphasis of the Great Goddess and her Consort in their own version of Hinduism, and have reverence for the names Shiva and Shakti, which implies that these are indeed the names of the Sind deities. The link between Hinduism and the God and Goddess of Sind has been noted also by many historians, yet the focus is primarily on Hinduism, rather than on the Sind religion that predates and was incorporated into Vedic Hinduism. The direction of these new influences over the past 2,500 years alter the perspective by adding a political twist to the spiritual broth, however. For a better look at the earlier version of Paganism, we need to strain out the Aryan aspects and see what is left.

Of the two sides of Deity, it was the female that received many different names to express her various attributes, but the male retained his name and had the attributes listed afterwards. There is Shiva Nataraja (*Lord of the Dance*), Shiva Ardhanari (*Half Male and Half Female—Androgyne*), Shiva Digambara (*Sky-Clad; Clothed in Space*), Shiva Pasupati (*Lord of the Animals; Lord of the Beasts*), Shiva Linga (*Phallic; Creator/Fertility*), and Shiva Mahayogi (*Great Teacher; Great Ascetic*), to name just a few of the one thousand listed names of Shiva (*Beneficent*).

The Goddess, however, became known by specific names. Shakti is *Power*; Devi or Mahadevi is *Goddess* or *Great Goddess* and is the Supreme Being; Durga, *Inaccessible*, is a War Goddess; Anapurna is the *Bestower of Much Food*; Jaganmatri is the *Divine Mother*; Parvati is the *Earth Mother*; and Kali is the *Black Mother*, an aspect of Devi who represents the dark side of Nature, for all life passes through death to enter into new life, and Kali is that passage. This, too, is only a partial listing of the numerous names for the Goddess—yet all the names belong to one deity.

The Goddess name UMA is the one that most clearly demonstrates how the religion of the Indus spread throughout the Near

East. Each letter of the name has significance, and UMA is the name of the Dravidic Great Mother who rules humans, animals, and plants, and is considered a liberator through spiritual transcendence. She later came to be associated with the lion and a mountain, perhaps due to the influence of early Vedic invaders as they moved across Sind and the Near East. This goddess name is popular in the Southern region of India and the Punjab, areas of Dravidic concentration. UMA became the Sumerian Goddess Uma, whose father was named Sin, which forms a literal interpretation of her origin, for she did in fact *come from Sind*. Uma then became the primal goddess of

UMA Parvati, the Goddess, in her form as Earth Mother.

the Babylonians who adopted the Sumerian religion. When we consider that the Sumerians were early settlers from Sind, the connection between the Mesopotamian religions and that of the Indus Valley is all the more obvious.

The Horned God, Lord of the Animals, so familiar in modern Pagan traditions, was in India and the Near East matched with the Lady of the Mountain. Shiva and Parvati (also called Uma Parvati, so the source of the Goddess remains known) are seen in Crete as Zagreus and Cybele, and throughout the Near East under various names. Their symbols, the bull and snake, the phallus and vagina, and in some areas, the tiger and lion, are prevalent from the Neolithic Age onward.

By contrast, the emblems of the Aryan deities related to natural phenomena such as lightning, fire, and rain, and to a personification of what were considered human virtues such as honor, sharing of goods, etc. The oldest religion of humanity addressed the people's place as part of the cycles of Nature. The Aryan development centered on humans as apart from their natural surroundings, with the gods being called upon for security and success in dominating others. The newer concept made Nature something to be propitiated through sacrifice rather than to be celebrated as part of the unity of humanity and the Universe.

Shiva was also called Ann in prehistoric India. This name was sometimes shared with the Goddess, and can be traced through the Hittite Ann, Canaanite Anat, Celtic Ane, but also is seen in the Sumerian Anu. Ann has become Saint Anne in Brittany, and the name appears as the mother of the Virgin Mary. This quality of Shiva to be sometimes identified as female is most likely due to the Ardhanari aspect. From the Christian point of view, perhaps the most surprising name applied exclusively to Shiva in Hinduism is Isha (*Lord*), for when the gospels of the New Testament were being translated from the Aramaic to the Greek, it was this title for Shiva that became translated as the name, Jesus. The connection between Shiva and Christ will be covered later, but suffice it to say that

Christian tradition also recognizes that there were many names given to the Son of God, including Joshua.

I generally refer to the primary deities of the Indus as Shiva and Shakti, or Shiva and Uma Parvati, but over the millennia the aspects and descriptives of both deities, particularly those of the Goddess, have come to be proper names. This does not reflect a multitude of goddesses or gods, but one Goddess and one God, cojoined and approachable in different ways, for different purposes, under different names depicting various aspects. The duality of the God and the Goddess is a monotheistic approach that recognizes the inherent oneness in nature resulting from a natural twosome—a whole has two halves, yet remains a whole, and the whole may be divided into numerous segments (aspects), yet remains a whole. Shiva and Shakti are independent; as Ardhanari they are One.

Just as the letters of the name of the Goddess have special significance, so do the letters of the name of the God. To understand either one, we need to look at them both. The Tantric definition of AUM (the collective sound of the name of God pronounced to include all vowels) gives meaning to each letter. The A is Grace and is male, U is Power and is female, M is the All and is both male and female in union. The letters of UMA have the same definition, but it is the U that comes first to express the Goddess of Power, then as M in union

The figure of Om or Aum is depicted by the artist as a blended figure with connecting appendages.

with her Consort, A, the God of Grace. Either emphasis is acceptable—it depends on your needs and preferences. To contemplate
the Two as One, you would focus on the M as Shiva Ardhanari. Or if
you listen to the sound of M, you are also sounding the U and the A,
which then can represent the Mother Goddess pregnant with the
God as her unborn Child. This system of using letters to represent a
being or attribute of deity was passed along to the religious traditions of other peoples through Dravidian contacts, migrations, and
later Aryan conquests.

Shiva Ardhanari, the
God in androgyne
form as half male and
half female.

The mythic patterns of the God and the Goddess spread from the Indus with the symbols of each intact. The concept of Trinity, for example, was derived from both deities. Shiva had the Trident, and is still portrayed as three-faced (Shiva Trimurti, with murti referring to form or embodiment) and in this "three in one" aspect can be found the source of modern Christian belief. Some scholars believe that the Christian Trinity was derived from the Vedic, with God the Father as Brahma, Vishnu as God the Son (that aspect of Deity which becomes incarnate from time to time), and Shiva as the Holy Spirit, the element of Divinity that makes all the rest possible and which in the Judeo-Christian tradition is not to be blasphemed. One may curse in God's name or that of His Son, but *never* by the Holy Spirit. Thus is the reverence of Shiva preserved today in the West.

Shiva is also called three-eyed (capable of destroying or creating) and this relates again to His position as the source of the three aspects of the Trinity, but it is Shakti who is more frequently manifested in terms of Trinity. As Devi, She is the Mother of the Universe who divided Herself into three Mother Goddess forms: Sarasvati, Lakshmi, and Parvati. She is also Maiden, Mother, and Crone as Sati, Parvati, and Kali. A number of female Trinities have come down to western civilization, including the Three Fates (Lachesis, Clotho, and Atroppos), the Morrigu (Ana, Badb, and Macha), the Norns (Triple Moon Goddesses Diana, Selene, and Hecate), and the Triple Earth Goddesses (Kore, Persephone, and Demeter). Kore, being a child-like maiden aspect of Persephone, was not always part of this triad. Instead, Hecate was traditionally included for helping Demeter search for Persephone, stolen away by Hades to the Underground. Persephone then is the Maiden, Demeter the Mother, and Hecate the Crone. Hecate holds a dual position of Earth and Moon, for she represents both the Earth (crossroads are sacred to Her) and the magic power used to direct the Earth's energies as the Moon directs the earth's tides. The original female Trinities entered into the later Aryanized religions of India and the Near East, and resulted in a conflict between Goddess worshippers and Aryan conquerors.

In the purest form of the Aryan religions, the only thing that could remotely be considered a Trinity involved three male deities—the Father God, the God of Law, and the Warrior God. In Vedic Hinduism, these were initially Brahma, the Creator; Vishnu, the Preserver; and Indra, the Great Warrior. Then, as the religion merged with the Dravidic, Indra was deposed by Shiva, as the Destroyer. As early as 1915, however, scholars were writing about the incorporation of Dravidic deities into modern Hinduism. In the Pagan system of Northern European, the Gods were Odin, King of the Gods; Tyr, the Lawgiver; and Thor, the Great Warrior. No Aryan goddesses of power were recognized in India for a time either, until the Dravidic Goddess began to infiltrate Vedic Hinduism at the side of her Consort, Dravidic Shiva.

For centuries, the elevation of the Goddess in the Dravidic strongholds of India was considered a heresy. Between 700 and 1000 C.E., worship of Shiva predominated in India. Subsequently, there were chronicled numerous religious purges in various regions of India depending upon which emphasis the ruler followed. Followers of Vishnu slaughtered those of Shiva, and when the Shivaites came into power (particularly from the fourteenth thru seventeenth centuries C.E.), the slaughters were reversed. The few females that had been deified by the Vedic Aryans were generally presented as dutiful mates to the Gods and tending to domestic chores, just as was mainly the case in northern Europe.

In the days before their expansions, the Aryan tribes had an earlier tradition of honoring the Mother Goddess. This is a another vast field of study, but Marija Gimbutas wrote extensively on this topic as it related to her archaeological studies (see *The Civilization of the Goddess*, New York: HarperCollins, 1991). After the Vedic conquest of the Indus, however, it was not politically possible to revive the older Aryan goddess tradition. Glorification of the female aspect of Deity would have weakened the position of power and elitism that

The Trinity of the Godhead encompassed by the Great Goddess.

had evolved among the leaders and warriors in Aryan society, and so worship of the Goddess in the conquered lands had to be eliminated. This is the background that led to the diminishing of the Goddess in favor of the God in the Near East religions. It was a practice echoed by the Northern tribes of Goths, Teutons, Germans, Anglo-Saxons, and Gauls in Europe.

The Vedic Hindus were an Aryan tribe who worshipped the sacrificial altar (the Vedi) and emphasized the importance of fire and the ritual maintenance of a fire in each home (which, in the intense heat of parts of India, is not a pleasant chore). Ritual was applied to nearly all aspects of life, and this was typical of all the Aryan tribes. To be valid, religious duties had to be correctly carried out with complicated and detailed instructions. These duties were the responsibility of a designated, hereditary priesthood who received exhorbitant gratuities from the people they ruled in exchange for their services as intermediaries to the Godhead. The elite status of the priesthood was enumerated in law, and maintained by required separation and restrictions in marriages to those of their own class, or caste. They originally had contempt for images and temples (coming from a mobile background), but in India, with the blending of the Dravidic and Vedic traditions and the opportunity to become a more settled people, a new religious form was created, overriding the earlier admonitions to become modern Hinduism. It was this accession to images and temples that the Levite Aryans later sought to eliminate.

The God and the Goddess of the Indus were represented by the Sun and the Moon interchangeably. This was acceptable because they are One, and it depended upon which aspect was being considered as to whether the Sun or Moon served as the best emblem. Joseph Campbell, in studies and lectures on mythology, has said that in general the Sun and the Moon designate the God and the Goddess respectively in the West, whereas the opposite is true in the East. Nevertheless, there are a sufficient number of exceptions to this concept that I feel the matter is ambiguous in both East and West.

Vedic Shiva is typically depicted as wearing the Crescent Moon in his hair, but this may have come from the Aryan influence showing the Moon Goddess as a smaller part of the male deity. Yet Shiva is also described in Hinduism as being like a million suns. As the Sun God, he brought Parvati into Hinduism as a part of himself. Fertility, seasonal changes of solstices and equinoxes, phases of the Moon, and agricultural schedules all became part of the cycle of life that was the basis for the first religion in Sind. Nothing has changed—not since the original idea from at least 28,000 B.C.E. The names of the deities may be altered, the reasons for the observances redefined, but it is still the same whether, for example, the Winter Solstice is the Wiccan celebration of Yule, the Christian celebration of Christmas, or the Jewish Festival of Lights (Chanukah or Hanukkah)—it is the return of the Sun that is celebrated. This applies to most of the other religious holidays of today.

From the Aryan point of view, the worship of a phallic god was disgusting. They failed at first glance to recognize that there was a greater idea involved than mere penis worship, one that encompassed the veneration of the Creative Forces. The male element as Linga could be represented by anything from a sacred river stone to a standing stone or a tree stump, and was the symbol of the creative

This depiction of the Lingam, enshrined as an object of worship, was probably worn as a pendant.

energy that dances in each and every living thing in the form of dynamic molecules. The female element as Yoni, generally represented by a ring stone or one with a depression or a cleft, gives expression to that energy in the shape of the life produced. The whole concept was not vulgar, and most modern Hindus would be at a loss to understand why anyone would deem it so today. Although there are some Hindus who have had contacts with westerners and experienced this reaction to the Linga, they have expressed consternation at their religion being considered primitive by westerners who see an executed man as an image of God.

The Linga depicts an understanding of the workings of Nature and the Earth on a cosmic and microscopic scale. The Dravidians were not ignorant—they had sciences that are only now being rediscovered after centuries of burial under restrictions imposed by religious rulers. Shiva's dance is the motion of cosmic energy, just as it is now known that the molecules in everything that appears to be solid are actually in a state of constant excitement. Shakti, through the Yoni, defines the form of these dancing molecules—be it a tree, a rock, or a person—and thus everything that contains this energy is alive in one way or another, even "living rock." Today, science knows that molecules are constantly being traded off between objects; that there is a constant interaction between molecular structures, which makes pantheism all the more rational.

The concept of the Linga and Yoni are seen in the Chinese Yin and Yang, indicating that the religion of Sind may have traveled there as well. The ithyphallic Horned God, sometimes seated in a Yoga position on a low throne or stool, has been found across Europe from 6000 B.C.E. At times the deity is depicted as a bull, a bull with a human face, or a phallus with a human face. There are ancient burials at Lepenski Vir in Yugoslavia near the Danube that are made in the yoga position, and aspects of the Dravidic heritage are reflected in the religions of Cambodia, Java, and Bali. The images of the Linga and Yoni are thus directly connected to the first civilizations and beliefs of humanity, radiating outward both east and west from the Indus Valley.

From the Dravidian expression, the Linga is the source of the energy, while the Yoni determines what that energy creates, for the Goddess takes that energy into Her womb and gives birth to all things. For this reason, She is called Power. Because the Goddess had control over matter, it became evil in the Aryan-based belief system and cosmologies. The pre-Vedic system saw that energy and matter were interrelated—God and Goddess in union—and that matter was not evil, but the form the God took in substance. The modern quandary argued by theologians over matter is that by labeling it as evil, God's creation becomes evil, which would make God unworthy of devotion. This problem has tormented the Judeo-Christian-Moslem theologians for two thousand years, causing torturous stretches of rationalization to turn the situation to be less unfavorable to God. Two unfortunate side-effects arising from the denouncement of matter are the subservience of women for bringing life into substance, and shame for the human body. Indeed, the love-hate relationship in these two areas is a conundrum of the modern world.

The tarot contains a card that addresses the dilemma faced by people who reject Nature and the expression of the natural element. Such people are in a bondage that requires the voluntary rejection of Nature; the fear of accepting their bodies; and the regarding of the needs and actions of their bodies as offensive. This problem is expressed in the original depictions of the Devil card showing a man and a woman chained to the New Religion's renamed image of Pan, the Horned God of Nature. But the chains are of their own making—they can release themselves at any time. To understand how this could be, you only have to consider the prim notions of modern America, where nudity is considered offensive, sex is a dirty word, and people may be prosecuted when they seek an outlet for their repressed natural sexual desire.

Previously, we have invoked the Seeker in the Hermit card as we pursue the roots of our Pagan heritage, so let us look to Pan, once called The Great All, for understanding of our link with Nature and our ancestors' embracing this driving force of untamed Nature. To confront this "devil" is to face that aspect that causes shame in yourself. It is only pretense to hide sexuality and bodily functions, and that pretense is based in fear.

The Aryan tribes coming from the area that is now called the Ukraine arrived as conquerors who had turned away from Nature. Their religion had undergone changes that attested to their right to assert political dominance over other peoples. Their vision of the Divine served their social order and the political reality. Since those they conquered were at one with Nature, the Great All became shameful. The Aryan gods had to be superior so the invaders could

The Devil Card in tarot, in this deck designated as The Horned One. (*The Witches Tarot* by Ellen Cannon Reed, Llewellyn Publications, 1988; used with permission of publisher.)

XV   THE HORNED ONE

claim superiority, thus justifying their aggressive actions. The Dravidians, then, were the inferior people of an inferior God of Nature. The Aryan religions of the various tribes had already incorporated this fear of Nature through the fire sacrifices intended to appease the forces of Nature. The step to disavowing the Nature in humanity was a logical one to follow since the Aryans envisioned themselves as separate from the forces around them. Denial of the Nature that is part of the human bodily form generates feelings of self-loathing, fear of discovery/embarrassment, and repugnance of the body so evident in the lives of the prophets and saints of the new religions.

In some of these saintly writings there are rather ludicrous panics over sexual desires, embarrassing erections, and humiliating diarrhea! This idea of the body, the flesh, as dirty, evil, and shameful has become imbedded in the psyche of modern humanity. Shame of Self—indeed a religiously and socially mandated shame of Self—permeates our consciousness almost from the moment of birth. This is a major reason why so many women are constantly dissatisfied with their bodies, yet feel guilty when they lose weight, get their hair done, or add implants to enhance their appearance. The end result is that while on the one hand they strive to make themselves more attractive, on the other hand they are criticized for inciting base instincts in men. So a woman cannot please—if she is plain she is scorned as such, but if she is sexy she is a tramp.

It takes a great deal of courage to free ourselves from the bondage of the neurotic but socially accepted attitude of shame for our bodies. It is our imbedded lack of understanding of our natural selves that we need to overcome. At this point in our journey, we ought to pause and determine if we are willing to release ourselves from the bondage of self-shame.

Here is a meditation that may help you to face your Natural Energy and draw upon the power within. When we can accept that we are *of* Nature, we become truly one *with* Nature. By releasing our fear of being part of Nature, our creative energy is released from bondage and our spirit is set free.

Facing the Devil Meditation

You will need the Devil, Sun, and Moon cards from your favorite tarot deck, a card that signifies yourself, a brown candle, a dark green candle, and a white candle. Incense should be something earthy, such as patchouli or a blended scent evocative of the forest or rain. You may want to drum or shake a gourd rattle gently in your hands.

Cast your Circle and set up your altar or sacred space with the brown and dark green candles at the right and left sides (God and Goddess sides), and the white in the center (Both). Spread the four cards so you can easily pick each one up as you go through this meditation. You should make yourself comfortable, sitting either on the floor on a cushion, or in a chair with your feet flat on the ground, hands resting lightly in your lap. Light the incense.

As you light the right candle say:

> *This is the candle of the God of Nature, brown for the animal nature that links me with the creatures of nature and him.*

Light the left candle and say:

> *This is the candle of the Goddess of Nature, dark green for the vegetation nature that links me with the green growing things of Nature and her.*

Lay the Devil card and your significator card beside one another in front of the unlit white candle and say:

> *This is the candle of the God and the Goddess of Nature, white for the purity of Divine Love and Radiance, that links me through Nature to the Divine.*

Place the Sun card in front of the God candle, and the Moon card in front of the Goddess candle. Then begin a breathing exercise to relax and clear your mind, such as inhaling to a count of two, holding your breath for a count of two, then releasing for a count of two. Do this until the mind-chatter settles down and you are focused on the burning candles and the Devil card before you. You may be drumming or shaking the rattle during this time.

Look at the image on the Devil card and consider it in all detail. Most people do not really examine this card, they are so frightened of it, but you should do so now. Does the Devil have a hand raised in blessing (two fingers raised)? Is his blessing depicted as a false hand on a wand? Is your card one depicting the God Pan? How are the people bound and to what? Is it a dry fountain? A chain-bound treasure box in the tunnels leading to Hades? Is it a plinth upon which the Devil stands? Or is it an image of the Wild Man, celebrating the raw thrill of life? How do you feel about this card? What is it here that frightens you? What is the message of this card? Does it tell you that the blessings of Nature are false? That the blessings of the God of Nature set you free into the world? That freedom or bondage is yours to decide? That bondage is the dry well of creativity denied?

As you consider the images that come to you from looking at this card, formulate a thought question that addresses the fear you feel. Then when you feel ready, ask it:

> *Great Lady and Great Lord, Rulers of Nature, the Cosmos, and the Spirit, answer me as I seek my connection with thy creation.*

Then state your question:

> *Is Nature false?*

> *Is creativity a gift of Nature?*

> *Have I repressed my feelings and let myself become emotionally barren?*

> *What do I fear about Nature and the Divine in Nature?*

Or whatever other question of this card you have. Now wait for the answer. Look upon the candles and realize that the brown and green of Nature are part of the white, unlit candle that represents the Divine Presence.

See the images of the things you find shameful coming at you, then see them against the backdrop of the Universe represented by the Moon and the Sun.

See the stars of the spinning galaxies, the colorful, gaseous nebulas of newborn star systems, the passage of eons of time, the birth and death of stellar bodies, and know that in relation to all this, your worries are truly insignificant. Why do you fear? What shame do you imagine exists in being?

The Divine will let you see now how meaningless it is to abhor what you are. You are their child, they love you and hold you as part of them. You are as they have made you, complete with your desires and earthly form. Think on the meaning of this, then make a new commitment to accept yourself.

> *I am loved by the Lady and the Lord, what should I fear? I cast from me the feelings of inferiority and shame for being human. I am a child of the Divine.*

Light the white candle:

> *I am a child of the Divine, of the Goddess and the God, therefore I am also Divine. As the Elementals are of the*

The Moon

The Devil/
The Horned One

The Sun

*Divine, and exist in all things, all things are of the Divine
and we are kin to another, and to the Earth, the Moon, the
Sun, and the Universe.*

Place your significator card on top of the Devil card and say:

*I affirm my oneness with the Divine, and I cast aside my
chains. I am free to live and be one with Nature and the
Universe.*

Let the image of Divine love and acceptance flood your being as
the white candle burns, and release your fears.

Snuff out the brown and dark green candles, then the white, and
put away your cards. If the pressures of society to feel ashamed of
your body overcome you, return to the meditation of the card of
Great Pan, the *great all.*

The Mythology of Shiva

The Vedic Hinduism of today is an orthodoxy that was formulated
over the years from 1000 B.C.E. through 500 B.C.E., blending Vedic
Aryan and Dravidic traditions. Prior to that time the two systems
functioned as rival denominational factions, with the latter being
considered inferior by the ruling Brahmins, and with many regulations of the Vedic tradition being imposed upon the Dravidic. The
progression of Shivan mythology—myths that cover the same themes
over and over but with slight variations—shows a gradual improvement in the status of the Dravidic God, with subsequent improvement for his Consort, Shakti. This has resulted in an Aryanization of
Shiva/Shakti, as evidenced by the Puranas—written instructions for
the worship of Shiva that date from between 900 and 1100 C.E.
There has also been a "Dravidicization" of the Vedic Aryanism, as is
apparent from the alterations in accepted Vedic mythology. But really,
it is inevitable that there would be some kind of change to accommo-
date reality over several thousand years, and these changes take us as
Seekers further into our journey of discovery.

The original religion of Sind, while not the same as Hinduism, can nevertheless be found in the religions influenced first by the original Dravidic faith, and then later by the Vedic distillation that followed and migrated with the Aryan tribes. Hinduism has many denominations, but unless that denomination is Tantric (dedicated to the study of universal power, Shakti, and its expression) or Shivaism (often spelled Saivism, and dedicated to the God Shiva), the basis has a pronounced Aryan influence. The sects dedicated to Shiva and Shakti simply have less Aryanism than Hinduism in general, but the influence is still there.

There are several primary themes in the overlaying of myths that are reorganized over time with different results by various religious schools of thought. In one case Shiva is ordered by Brahma to create the world, but he takes so long in preparations that the job is turned over to Vishnu, a clear slam at Shiva's creative powers. Yet in a later myth, the same story has a different twist; the reason Shiva's preparations were taking so long was because he was going to make humans perfect and immortal, but Brahma was afraid of competition from humans and wanted to be worshipped, so Vishnu was given the task, and carried it out quickly so that humans were mortal and had bodies susceptible to any number of frailties. The result of this myth is to elevate Shiva as a selfless god who wanted a perfect creation, but Brahma becomes selfish and cruel in his need for worshippers. Vishnu comes across as either a shoddy workman or a toady for Brahma in the revised myth. Indeed, a subsequent myth has Shiva so annoyed at how Brahma has messed up creation that he condemns Brahma to have no worshippers. Today there is only one small and neglected temple in India dedicated to Brahma.

One can see the interplay between Aryan and Dravidic elements in these myths. Each side tries to elevate its own deity while diminishing the other's. So Shiva curses Brahma, and naturally, the follow-up myth by the Aryan faction has Brahma curse Shiva so that his Linga falls off, terminating the creative symbol of Shiva. But then, as the next version states, Shiva, called "The Unperturbed," only allowed that to happen because it gave him a chance to show his greater power by restoring the Linga. And on it goes until at last, in one myth, Brahma and Vishnu both worship the Linga of Shiva.

As the mythology improved the status of Shiva, and therefore, Shakti (especially as Parvati and Devi), there was a reaction from the Brahmin caste against the Dravidic incursions into the Vedic Aryan faith. The initial intent of the conquerors was to establish their dominance over the large population they ruled through the use of precise and complex religious rituals that invalidated the old religion of their new subjects. The local deities were mocked in mythology and degraded in terms of what they represented. Parvati was described as being ridiculed even by Shiva for her dark skin, and she then had to practice Yoga to acquire a golden color that pleased her husband. Shiva was described as a lord of vampires, terror, and thievery; one who haunted the burning places (Aryans cremated their dead and imposed this practice on the Dravidians) covered in ashes. He was a beggar and a seducer of women, unfaithful to his wife, and yet too intent on Yogic practice to create the world when ordered to do so by Brahma.

The association of Shiva with the Aryan god Rudra is one that has continued to confuse people learning about Hinduism and Shiva. Rudra is often called a terrible or more primitive aspect of Shiva but Rudra was actually an early *Vedic* deity. The train of events appears to have been that the various Aryan tribes had their own major or totem tribal gods, and Rudra ("Reddish") was one such god. The qualities of Rudra were assigned to the Dravidic Shiva, so that by the time the Vedas were being written, the two had been incorporated into one god. Yet Shiva is described, not as red, but as white or silvery. To see Shiva as evolving from Rudra is to miss who Shiva is. Shiva predates the Aryans and their deities; Rudra is an Aryan deity of comparatively more recent lineage.

Although depreciated in mythology, the very fact that the myths were passed on to the people of Sind caused the myths to never end in the way they were originally presented. Somehow, Shiva and

Parvati always managed to turn things around to their favor in the storyline, and the unpleasant aspects attributed to them simply did not have the intended impact. Although Shiva failed to bring about creation, the myth was revised to say it was because he could only create immortal beings, and Brahma commanded mortal humans to worship him. The God of Grace has not been diminished, but shown to be more loving. The Vedic Brahma, however, deliberately makes humans suffer.

Shiva and Shakti have continued to be shown as deities of compassion, love, and understanding. It was as though they smiled with tolerance upon their enemies until, at last, Shiva the Unperturbed and Shakti the Great Mother overpowered the Vedic Aryans with kindness. This is not to say that there were not some sects that developed from the Aryanization of the two as demonic—there were indeed blood sacrifices and assassin sects formed from the initial meddling of the Aryans. Modern Hinduism has different denominations of Shivaism and Shaktism, and some of these were banned because of their brutality. Religious freedom is mandated in the Constitution of India, and there has been a widespread resurgence of the original Sind form of the God of Love and Goddess of Power, viewed with a positiveness unimpeded by Brahmin rhetoric.

The advent of Buddhism (624–544 B.C.E.) was the most recent concentrated attempt to remove Shiva and Shakti from the Vedic Hindu faith of India. The Aryan deities of supremacy have always been secular and political. They had come into being much later than the Lord and Lady of the basic level of the European Aryan religion, and had reflected the needs of a specific class of people—rulers and warriors—who did not exist in the previously communal organization of the tribes. By the time Mohenjo-daro fell in 1200 B.C.E., the Vedic Aryans had a completely organized system that relegated the Dual Deity of their earlier conquests into lesser deities designated for the masses, but not significant enough to ensure a pleasant afterlife. Only the priestly rulers had the power to communicate with the gods of consequence. While the fertility deities could still be honored by the ordinary people, for such important matters as life after death the male triad of superior gods had to be addressed through the designated priesthood, who alone knew how to perform the complex rituals. These deities were created for the political purpose of sanctioning the social power of the rulers and the warriors who supported them.

The Buddhist reform movement sought to purge Hinduism of its Dravidic elements, coinciding with the reformational writings of the Pentateuch occurring shortly thereafter. Buddhism is today considered a heresy of Hinduism, which is why there are not many Buddhists in India and why there is warfare between Buddhists and Hindu Tamils (ardent Shivaites with an ethnic Dravidic background) in Sri Lanka. The earlier shunning of Shiva and Shakti did not prevent the people from slowly elevating their native deities within the imposed worship system, and today Shiva is seen as the One Alone—having successfully moved from the role of ridiculed outsider to that of Supreme Deity. He is considered the one in whom resides all aspects of matter and being, and in whom the Universe dissolves and appears in many forms. But Buddha (and other Brahmins like him) was dissatisfied with the inclusion of Dravidic influences in whatever form because this undermined the position of the priesthood. In time, Buddhism, too, developed new forms, but even with the return of Sind elements in the practice of Tantric Buddhism, the role of the female is diminished in accordance with the Aryan tradition.

The Vedic mythologies, meant to uphold the power of the rulers and the warriors, had progressed to the point where Brahma was minimized and Shiva glorified. Vishnu also came to a secondary place—as the devotee of Shiva. This is illustrated in the myth about Brahma and Vishnu arguing over which of them was supreme when a fiery pillar appeared before them. To investigate this phenomenon, Vishnu traveled downward as a boar and Brahma traveled upward as a swan, but neither found the end of the pillar in either direction. They met again and Vishnu admitted his failure, but Brahma lied, claiming he had found the other end and was therefore the Universal Lord. At that point, the column of fire opened and out stepped Shiva, the Infinite, praising Vishnu for his truthfulness and placing Vishnu as second to himself. Brahma was reprimanded for his lie and condemned to remain without worship from then on. This tradition was carried over to early Christianity when cathedrals and churches were named, not after God, but after members of the Holy Family and saints.

Buddha restated Hinduism with an emphasis on the caste system, multiple forms of sexual discrimination against women, domination of women by men, alienation of women from religious participation except as subservient to men, and the superiority of the ruler and warrior caste over everyone else. All of these elements are absent in devotion to Shiva, but can be found in Buddhist societies, such as Japan with its Samurai tradition and low status for women. The later development of a Tantric Buddhism is considered a heresy as it attempts to bridge the Aryan and Sind ideals. The concept of any power being in the female, however, was unthinkable to the original Buddhism movement.

The Brahmin religious rituals were secrets handed down from fathers to sons, and the sons were required to carefully learn the proper procedures for each ritual, lest anything be done wrong and ruin the ceremony. If the words were garbled or stumbled over, if one thing was done out of proper sequence, the entire ritual was ruined, no matter how far along it had progressed, and it would have to be started over from the beginning. These ceremonies could be very costly and time-consuming as it was, but to repeat them could be more than the participant could afford or endure. The very fate of the souls of the dead depended on the ceremony for cremation, with the preliminary rites, and later benedictions being done exactly right, or the departed would suffer the consequences. The same rigid adherence to detail has been passed along into the methodology of kabbalah magic, rituals in ceremonial magic, and the celebration of the Catholic Mass and other sacraments.

Buddhism was all but exterminated in India, with many Buddhist priests being tortured to death or consigned to vats of boiling oil, and Hinduism was able to continue its development toward an even more Dravidic acceptance and emphasis. The denomination of the "Heroic Shiva" (the self-realized adept sees the whole body as the expression of various aspects of the Divine) arose between 1100 and 1400 C.E., and took on a program of economic and social reform that included the abolishment of caste and sutee (the burning of living widows on the funeral pyres of their dead husbands), and a return to the Sind practice of burial of the dead. A strong missionary movement was launched (just when Europe began to experience its first "Renaissance" in the twelfth century) by this Lingayat denomination (so-called because its adherents wear a Linga symbol around their necks, much as Christians wear a cross), and its impact is still being felt today.

The Lingayats could have originated as an attempt to return to a purer Dravidic faith—just as the Brahmins had tried to restore the Aryan elements of faith in Hinduism through Buddhism—but the Heroic sect gained power in various regions, and became the state religion in the province of Mysore in 1498 C.E. Denominational warfare existed in various parts of India as the followers of Vishnu and those of Shiva disputed over which deity was supreme. The mythology became convoluted, and the success of either god in the same myth depended clearly on where it was being presented. If the region was dominated by ethnic Dravidians, the greater was Shiva; if the region was dominated by the ethnic Aryans, the greater was Vishnu. Yet the Shivaite principle of freedom of worship has been officially accepted in modern India, although the actual practice is always a point of dispute—as it is in most of the world, including America.

The presence of AUM and UMA can be traced through the religions that came after them because their influence has been strong and enduring. The changes made in the basic naturalistic religion of Sind make a fascinating study as the ebb and flow of societies have taken the basic concepts, reshaping and redefining them to suit the needs of the worshippers. The politicalization of religion was an Aryan innovation that required the invention of virtually secular deities, and from that has come the heritage of the religious wars that have plagued humankind for two thousand years.

With the renewal of interest in our Pagan past and religious roots, matters of conscience and the spirit are returning to the control of the individual. We have traveled to the distant past, shrouded in the gray gossamer mists of time, to find the emergence of a recognized spirituality, and moved forward apace to see the arrival of a new religious direction based on social changes. Now we turn our gaze to the twists and turns of the road of spiritual development, and we hold up the Hermit's lantern that the light may shine to show us how the religion of the God and the Goddess bears an influence on modern religions. We find this by looking at how the Aryans reacted to this Indus faith when they encountered it in regions other than India. Like the Dravidians, migrating in waves from the Indus, we move to other lands, searching for the clues of their passage.

Chapter Three

Aryan Orthodoxies and Sind

The Wheel of the Year is ever turning, through sun tides
and moon tides, through seasons and harvests, for plants,
animals, and people; for all life moves within the Wheel of the
Year from life to death to life again. The balance and the
harmony of the dance of life is the spiral dance of energy eternal.
—Green Witchcraft: *Mabon Sabbat*

We can trace European Paganism to that of Crete, but here, too, the Minoan Civilization of Crete contains the elements of the Indus worship of Shiva, with bulls, snakes, phallic images, horns, circular domed funeral chambers built like those of the Indus, and Yoga positioning of the dead (as is still done in modern India among the Shivaites). Even the famed Minotaur of Crete is a creature of Shivan background, a guardian that can be seen in Shivan temples in India. The Achaean Aryans conquered Crete around 1600 B.C.E., took the Minoan version of the religion of Shiva to the Peloponnese Peninsula, and from this religious synthesis came the basis for the Mycenaean culture.

When the western religious experience is viewed as a whole, it becomes apparent that there are two basic patterns of belief at work. At one time, at the earliest level, there was only one pattern—that of the Dual Deity—which evolved naturally and reflected the environment of nature and the place humanity held within it. From the beginnings, just as is indicated in the biblical book of Genesis, humans were one with the world in which they lived. It was a sort of paradise, not because everything was perfect, but because humans knew who they were and how they fit into the scheme of things. This was a triumph of human metaphysics. It was also the religion of a communal society and the religion of Sind.

Not until the formation of a ruling and warrior class did the concept of deity change. For this reason, the Father God/Lawgiver and Great Warrior God are not a natural, but a *political* development that reflected the need to legitimize the change in society from communal to hierarchical. Aryan tribal societies altered to meet the challenges of population growth and subsequent territorial expansion. Leaders were supported by their warriors, and in time, the society became segmented between those who fought and those who tilled the earth, tended the animals, and created the goods necessary for living. For a time, women and men were equally mobile in Aryan society, with farmers and women capable of bearing arms for the ruler, but over the centuries, laws were created that stifled this and tied some members of society to the land, others to service, and others to males. These laws had the effect of distancing the practice of worshipping the natural deities from that of worshipping the political deities.

All segments of society initially practiced the same religion, but with the advent of a political system, spirituality became a politicized theology. Those who were not in the top segments of the political structure of rulers and warriors did not have ready access to the deities of these classes. As the power of the upper classes increased, so did the powers of their gods, until at last, the Dual Deity became a lesser form of religion in Aryan societies, and the ordinary people could only approach the greater gods through their emissaries, the warrior priests and the Divinely appointed king.

The priesthood that came into being was required to administer the sacred duties that ensured the obligation of the common people for obedience to their rulers. Since the God and the Goddess were obvious in Nature, it was necessary to create a reason for people to turn to another set of deities, and from this need came the concept of *salvation*. This meant that the Goddess and the God of Nature were no longer sufficient for human religious expression and they were pushed aside in Aryan theology. During conquests of other lands still practicing the original form of worship, the different Aryan tribes—be they Vedic, Luvite, or Dorians—treated the local religions as anathema (cursed, damned, and evil) and worked hard to excise the older deities from popular veneration. In Greece, the oracle goddess temple of the Pythias was overthrown and turned over to the god Apollo. The python was described in the new myth as being destroyed by the Aryan god, and this center of prophecy, the Oracle of Delphi, was turned over to him. Yet priestesses still were required to actually sit on the tripod over the fissure of volcanic gasses and speak the words of prophecy that would then be interpreted by the priests of Apollo.

The power of the priesthood depended upon the power of the rulers and warriors, and they were all members of the same class. This is seen in modern India as the caste system, while in medieval Europe it became the nobility or aristocracy, as the Church was considered a good place to put extra sons who could not look forward to a legacy and were insufficiently skilled to support the King at arms. There were variations, with some members being inferior to the nobility (friars), others similar (bishops and archbishops), and some superior (cardinals), even to the secular ruler (the pope).

In Europe, the original religion was relegated to a position of a tolerated but lesser faith—a faith of superstition and old practices remembered by country folk: the *pagani*—rather than the elevated level of religion of the higher strata of society. Even in the days of Imperial Rome, the worship of local deities of the pagani was not permitted within the vicinity of the sacred city.

Much of the policies of the various Aryan tribes can be distinguished by a marked dependence on militaristic single-mindedness. Conquest and dominance are the major themes. But in India, the Vedic Aryan faith became infiltrated by the religion of Sind. This happened because the conquered Dravidians were not part of the

Athena, also known as Pallas, was one of many deities worshipped by the *Pagani*. All the ancient statues of Athena show numerous serpents adorning her breastplate.

evolving Aryan society. They did not function and grow with that class system, and they were the original inhabitants of the land wherein the ancient religion of the God and the Goddess evolved and flourished. By the time the Vedic Aryans arrived in the Indus Valley, Shiva and Shakti were the living and socially entrenched deities of the Dravidians. By remaining in the Indus, the Vedics became more settled and found their religion changing to adapt to the land and its people. But other Aryan tribes did not stop in India; they found their way into Asia Minor, the Near East, and into what became known as Greece and Rome, taking the lessons of the Indus with them.

The great divergence that takes place, then, did not occur in Europe where country faith and noble faith, natural religion and political religion forged a livable arrangement of tolerance, nor did it occur in India where the ancient beliefs held fast and merged with the Aryan faith over time, to the point of reestablishing the Dual Deity as Supreme. It happened in the Near East. This third approach to spirituality becomes the heritage of modern western religion—the battle between a pure form of Aryanism such as did not even exist in the tribal homelands, and the religion of Sind which had previously spread throughout the Near East. From this conflict evolved the Judaic, Christian, and Islamic faiths, yet their basis is not Near Eastern, but a branch of Northern European, devoid of the naturally evolved Deities, and based solely on the secularly created gods of the nobility.

Achieving a pure Aryan religion with the God of the Brahmins (the Vedic Aryan aristocracy caste), required the repudiation of the practices that had undermined the Vedic system in the Indus Valley. It is not a coincidence that the Judaic tradition is descended from a Brahmin—Abraham. Nor is it a coincidence that the timing of the historical beginning of the Israelites (1232 B.C.E.) is soon after the fall of the Mycenean Kingdoms (1250 B.C.E.—remember time moves in the other direction in terms of B.C.E., so that the smaller numbers are closer to our own time, and the larger numbers are further into the past). By looking at a wider picture, rather than focusing only on the Near East and Mediterranean regions, it becomes clear that after the continued invasions of the Indus (from 2150 to 1250 B.C.E. until the last Indus city, Mohenjo-daro, fell to the Vedic Aryans in 1200 B.C.E.), the sudden break in the last line of resistance allowed Aryan tribes to spill into the Near East at a tremendous rate. Until this final collapse, the nomadic Aryans had moved in waves, but now they came as a deluge. The Aryans overflowed the Indus Valley into Mesopotamia, and by 884 B.C.E., they founded the Assyrian Empire.

The Aryan tribe of Luvites moved across Anatolia into the land of Canaan. There they encountered the Canaanite refugees from the fall of the Mycenean Kingdoms—*Israelites* who made calf artifacts of worship, revered snakes, and had reestablished themselves on hilltops after deserting their cities in the valley. The Levite rulers of the Hebrews were derived from Luvite Aryans, and so religious leaders claimed religious leadership through Aaron's descent. Two centuries later, the Aryan Buddhist reform movement began in India, during which time Jewish colonists were known to be living in Egypt, where a missionary branch of the Buddhists was located in Alexandria. It was after this contact that the Levites decided to hold their own conference of leaders and create their own holy writ.

The succession of historical events involved great activity from the Aryan people, including the rise of the Persian Empire, whose people are today's Iranians, and acknowledged by historians and anthropologists to be an Aryan race. The building of the Temple in Jerusalem was actually constructed under the rule of the Persians in 520 B.C.E., and fits in perfectly with the need to promote the Aryan faith and dismantle that of the God and the Goddess of Sind. The Persians had already come up with their own salvation religion and dichotomy deities of good and evil in Zoroastrianism, so the Temple was a concession to the needs of the Israelites being ruled by Aryan Levites.

The Levites themselves were separate from the other Israelites, and like their Vedic kin, they were forbidden to intermarry with the people they ruled; they received the first fruits of all harvests; had property rights that amounted to fiefdoms; and were by law the only ones permitted extravagant dress and displays of wealth. These are the same regulations that applied to the Brahmins of India to keep them segregated from, and in power over, the conquered Dravidians, and naturally enough, the idea of special rights and privileges for the Church leaders appeared in the developmental stages of Christian Europe and lasted into the eighteenth century. Today, vestiges of these rights and privileges continue to exist in such matters as nontaxation of church income and legal confidentiality privileges in a confession of sins heard by a pastor or priest.

The myths and symbols of the deities of Sind had come into the Near East and lay at the foundation of Near Eastern religion from the time of Uma of the Sumerians in 3600 B.C.E. The earliest Bible stories of the Old Testament can be traced to those of Sind circa

5000 B.C.E., with stories from the Sumerians, Babylonians, Egyptians, and Syrians further building this tradition, yet the tales are erroneously believed by many people today to be of Hebrew origin. The story of the Creation in seven days came from Sind 7,000 years ago. Egyptologist James Breasted traced the tale of the seven years of plenty and seven years of famine as coming from Egypt in 2980 B.C.E.—two centuries before the first pyramid was built. Much of the Ten Commandments was lifted nearly word for word from the Sumerian law codes created between 2474 and 2398 B.C.E. Hammurabi took these Sumerian laws and adopted them for Babylon during his rule from 2123 to 2081 B.C.E.. Today, many historians are more ready to compare the similarity between the commandments and Hammurabi's Law, but footnote or ignore the origin in Sumeria. Why is this? Perhaps because Babylon is linked to the Hebrews, while Sumeria is linked to the Indus?

There is a Sanskrit root word connection between such other lawgivers as Moses, Manes, Minos, and the Assyrian Mises. These names are not individuals, but positions of authority in the Aryan societies. From the Egyptian literature of 1580–1100 B.C.E. come the prototype of Solomon, the story of Lazarus, and the tale of the feeding of the multitude. These various non-Hebrew myths were borrowed and restated as the Word of God by the early Levite writers of the Old Testament beginning in 621 B.C.E., but to understand what the Old Testament is about, you have to understand the purpose of its being written and the identity of the enemy of the Aryan God.

One of the symbols of Shiva and Shakti that was incorporated into the religion of the Sumerians, and then carried forward through time with the religions adopted from the Sumerians, is the Tree of Life and Knowledge. The tree imagery has been carried into the present time by the Book of Genesis and the story of the Garden of Eden. The Tree was supposed to be located in the midst of the Garden, which may imply that it lies at the center of the beliefs, or the location where the beliefs are centered—hence in the midst of the Sind religion in Kashmir, the first region of the subcontinent encountered by the invading Vedic tribes. There is evidence to suggest that this is the deeper meaning, and we will shine our lantern's light into that corner soon.

The Dravidians believed that knowledge was to be valued and was the source of immortality, and they represented their God and Goddess as trees. By Talmud tradition, the Garden had two trees, not one, at its center—She of Knowledge, and He of Life. If one knew the interconnection of all life in energy, one would understand that humans were naturally immortal and that death was only a passage from one form of life to another—no salvation was needed for there was nothing evil about the functions of life. This is the meaning of the term *"Original Sin(d)"*—not being ashamed of being human and alive—the original religion of Sind.

The Indus people cherished learning and enjoyed a life free from guilt and priestly rulership. Wisdom became associated with Sind early on, and being called a thing of "sin" was to be denounced by the Aryan warrior-priesthood whose power depended on their control of the people they ruled through requiring fire sacrifices to appease their god. In fact, just about anything from Sind was recognized as such, and thus the term for something non-Aryan was Sind, or sin. The customary etymology for the word "sin," which evolved from the German *die Sintflut* ("the Great Flood"), is to the Aryan contact with Sind, from which India derives its name. The name "Sind," derived from the native word, *sindh* ("river"), was translated as "Hindu" by the Persians, and then "India" by the Greeks.

Today, except for Sind in modern Pakistan, the progression is no longer readily apparent. Modern Indians still see their land as stretching from Sindhu to Sindhu, meaning from the Indus River to the Bay of Bengal. The region known as Sind today, in the southern portion of the Indus Valley, is subject to frequent flooding; and indeed floods there killed over 100,000 people in the autumn of 1992. The German and the Indian come together through the Levites' reporting not about events in Mesopotamia, but in Sind.

In Hindu tradition, it was at the source of a Kashmiri river Sind, near the Cave of Amarnath, that Shiva let Uma Parvati in on the secret of creation. Thus, the very crime of Eve—seeking knowledge (and thereby immortality) from the beautiful god who is always depicted draped in the snakes of wisdom—was originally a gift from the God of Sind to his Goddess. This is Energy explaining to Matter how it all works. One must keep in mind that Hinduism is a combination of Aryan Vedic and Dravidic Sind traditions, and thus, to the Levites, what was accepted in this amalgamation of mythology in India was seen as an impurity to be denounced by true Aryans and something to avoid in Canaan.

The Serpent of Eden is therefore another image from Sind, possibly one that indicates the earliest known use of snakes as a means of attaining an altered state of consciousness for the purpose of shamanic divination and expanded awareness. Snakes were

Symbolism is universal—in this woodcut the Chinese god of immortality is shown with animal figures reminiscent of Cernunnos and Shiva.

associated with the Dual Deity, but particularly with the Goddess, and it seems (from ancient engravings) that women were the first to use them for prophecy. It is known today that if a person has received small doses of venom to build up immunity, the venom from certain snake bites will produce the effects noted in classical writings describing oracles. A man who worked at a lab in Florida collecting snake venom for medication was bitten accidentally and recounted the sensations that overwhelmed him. His hearing became acutely sharp, he heard sounds like that of many birds chattering (and birds are associated with the Goddess and prophecy—to become in modern times the quip, "a little bird told me"), and he had visions. For him the experience was intense and profound. This man was not Pagan, but for a short time, he crossed over to an ancient Pagan practice and told about it in terms unaffected by religious influence or restrictions.

You can reach out to this ancient Pagan experience through meditation. See yourself on a journey to Delphi, the site that was sacred to the Goddess for over 3,000 years. The symbol of her wisdom was the python, which the much more recent mythology claimed was slain by Apollo. The temple did transfer hands from the priestesses of the ancient Great Goddess to the priesthood of Apollo, but even then, only a priestess could act as a channel between the worlds. Imagine yourself on a trip to Greece, traveling with other tourists, and yet silently seeking connection with the ancient heritage of your ancestors. Not everyone can go abroad to visit the sites of their Pagan roots, but through reading and meditation you can still evoke the sensations that draw us to a renewal of the ancient ways.

A Visit to the Oracle of Delphi

During this meditation, I recommend burning mugwort leaves in a ventilated area to open the subconscious. Suitable substitutes include sage, lemon grass, burdock, rosemary, and woodruff. You

will also need in your cauldron, or similar container, either a charcoal disk for burning incense or a votive candle (black or purple)
into which you can drop the herbs. Cast your Circle and call upon
the Elementals. If you use candles at the Quarters, these should be
purple. Sit before the cauldron and add some of the herb, watching
it smolder. You may want to drum or use a gourd rattle as you let
yourself drift back through time.

The Oracle of Delphi was closed by decree of the Christianized
Roman Senate, and the entrance was sealed, so that to this day people are forbidden to stand over the entry to the Oracle. In the
underground chamber is the fissure in the bedrock from which
issues vapors, perhaps from volcanic gasses. For thousands of years,
and into the early centuries of Christianity, a priestess sat upon a
tripod over the crack, inhaled the fumes, and uttered her prophecies. Her words were generally unintelligible, but another priestess
(until the Oracle was taken over by the priests of Apollo) would
interpret the words.

As the fumes of the herbs drift upward, look through the smoke
and relax. See your surroundings change into the stony walls of a
cavern; listen for the distant sounds of people, a chirping bird, and
the wind moving through the poplars outside. Envision the shad-
owy room as circular, a python in relief upon the walls and glimpsed
in the torchlight reflecting off the smooth, polished stone. The floor
is worn from thousands of years of use, but uneven as the natural
bedrock of Mother Earth. Think about the symbolism of the Goddess as Womb and Tomb in this secluded place. She is Earth, and
She is Passage—Crone of Prophecy and Mother of New Life. The
ancient snake goddess, Rhea, famous in ancient Minoan artwork as
holding serpents in Her outstretched arms, can be touched here.

Let your thoughts drift with the drumming/rattle of the gourd.
See the brass tripod glinting in the torchlight. It is empty, awaiting
the priestess. Now move toward the tripod and ascend. It is there
for you, for you are the one who inhales the essence of the Divine,
and allow the Divine to speak through you. You are now poised on

the "seat of wisdom" and new sounds come to your awareness. No longer do you hear the breeze stirring through the leaves of tall poplars or the shuffling of feet, but instead, the chirping of birds seems somehow strange and close to your ears. You think of the bird images of the Goddess—crow, raven, owl, dove, peacock—all these are Her totems, and now you understand that this means the voice of prophecy comes as bird chatter onto your awareness.

Now the sounds change, and there is a babble of words, colliding in a cascade:

Areth; amoad; aneadi; careth; imionee; trianeth . . .

and on the words go. At first you hear a confusion of sounds, then the meanings of the words come clear to you on a subconscious, psychic level, and you realize they are coming from you. You are speaking the words of the Goddess, and you are Her priestess! The cavern is filled with the ecstasy of your speech, and you hear what the Goddess tells you and what she reveals to you. Through the Womb/Tomb of the Oracle Cave, you realize that no human power can legislate against the Lady, for she lives—is life—gives life!

The Oracle of Delphi. This poetic interpretation lacks the tripod stool over the gaseous fissure that is described in ancient records.

As the sounds now start to fade, you remember that you are not allowed to physically visit the sacred site of the Goddess, but then her voice comes to you and offers comfort:

I am in all places of the Earth and I am in your heart.
Take the tripod into your heart, and whenever you have
need, sit and speak with me, for I am everywhere, and I
am with you always.

You understand now that the whole of the Earth is her temple, and that knowledge opens the way to communication whenever you seek the presence of the Lady.

Take a deep breath and release it. The sounds of the chamber begin to fade. Take another breath and release it, and you are back in your meditation circle. Have something to eat and drink, then open your Circle and put away your tools. Touch the floor with the palms of your hands to drain off any excess energies, and resume a normal routine.

By entering the Oracle Cave, you connect with the tradition of priestesses of the Goddess from multiple millennia past into the present. That the cave is sealed today is no longer important, for the cave may be accessed by the mind and the spirit. The physical limits have been transcended and made intuitive, only to have the intuitive manifested through the energy of the Practitioner of the Craft. The Age of Aquarius is the manifestation of the power of psychic energy, and the more people who embark upon these types of meditations and visualizations, the stronger the manifesting power. In time, the Oracle of Delphi will be reopened to the public, and a priestess will again be seated upon the ancient tripod, and the voice of the Goddess will be heard by all who come to marvel at this sacred site.

The idea of a *Holy Land* also predates the Judaic application and comes from the Dravidic (and later Vedic Hindu) religion, being the land that extends from Sind to the sea. Hindu beliefs imply that a person cannot be really considered a Hindu until having visited the Holy Land—India. In some areas, certain stones, trees, hills, and mountains are centers for pilgrimages, which is a custom adopted into Judaism, Christianity, and Islam. Some archaeologists believe that the Holy Land of the Judaic tradition was actually centered around Kashmir, site of the earliest Aryan victories in India. Hindu Mystics have described Shiva as "milk and honey," and "the bright light" (He is considered to be ash white, but sometimes is portrayed as sky blue, or white with a blue throat, caused by His drinking a poison that threatened to destroy the human species), and by 621 B.C.E., when the Aryan Levites began writing the Pentateuch, they named for their own possession the land of milk and honey. In a sense this was true as the Aryans did rule the Indus Valley. It was not the land of the Israelites or Hebrews that was being discussed, but the land of Shiva—Sind; just as Eden, or Paradise was not located in Mesopotamia's Valley of the Tigris-Euphrates, but in the Valley of the Indus and its main tributaries.

The descriptions of Eden in the typical published Bible are not clear, and so interpretations are usually added that relate rivers and locales to familiar areas around Mesopotamia. These names do not accurately relate to the text, however, and did not at the time of the original translations. Since the translators were working from the assumption of the Holy Land being in the Near East, they related everything in the Bible to that region. The main river of Eden, with its four branches flowing out of the garden, is more reasonably the Indus. In Genesis, the land of Havilah "where there is gold," through which the main river of Eden flows, is a reference that definitely fits the irrigated farmlands and the legendary wealth of the Indus Valley. One of the great Indus cities has a name evocative of the strange name used in the Bible—Harrapa. India's rivers provide 90 percent of the total gold production in India today, so that just as when Genesis was written, there are rivers of gold. When we consider the theory of consonantal shift, called Grimm's Law (1819), with the softening of the consonants over time and the systematic changes in words moving from one language to another, the development of *Havilah* from *Harrapa* is easy to see.

The river that flows from Eden and supposedly encompasses Ethiopia (which in reality has the White Nile on one side and the Red Sea on the other, and is not "encompassed" by either) is more likely to have bordered Kashmir, so that what is called Cush in the Bible is Kush, the passes of which were used by the Vedic Aryans to enter Kashmir.

Simply looking at a map and considering geographical features is sufficient for locating Eden, but archaeologist and author Holger Kersten traveled there and details the place names that are in the Bible, but located in India. The Indus, called Sind in Kashmir, has along its route all the places of Bible fame, and even the tomb of the Lawgiver, Moses. While he makes a convincing case for the Kashmiri origins of Judaic beliefs, that is only part of the picture. The Aryan invasions of the Indus Valley began around 2150 B.C.E. in the northern region which fell long before the southern region. That is why the Judaic tradition of Canaan did not get started until after the the destruction of Mohenjo-daro and the fall of the Mycenean Empire. The area of Kashmir would be part of the Levite tradition just as it was for the Vedic tradition.

Comparing the Bible's description of Eden to the map, it is immediately apparent that there are four distinct branches that pour into the Indus from the north of the valley, but the Tigris-Euphrates has no connection with the rivers around Ethiopia, nor are there four large rivers connected to these two anywhere in Mesopotamia. Nothing fits the description of the Garden of Eden and its rivers so clearly as does Sind with the Indus River, four large tributaries, history of wealth, religion of trees and snakes, and historic origins of civilization.

The biblical names of places are easily found in India. Remember, I said that today's visitor to Israel will find at least two sites offered for various biblical occurrences. This is because it is very difficult to find sites that match the descriptions. Kersten, quite accidentally, discovered that the place names existed in the much older regions of Kashmir, and these sites matched the descriptions. Biblical Mount Pisga,

Beth-peor, Heshbon, Moab, and Nebo are located in Kashmir, and called by the names Pishga, Behat-poor (today's Bandipur), Hasbal, Moab, and Mount Nebo, the latter of which overlooks Bandipur and the Kashmiri highlands. By following the directions given in the Bible and using a map of Kashmir, Kersten traveled to the sites and located the tomb of Moses, which is enshrined and identified as such in Kashmir. What happened in Palestine, then, is very much like what happened when America was settled by European colonists.

With the New World, the names of the Old World European towns were transported to the new colonies. Just as there are places in America named for sites in England, France, Spain, Holland, Sweden, Norway, and Germany, so there are places in the Near East named for sites in Kashmir and the Indus Valley. And just as one would be hard put to apply historical references of European places to those bearing the same name in America, the problem is likewise encountered in the Near East to make Biblical descriptions fit the places in Palestine, and thus the need to modify these identifications with "traditionally accepted as . . ." With Mount Sinai, our earlier example that in 1999 was being touted as located in Saudi Arabia (!), we have only to consider that the "ai" ending is Greek plural, and the source of the Ten Commandments reverts to Sin—carried into Assyria from Babylon (from the Indus colony of Sumeria of 3600 B.C.E.).

By listing numerous examples of words that are identical in spelling and meaning from Kashmiri and Hebrew, Kersten believes that Kashmiri is derived from Hebrew. But in dating this, the opposite is true—Hebrew is derived from the Kashmiri, and shows the connection between the Vedic and Levite Aryans.

The biblical concept of God, and later the Son of God, being the Good Shepherd with His devotees called his flock, was adopted from the earlier description of Shiva as the Divine Shepherd with His flock of followers. He is also the reconciliation of opposites, and forms the balance between Creation and Destruction—the natural realities of the Universe, the earth, and all life. This idea of balancing opposites has always posed a problem for the Judaic interpretation of God. The Judaic deity is supposed to be a god of grace and love, but also of wrath (which is a quality of Vedic Shiva), but Judaism has difficulty explaining why a good deity would allow bad things to happen to his faithful followers.

The Book of Job is a case in point, wherein it is observed that the good suffer, and must still give praise to the God that allows this to happen. With a total disregard for the individuals involved in this story, Job is supposed to be pleased because after God destroys his first family to test his loyalty, he then provides Job with a new one. Anyone who has lost a child knows that another child, while a blessing, is not a "replacement." In this Bible story, not much value is placed on the individuals. It is not a Satan or demonic force that wreaks pain and suffering on Job, but the very deity he is supposed to worship. This union of suffering with goodness, then, is what led to such extreme self-punishment as self-flagellation, pole sitting for years at a time, and mortification of the flesh by early Christians. It is still going on in small Christian sects, and is reflected on a wider scale in prohibitions against any form of sensual pleasure, including dancing.

This problem of reconciliation made its way into the stories of the early saints of Christianity. They were people who were otherwise comfortable in life, but were consumed by guilt for having a pleasant life. They engaged in self-mutilations and starvation fasts, exerted themselves to find new ways to demean their flesh through lack of bathing, covering themselves with dung, and committing other acts that would be offensive to the body and society. Early records, such as the writings of Tacitus, show that the average Pagan considered the first Christians to be bizarre and abhorrent cultists.

The Dravidians did not see pain as evidence of one's goodness, nor did they consider a pleasant life to be a cause for guilt. The Aryan dilemma arose because their negative Rudra aspects were added to Dravidic Shiva during the initial attempt at subverting his worship, and this was carried over into the subsequent attempts at purifying the Aryan beliefs. Prior to this, people were more pragmatic and accepted that bad things do happen through chance, or luck, or fate, but that people are also responsible for the consequences of their actions, either in the present life or in the next, in the form of Karmic retribution or spiritual advancement. The problem with such a concept, of course, is that it removes the need for a priesthood to intervene between God and the ordinary person. With the religion of Sind, there is no innate human guilt; but because the Judaic version of the religion of the Aryans exempts the Dual Deity, there is no innate human innocence. Thus, along with the other extremes of Medieval Christianity, it was believed that even a newborn would be denied entry into heaven if the baby died before baptism.

There are many points in the Pentateuch alone that show the connection with the earlier religions of Sind and Hinduism, but in searching for our Pagan roots, and finding their entanglement in western religions based upon the Judaic writings, we do not need to prove or disprove the validity of those writings. It is no more necessary to prove the reality of Vedic Krishna than it is to prove the existence of Biblical Moses. We need only keep in mind that the Bible is a compilation begun centuries after the Aryan Levites arrived in Canaan. Much was borrowed from the dominant cultures of the area—Egypt, Babylon, Assyria—and the admixture of literature, legend, and mythology, does not address historical personages in real time, but idea-images. Thus there are no pharaohs mentioned by name in relation to Moses and there are no dates to align Biblical events in relation to historic events. Unless the reader relates places and events to the Indus, where a tantalizing exploration can be attempted to match Bible stories with the various Vedic writings, there is little coordination between historical reality and the Bible.

The statement by God to Moses, for example, giving His name as "I am that I am," has long puzzled theologians, but is directly traceable to one of the Hindu names for the Supreme Being—Tat (*That*)—which puts a whole new perspective on the meaning of this mystical phrase. Indeed, it becomes a circular mantra. The Prayer of

Manasseh is one of the Apocryhpha—books usually not found in Protestant Bibles, but located between the Old Testament and New Testament of Catholic Bibles—as are the only books of real Jewish history, Maccabees I and II, written in 138 B.C.E. Manasa, however, is the name of the Snake Goddess whose worship is still widespread in India. It was Shiva who first was called "Beloved Father," "Highest Truth," "Grace," and "Good Shepherd," and these titles were moved into the Bible by the Aryan Levites to describe their deity. "Yahweh" may even be derived from the Sanskrit word for "everflowing," as a fiery stream of lava, which is appropriately Vedic.

The Star of David is another symbol of Sind, and is actually the Dravidic Star showing the dualistic union of Shiva, as the triangle, and Shakti, as the inverted triangle. In Hinduism, the two triangles are placed together to form a six-pointed star, and that star is placed in a circle to represent the Dual Deity in Time. It is no coincidence that this symbol appears in the Bible and is related to David, for David is Dravid, and the stories about Saul, David, Bathsheba, Solomon, and the Queen of Sheba are a metaphorical progression of the religious development of India being restructured by Aryan Levite reformists.

Saul is the name of a valuable and durable tree of India, and as a Tree represents the Goddess Devi (turned into a male as was customary in the writing of the Bible, just as the Goddess Ashtoreth was made into the God/Demon Astaroth, to prevent any taint of a female deity of power being a rival to the Aryan Mountain God in an Aryan Scripture). The name of Shakti as Devi (*Goddess*), was also given a sex change to become the male Devil. The mythological progression recounted in the Old Testament shows that the Goddess Tree had been deposed by the God—Dravidic Shiva—in the Aryan Hindu blend of religion, and he now assumed the position of Power. David's dancing before the Arc of the Covenant as it was carried into Jerusalem was frowned upon because this showed that Shiva, the Lord of the Dance, had literally entered Jerusalem in the form of his religion before an Aryan deity could be established as supreme.

David later wed Bathsheba ("Daughter of Shiva") showing that the female aspect is under his domination, and they had a son named Solomon. It was Solomon who represented the final stage of integration of the Dravidic into the Aryan. The Shiva aspect of wisdom was defined through Solomon, who becomes advisor to the mysterious Queen of Sheba. Her origins have been seriously debated for centuries, and she has been considered to have come from a variety of places, including Ethiopia and an area of the eastern coast of the Arabian Peninsula just across the water from the Indus Valley. It is not surprising that her homeland is a matter of dispute and confusion, for she is literally Shiva's Queen—Shakti—and the story is meant to prove the superiority of Aryan Judaism by their god receiving Shiva's wife as a petitioner to be counselled, and then sent off to an obscure mortal king to be his submissive and now mortal wife. The entire story denotes the diminishing and final banishing of Shakti, and the absorption of Shiva as an Aryan. At least this was the purpose of the story, although not the reality of the situation.

Throughout the history of Judaism, the Levite priesthood had to contend with the rivalry of the religion of Sind, and the council that put together the Bible included numerous baleful references to the continued practices of the Old Religion. There are admonitions about the women weeping for Tammuz at the temple doors; women dressing up in their finery, as did Gomer, the wife of Hosea, to worship Ashtoreth with sexual unions at the Temple—and of course, this shows that these actions were accepted by the populace, for they took place *at the Temple*.

The myths of Shiva and Parvati have been restated numerous times throughout the western world and were well known at the time of the writing of the Bible. It was because of the influence in Palestine of the Minoans Zagreus and Cybele, Greek Venus and Adonis, Thracian Dionysus and Kybele, Roman Cybele and Attis, Babylonian Ishtar and Tammuz, and Egyptian Isis and Osiris that the Aryan religion had to be codified and made orthodox. The Bible then is clearly not intended to be history, but a set of books that would sway people away from the purely Dravidic or the blended religious practices as found in India. By voicing recriminations against following the older traditions, the populace could be persuaded to accept the Aryan faith and thus secure the power of the Levite priesthood that ruled the Hebrews. The effort was never entirely successful.

It is interesting that while modern western languages have been traced back to the Indo-European roots of Sanskrit, history does not readily address the religious heritage that traveled with language. These concepts, like the words, come from the Indus Valley. By retaining a narrow focus on the Near East as the source of civilization, Western society falls short of identifying its own heritage from Sind, for humankind was indeed "born in Sind" as the Bible states. The mythology of the Bible is a pointer to the reality of the influence of the Indus deities in the Near East and the foundation of modern mainstream religions in AUM and UMA.

The Roman god Attis was familiar to the Levites as Tammuz.

The Judaic religion is both a repudiation of the early Sind religion and an attempt to create a pure Aryan worship form based solely on the God of the ruling class. The Aryan tribes that conquered the Near East were Medes, Persians, Vedics (Hindus), Hittites, and Luvites (in Asia Minor), and their kinfolk, the Levites (in Canaan). This latter group created the religious system and mythology still in use today, and designed it to ensure their power and destroy the God and the Goddess. Even so, the tradition would not disappear. The rule of a political God might be enforced, but the elements that went into the formation of the natural dual deities are evident and speak to us through the ages in Nature.

Talmudic and popular Jewish tradition have related these natural elements to Yahweh as the dual deities, Elohim and Jehovah. Again, God is venerated as male, but is described in terms of male and female aspects. The struggle continues to this day in Judaism, and the conflict has passed into Christianity.

Jehovah is actually a feminine aspect through which the Goddess may be invoked. Most Christians do not understand the Bible in the same way as Jews because the traditions are not ethnically inherent. It is because they are inherent to the Jews that the vast majority of those in modern Israel are not orthodox, but secular. In the past, most were adherents of the same Pagan traditions being revived today in the western world, yet their literature is Near Eastern and does not truly belong to European culture. It cannot be fully comprehended in the same way as it is in Israel today simply because the ethnic tradition is different and cannot be absorbed and taught in a European context.

Where the Jewish people existed in European society, they were basically segregated, living in their own communities, called ghettos. They were shunned and frequently maligned in medieval writings. Instead, the Europeans, with little understanding of the evolution of Christianity, fought for centuries over an "alien" and nonrelevant theology, while all but annihilating their own native and ethnic Pagan theological heritage. The reason Neo-Paganism is so attractive to people of European descent today is because it is relevant and innate.

The Roman Catholic Church early on adopted popular Pagan elements to attract and retain followers, and remains today more popular than all the Protestant sects combined. While the strategy worked, it went against the very intent of the Bible of the Levites. Thus the accessions to the needs of the people by the Church in order to convert them to Christianity in effect distanced growing Christianity even further from its Jewish foundation. To draw in the country folk, the Church embraced the association of water, wells, and springs with purity and the Goddess-image of Mary. The Pagan shrines were rededicated to Christian saints and Mary, and a number of Pagan deities were renamed as Christian saints (Saint Brigid is a familiar example, being the goddess Brede or Brighde). Pagan holidays and practices were also adopted by the Church, but with a Christian slant.

The Roman Yule holidays of Saturnalia and Juvenalia were revised to become Christmas, and the Saxon spring festival of the Goddess of spring, Oestar, became the Christian holiday of Easter honoring the death and resurrection of Jesus, but the trappings of rabbits, eggs, baking of phallic cakes, and even the proper name of the Goddess remained. The baking of phallic bread at Easter was done in Italy, Germany, and France until recent times, and the "Sacred Member," a large phallic image, was carried in the Easter procession near Naples until the eighteenth century C.E. The August harvest festival honoring Artemis (Goddess of the Moon) as Virgin/Mother, or Hecate (Goddess of the Dark Moon) as the Protectress and Teacher of the Secret Arts, became the feast of the Assumption of Mary into Heaven. The gift exchanges celebrating the rebirth of the God at Winter Solstice as a baby to be nurtured by the Mother Goddess have been redesigned as relating to the gifts of the Magi to the Virgin Mary and Baby Jesus, even though in the Bible story, the Wise Men arrived when the baby was two years old. The inconsistency is brushed aside.

The New Testament Gospel of John begins the lineage of Jesus with, "In the beginning was the Word, and the Word was with God, and the Word was God." This is a reflection of the Goddess, however, for the name "Parvati" is derived from the words for "Earth" and "The Word." John describes the beginning as the time of the ancient Mother Goddess with Her Consort, who is with her, and as Ardhanari, is her. She then is "the Word brought to Earth," or "made Flesh," and thus does the Jesus of religion become the representative of the Goddess and the androgyn combination of the dual deity. The problem with the New Testament, of which this is but one example, is that the people who wrote the various books and constructed the Christian theology did not have as firm a grip on the meanings behind the theology of Judaism as did the early Levites. They took the symbols and combined them to meet the political realities of their times, which has resulted in theological arguments ever since that time. The unfortunate problem with the insistence on an orthodoxy, in the Aryan tradition, is that religious wars erupt. Millions of people have died during the nearly 2,000 years of Christianity because of disagreements over the interpretation of incongruous passages culled from revised and discarded sources.

The innovation of Islam was in the removal of any proper noun that can be associated with God—in other words, since all the names of God relate to the Dual Deity, God has no name but God—which is a more accurate translation of the Arabic. There is, however, the suppressed but nevertheless existent sexual opposite of Al-Lah in Al-Lat, the Goddess, who was worshipped before the start of Islam. In the very structure of language, the female aspect cannot be denied any more than one can realistically state there is "right," but only "right." The very existence of this polar word implies its opposite, be it "wrong" or "left." There is no neutral, genderless word for God, but there is Ardhanari for both genders.

The ultimate goal in the worship of Shiva is to achieve the level of knowledge that makes it no longer necessary to practice rituals or duties, meditate, or proclaim the faith in any way, for the body itself is the temple of God, and life is the ritual therein. Instead, one may act as a child or as though insane because of ecstasy, with outbursts of singing, dancing, and wild abandonment. These actions are all signs of having reached the knowledge of truth; the Self experiences the Universe as identical, connected. The belief is that Shiva does not require ritual, but allows it for the benefit of the less enlightened. His love for people allows him to let them display their love for him—it is a mutual obligation borne of love, much like a mother loves her child's messy Valentine card because it is the expression of love for her from her child. Shiva simply *is*, and it is expected that all who love Shiva will love all beings as part of him. This theme, too, is an aspect of Christianity that has been expressed in the ecstasy of saints (like Theresa) and the theology of various denominations (such as the Shakers and "Holy Rollers" of colonial America, and the Pentecostals of today).

Shiva is described as having stretched out the Earth and as dwelling in all places and objects. He is in the stones, plants, and animals of the Earth; the Master and Lord of all creatures and the Universe. It is believed that he grants favors, dwells in the hearts of good people, and appears in a form because he loves people and wants to free them from continuing rebirth into the world due to Karma. He is called the Great Physician, the Killer of Death, and the Victor Over Death. All these attributes might sound strangely familiar—they are themes borrowed and placed in the Old and New Testaments of the Bible. Just as the idea of freedom through study, ritual, austerity, and virtue has been incorporated in the Judaic and Christian system through an emphasis on religious education, service to God through good works, and membership in a religious community, the theme of salvation from sorrow coming from both one's own efforts and the grace of Shiva is echoed in the injunction that one is saved by the grace of God, and good works are the proof of this.

This incorporation of Shivan ideals into Christianity is really not surprising. I said earlier that there was a connection between Christ and Shiva, and it lies in the very name. Again, it is the Aramaic translation into Greek that gives us the clues as to what the early

Christians were all about. They were a heretical sect of Judaism after all, and the name Christ is the Aramaic form of the name Krishna. There are scholars who posit that the historic personage of Jesus was engaged in missionary work for Krishna in Palestine, and in the oral preachings that came to Rome he became inextricably associated with the God he was preaching about. All the themes and mythological patterns of Krishna (which predate Jesus by as much as 500 years), from the Star of the East to the Wise Men and so forth, have been assigned rightly to *Christ,* but wrongly to *Jesus.*

Krishna is considered to be an incarnation (avatar) of the Vedic God of Creation, Vishnu, but he was a lifelong devotee of Shiva. Remember how the development of the mythologies ended with Vishnu being made second to Shiva? The story of Krishna takes this one step further, and this is what was being carried to other sites with missionary zeal. Indeed, the appeal of Krishna remains to this day as missionaries travel the world converting people to his worship.

Krishna's initiation into Shivaism is described in the *Mahabharata.* In this account, the idea of why Krishna and Shiva are the same is presented. As an incarnation of Vishnu, Hari Krishna, *Yellowish-green One* and Hara Shiva, *One Who Takes Away* are One in the same sense that God and the Son of God are One. Shiva is considered to be All, and is the God, while Vishnu is an aspect of Shiva that is manifested from time to time through incarnations. The "Hari" refers then to those incarnations upon the Earth through the Earth Mother. With Christianity, Christ is born of the Earth Mother (Mary) as the Son of the Heavenly Father (Shiva as All). But the preacher Joshua was translated into the Greek as the God Isha to become Jesus, and was thus assimilated as the deity Christ (Krishna)—which is why people of Nazareth who are said to have known the preacher in his youth, and his human family, did not consider *him* a deity.

While Shiva is revered as a "personal God" (a usage later adopted by Christian theologians who had access to Indian theological works), the personal aspect of Shakti is Ishtha Devata. This name became blended in India to create Ishvari, the "Queen of All," whose name then spread to Mesopotamia where She was worshipped as Ishtar, Astarte, and Ashtoreth, and despised in the Old Testament of the Bible as Asteroth. Shiva is also called Ishana in India, which may well relate to his female aspect as Inanna, and he is called Hara, which could be the source of the Goddess Ishara. The name Shiva is preserved in the Judaic tradition as both the name of a calendar month and the term for mourning, while Ishtar has been renovated as Esther and made into a proper Jewish maiden. The mourning term for Shiva was derived from the early Aryan myth that placed him as one who haunts the burning places of cremations. The Vedic Aryans at one point even tried (with some degree of success) to confuse pre-Vedic Shiva with their own deity, Rudra, the "Howler," a God of aversion to be feared and placated rather than adored. Shiva is a deity that is very approachable by men and women alike, and this was not acceptable to the Aryan.

The Christianization of the Judaic religion resulted in a dichotomy. The European Pagan Mother Goddess is revealed as Mary, the Mother of God, and the titles and adulations that once adorned the Goddess now belong to the Virgin Mary. As Queen of the Universe, she liberates her devotees from fear, suffering, and evil. According to Catholic tradition, if you pray to Mary with the rosary (prayer beads being an ancient form of Shiva worship), she will be with you at your death to ease the transition into the next life. This is literally so by Pagan theology, for Mary is both Kali and Shakti. The processions and feasts dedicated to the Goddess have become those of Mary, and like the Goddess she is associated with the Elementals Water and Earth. The Hindu tradition grants that Shakti incarnates in different ages, and so it would not be difficult to consider Mary as an example of this mythological motif being redirected.

Today the influence of Sind is barely recognized in the orthodoxies that have come down to modern times. Shiva's dance is the visualization of an ancient concept only recently recognized by science, that of the periodic dissolution and recreation of all life. This ceases to be disturbing when you realize that you are fully and naturally part of the process. Neither fear nor salvation apply because of the Grace and Power—you are a participant in Nature. It is the Indian idea of Oneness with God that is aspired to by western religions, but hindered by the preoccupation of segregation of believers into groups of *saved* and *unsaved; them* and *us*. Fear over who would survive the dissolution of the Universe has led to unnecessary hatreds, resentments, and war—unnecessary because science has already proved that *all survive* since energy cannot be destroyed, but is, just as Shiva is.

In the Dravidic tradition, devotion is a personal matter and an individual responsibility. This is the reality of any spirituality, for whether you are a member of a religious organization or not, *beliefs* are internal. Even the understanding of orthodox theology is unique to each individual, no matter how similar the rituals enacted while functioning within a group. This is how people have clung to the Old Religion while attending the services of the New. The votive candles become the avenue of spells, while the incense-filled cathedrals become the sanctuaries for charms, watched over in many European churches by my favorite portraiture of the Great Goddess: Mary smiling, in the flowing blue and white draperies (the colors of law and rulership), her head crowned by stars, her unbound wavy brown hair billowing around her white shoulders in the wind as she stands triumphantly with one bare foot upon the Horned Moon, with an adoring snake in attendance.

The priestly status of clerical representatives before God is an Aryan innovation whose purpose has long been outlived. The world order is moving toward elected representation in governments, and this may well fuel a reconstruction of religion to make it relevant, to reflect the secular reality. The result may be a genuinely new form of Paganism, one in which individuals take back responsibility for whether or not they hold religious observances, and determine their own rites based on need and appropriateness under societal laws which they themselves create through representative government. We must come to terms with reality. The time for a purely upper-level Aryan religion has passed, just as has the time of a purely Dravidic religion. Neo-Paganism is at its best when taking the wheat of the past and discarding the chaff.

The modern resurgence of Paganism is often related as an outgrowth of old European traditions, but for people who are distanced from their ancestral heritage by the fact of living on another continent, such as Americans, Canadians, and Australians, the old traditions have either taken on a New World flavor of their own, or are intrinsically lost. Even traveling to Europe, observing modern versions of ancient Pagan traditions—the Abbots Bromley Horn Dance, the Fools Parade, the Morris Dancers—and visiting Pagan sites such as Stonehenge, New Grange, and Chalice Well, are not the same thing as growing up in a region and being saturated by the continuous flow of that region's history from your infancy. For this reason, many people in the New World experience a sense of yearning, of nostalgic disassociation with their heritage—and perhaps even a tinge of envy for their kinfolk remaining in the Old World.

Neo-Paganism is the term more widely applied to religions that venerate Nature and see humanity as an integral part of the whole. The three main belief patterns of both ancient and modern Paganism are polytheism/Divine plurality; the Divine manifested in Nature; and the duality of Divinity as both female and male—the Goddess and the God. Non-Europeans can take the past and create a viable Pagan synthesis with their own particular heritage and regional flavor. Hence, as an example, the incorporation into American Wicca of such things as Pennsylvania Dutch hex signs, hoodoo, New England spiritism, and Native American sacred sites and spirituality.

The power shift coming from a rising interest in Neo-Paganism is already being fought by organized clergies of the world. The televised antics of preachers casting out devils and saving women who profess to be devil-worshipping witches for the cameras are the kind of spiritual untruths being used to combat the revival of Paganism in America. The threat of eternal damnation is hurled at any who dare to explore a new spiritual approach, yet it is through the entrenched religious systems that excuses are found for wars around the world. The political arena of world affairs is given Divine sanction through the political deities of class, caste, and orthodoxy. Reason, knowledge, and accessibility of information are the enemies of an orthodox priesthood, but the age of instant communication is already upon us. The world is currently experiencing the travails of a process in which religion is in competition with numerous sciences and open knowledge. Even syndicated newspaper comic strips are beginning for the first time ever to include information on the Pagan origins of popular religious holidays. Changes in perceptions about the earth, Universe, and life itself are being felt, and any power structure based on ignorance and dogmatic interpretation will naturally suffer. As we swing our lantern to light the path into the future, we can only peer into the hidden recesses of the winding road ahead of us and wonder whether the Neo-Pagan revival will continue to gather momentum to become the new spirituality of the New Age.

Chapter Four

Pagan Roots Get Tangled in Europe

Why do we call people snakes when we intend to insult them?
And why should people feel themselves inadequate? Think about
the snake and what it symbolizes. The snake is called a lowly
creature, and it does slither on the ground, but it also winds its
way through rocks and treetops, and it swims in the water. It is
called slimy, but it is not. It is called evil, but merely lives its life,
doing good in controlling rodent populations. It is despised, but
is noble and beautiful. Then what did the snake symbolize to our
Pagan ancestors? It is the spirit reborn. The snake is regenera-
tion and wisdom. And it is the symbol of the Goddess and of the
God. Held by Cernunnos, draped over Shiva, worn by Athena
and Minerva, source of prophecy and oracular vision, adoring of
the Goddess, the snake is the noble companion of the Divine.
Is that an insult then?
—From a Meditation

Tracing the Pagan aspects of modern orthodox religions, we can seine out what relates to the pre-Aryan paganism and what does not. We can do this by matching known Pagan themes and elements in modern religions, and by removing, or deducting, known Aryanizing themes from Paganism.

I stated earlier that Catholicism is more popular than all the Protestant sects put together (excluding Mormons who are not Christian in the traditional sense). The very things that Protestant groups rebelled against in Catholicism during the Reformation and its aftermath are what draw people to this religion: veneration of the

Mother of God, holy water, rosaries, miraculous statues and images, incense, candle-lighting, sacred shrines, holy wells, retention of pagan holy days as saints' days, and so forth. There are many who feel "at home in the Holy Mother Church" simply because they are feeling the cultural ties of their Pagan heritage expressed in socially accepted terms. The one aspect that continues to detract is the demeaning position allotted to women in general, even while reverence is given to the Virgin Mary, whose original aspect was meek and submissive.

It was at the Council of Ephesus in 431 C.E. that Mary was elevated to fill the role held by Diana-Artemis. This Greek city was the ancient site of the temple of Artemis, the Great Mother Goddess. Her temple was the focus of pilgrimages from distant lands. People traveled to Her sanctuary from throughout the Near and Far East, from the Mediterranean, and Eastern Europe, seeking miracles and paying homage to the Great Mother. Her shrine, closed by law, was decorated with numerous tokens of Her healings—little figurines and appendages that testified to the miraculous cures. The statue of Artemis is called "Many-Breasted," although the numerous pendulous breasts draped around Her are more like ostrich eggs—a spiritual symbol of rebirth in the Near East. This statue, which was found in excavations of the temple site, was clothed in rich garb just as is done today with statues in Catholic churches, particularly those in Europe.

Isis nursing Osiris. The image of a maternal Isis was popular throughout the Roman Empire and was adopted into Christianity as Mary and child. Here she is shown related to Hathor, Goddess of the Universe.

When the Council of Ephesus met to determine the orthodox meaning of the Holy Trinity, they were surrounded by angry locals who demanded the reinstatement of their Goddess. The Council deliberated and then rededicated the temple of the ancient bear-goddess, Artemis to Mary *theotokos*—god-bearing.

She was officially the Mother of God. This was when and how that title came to the Christian Virgin Mary, and the rituals of Artemis were given over to Mary. So when I say that Mary is the Christian version of the Mother Goddess or the Pagan Great Goddess, it is because of actions such as this that deliberately align her with the Pagan tradition, and thus made the transition from outlawed Paganism to legal Christianity less painful for the population.

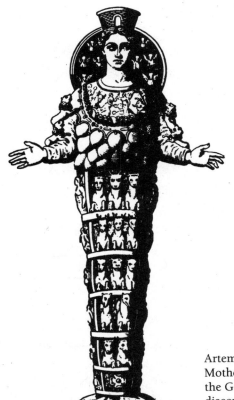

Artemis, in her aspect as the Great Mother Goddess, who became Mary, the God Bearer. This statue was discovered in excavating the site of the temple of Artemis at Ephesus.

Nevertheless, the emphasis of the gentle aspects of the Goddess results in an Aryanized Mother of God. Her powerful aspects are denied or muted, at least in the official stance of the Church, while not to the populace. When the dual sexual attributes of the Pagan Divine are viewed from the female perspective, the Goddess becomes capable of war and violence—a Kali or a Morrigu—for in Pagan tradition, the Goddess of love has often been equally a Goddess of war and aggression. The different sides of the Divine Androgyne remind us of the different sides of Nature, but with the Aryanization of the Goddess, half a person is created. This is the denouncement of Eve seeking wisdom and immortality in favor of Mary as the obedient handmaiden. As Virgin Mary, the Goddess becomes the symbol of the perfect, dominated female with total submission to the Aryan Lawgiver Godform. Meekness, then, is the woman's role, not assertiveness or power, and this is a theme found throughout the Aryanized vision of the Goddess. They are spouses, hearth-keepers, and domestically inclined. This is not to say that the domestic skills are not to be revered, for they certainly are, but that this does not alone define the female either in humanity or in the Divine. Uma Parvati is often depicted as the devoted wife of Shiva, yet she is also Kali.

Regarding the Scriptures of Christianity, much is owed to the early Greek writers for their form and substance. We have already explored some of the connections with the proper names of Jesus, Isha, and Shiva, but it gets even more interesting. Although the western world does not dwell on this very much, the Greek Church came before the Roman Church, so to find out what was happening in the writing of the New Testament, we do need to focus on the Greek contributions. Later translations from the Greek into the Latin, then into the common languages of various nations, the vernacular, resulted in some literally correct words with mistaken meanings. For example, the word "rejoice" in Greek usage actually means "hello." Because the new Jewish sect was attempting to establish itself among Greeks, many sacred attributes and Bible stories were lifted from the Greek Pagan tradition—in particular that of the immensely popular resurrection god, Dionysos. The religion of Dionysos predates the Old Testament by many centuries, coming to Thrace from India, then being carried into early Greece. His religion continued to flourish until around the fifth century C.E.

It becomes clearer that the Greek influence really is everywhere in the Old and New Testaments when comparisons are made to the stories of Dionysos. He crossed the Red Sea dry-footed, had armies led by pillars of fire, had rays of light streaming from his forehead (as typical of depictions of Moses) or from a third eye (as typical of Shiva—Alexander saw Shiva and Dionysos as the same god), and he descended a mountain with a code of laws inscribed on stone—all of this centuries before any written account of Moses. In the case of the laws, this myth exists in a number of other pre-Judaic sources such as King Minos of Crete descending with the laws in stone from

Dionysos, the resurrection god, who is sacrificed, then returns to ensure the fertility of the next season, as Jesus died to save humankind.

Mount Dicta, Hammurabi of the Babylonians receiving his laws in stone from the god Shamash, and Zoroaster of the Persians (660–583 B.C.E.) returning from the mountain of Ahura-Mazda with his laws in stone after God appeared to him amid thunder and lightning a mere forty years before the writing began on the first books of the Old Testament. Remember, too, that it was the Persians who built the Temple in Jerusalem, which the Levites pronounced to be the second temple.

As with Moses, the myths of Jesus are also borrowed from Dionysos. The symbols of the miraculous birth, the baptism, entry into a holy city on an ass, the Last Supper as a sacrament, suffering, death, and resurrection are all from Dionysos and can be traced back to India, from where, as Danielou reports, even the myths of Dionysos say he came. The first miracle of Dionysos and Jesus involved turning water into wine, and the Holy Communion is also seen with Dionysos. By the association of Dionysos with Shiva, and Jesus with Dionysos, the connection between Jesus and Isha (Shiva as Lord) is not difficult. Kersten, in his travels in Kashmir, located the tomb of the man Jesus in the town of Srinagar, marked in the traditional way—a large stone carved to match the feet of the deceased. The marker indicates nail holes in the feet of the prophet from Palestine, a man named Yuz Asaf. One of the traditional names ascribed to Jesus is Joshua, and with the softness of Hindu pronunciation, the link between the two names is obvious.

Kersten's premise was that Jesus, or Joshua, was a Krishna devotee and missionary who survived the crucifixion through yogic training, preparatory drugs, and reaction to the drug given him when he said he was thirsty. He was then revived and returned to the Holy Land—Kashmir—where he died in his mid-eighties. For Kersten, the study of the missing years of Jesus led him to Kashmir, and the Sind, where he found and brought into English print details and proofs from Indian sources that were available to educated people two thousand years ago. The Jews in the early days of Christianity were annoyed with the deification of Jesus, and the early critics of Christianity considered it a religion of the ignorant. The prospect of Jesus being involved with Hinduism and Buddhism has been suggested over the past century by several historians who note the Vedantic similarities.

In Dionysos, we are looking at a Pagan deity with a traceable heritage, and there are historians who make a strong case for the connection between Dionysos and Shiva. Dionysos came into Greece from Thrace first as a fertility goddess, then as the horned god fathered by the Aryan deity, Zeus, with his daughter Persephone. There is a similar Hindu myth of incest between Brahma and his daughter, the Dawn.

Over the centuries, the mythology of Dionysos developed into the Son of God who dies to save humankind. His mythology related to the crops, with mourning for his sacrificial death followed by celebrating his resurrection. The god was very popular in both Greece and the Roman Empire, and his worship even included a forerunner to the Easter sunrise service, with women going into the hills to greet the reborn god at dawn. The story of the suffering, death, and resurrection of Dionysos was ritually repeated just as is that of Jesus in Christian churches at Easter, and his followers believed that they would never die because of him. The recitation of a litany and the acting out of roles as with the Easter Passion plays (dating from medieval times to the present) in Christian churches are directly related to the older Greek religious practices.

As with the worship of Shiva, ecstasy was the prevalent form of worship for Dionysos, and the name of his followers, *bacchoi* (bacchants, with the "ch" pronounced as a "k" sound), is naturally similar to the Indian word for religious participants, *bhaktas*. It was a relatively painless transition from Dionysos to Jesus, since the former laid the groundwork for the latter as the seed reborn to a life of happiness, and so the early Christians also believed in reincarnation. Indeed the concept of rebirth in the New Testament initially emphasized the physical rebirth of reincarnation. This was only deleted from the Scriptures some 500 years after the crucifixion— 300 years after Christianity was made the only religion of the

Empire *by law*—at the Second Council of Constantinople in 553 C.E. At the insistence of the Byzantine Emperor Justinian and his wife Theodora, a former burlesque performer who made a habit of having her opponents murdered, reincarnation was eliminated from Church teachings to prevent people from saying that others would be punished for their misdeeds in the next life. John Romer presents an excellent study on the pre-orthodox beliefs of Christianity in his often-repeated television series, *Testament*.

In India during the first two centuries of Christianity, there was a resurgence of Shivan missionary work, at which time the Greek philosopher, Apollonius of Tyana, visited India to study. Tertullian refers to the Indians in his *Apologia versus gentes* in 197 C.E., indicating the Indians were an integral part of the Roman economy. The trade between Rome and India was a thriving one; India supplied the Empire with manufactured goods from textiles to wood and metal work, to exotic animals for the games. It is not as though India was isolated from the western world in the formative years of Christianity, and certainly not from the Near East during the formative years of Judaism.

The *bacchoi* of Dionysos, in legend comparable to the *bhaktas* of Shiva.

Christianity can be used to syphon off the Aryanized elements of Paganism because there are also connections with this Indian heritage through Krishna. I mentioned before that Krishna was a devotee of Shiva, but, just as there are miraculous similarities between Dionysos and Jesus, so there are a great many similarities in the life stories of Jesus and Krishna. At one time there were Chrestins in Asia Minor, and it was only after they had been destroyed as heretics by the Papal command that all the followers of Jesus were called Christians. The Greek word *chrestos* meant "anointed with oil," while *Krishna*, commonly pronounced in India as "Krishto," refers to one who attracts everything, and thus is the personification of God. For the Hindu, Krishna is an incarnation of Vishnu, whose own name refers to the light and energy of the Sun—formless until incarnated. The indications are that Jesus the historical person was a missionary for Krishna, and he became incorporated into the deity he preached about. All the themes and mythological patterns of Krishna, predating Jesus by five centuries, from the Star of the East to the Wise Men, have been rightly assigned to Christ, but wrongly to Jesus. The recognition of the difference between Jesus and Christ has been noted by numerous historians and writers, most recently by A. N. Wilson (*Jesus: A Life,* New York: Norton, 1992), but previously by Ernest Renan, Albert Schweitzer, Francois Mauriac, Geza Vermes, Joseph Campbell, John Romer, James Breasted, and Arnold Toynbee. Modern theological discussions at seminaries debate the *meaning* of Jesus and Christian teachings, and many religious writers continue to view themselves as good Christians while reinterpreting the Bible as metaphor.

There is another consideration that should be noted. The actual text writings of Krishna span 1000 to 500 B.C.E., and Emperor Ashoka of India sent out missionaries to the Near East and the Mediterranean around 250 B.C.E. In the Hindu writings themselves, the Vedas indicate their written date is around 4500 B.C.E., but the Indus Valley had not seen its first Aryan until 2150 B.C.E. This is an Aryanized version of history—the tradition of pushing back time to give validity to their theology was just as active in Vedic India as it was in Levite Canaan. The timing is obviously inaccurate, but deliberate. In this same way, the Levites made the history of the world begin at a time when in reality there were other thriving civilizations. This historic unreliablity provides a direct link between the Vedic and Levite Aryans. Yet historians still get tripped up and mingle myth with history, as when timing something historical with the nebulous description of "in the days of Solomon," or some other Biblical personage. So ingrained has the tradition become in western society of considering the Bible as an accurate depiction of literal events that to do otherwise is to risk censure.

The influences at work here show that the development of the Christian orthodoxy contains many pre-Aryan Pagan aspects. The religion also echoes Judaic tradition with the insistence that people have an inborn guilt (original sin). The theme is carried further in Christianity with the threat of a final judgment and eternal punishment. This atmosphere of terror is spurred by natural human sexuality rather than by the murders, rapes, or slaughters of war commanded in gruesome detail by the biblical God of the Levites. The Aryan God, then, is not offended by bloodshed and the degradation of people, but by the penis and the vagina—yet he is supposed to have created humanity and chosen its forms.

The Aryan disapproval of the phallic elements of the Old Religion did not prevent these from being incorporated into the newer religions, however. In Egypt under Hittite and Greek rule, the severed sexual organs of Osiris were still honored in special rites involving wooden replicas, and in Italy today, the "holy foreskin" of Christ is still venerated. In the Indus religion, the word "Linga" means "distinctive sign," and thus even formless objects in which the Divine presence is felt can be called by this word. The continuation of the pre-Aryan fertility associations are found in the many localized traditions of pillars and rough stones, tree stumps and megaliths, and in the Black Stone of Islamic veneration at Mecca.

The element of deity castration, either actual as by removal of the sexual organs entirely, or symbolic as by circumcision, is an Aryan characteristic that does not apply to Dravidic Shiva, whose emblem is the erect phallus. Shiva is unashamedly sexual and generative—he is both uninhibited pleasure and love. Shivan mythology makes it clear that the only men who fight against natural sexuality do so because of their feelings of inadequacy before the Source of the Universe. The need for Aryan-based religions to emasculate the phallic aspect of the Divine stems from the subordination of the earliest religious forms inherent in the Aryan beliefs. In order to establish the impotent political deities as supreme and alone in their power, the sexual deities of Nature had to be castrated. With Christianity, this is taken a step further. Jesus represents the normally ithyphallic Shiva as a *nonsexual* being in Christianity. The Son of God personally has no sexual practices, no sexual associations, no sexual references, and no sexual desires—not because of his divinity, but because his divine father is the Aryan Lawgiver rather than the Dravidic Creator of Heaven and Earth.

It becomes apparent in the Bible that there are two different kinds of God. One deity is a creative First Cause, but the other, more prevalent one, appears to be based on a typical local village/tribal deity who worries over the observance of religious laws and taboos. Again, this shows the difference between the original god of Sind, Shiva as creator and author of life through the Goddess, and the overlapping of the much later Aryan invention of tribal political gods of law and wrath, for whom ritual observances are the mainstay of the priesthood.

When you consider that the Aryan tribes swept down into India, Anatolia, Greece, Egypt, and the Near East in waves, beginning around 2150 B.C.E., you can visualize the waves of emigrants fleeing before them. The refugees of of the western and northern regions of India went in various directions, some of them into Southern India. By 1600 B.C.E. these cities, too, were feeling the pressure of Aryan encroachment. The cities entered into a period of siege mentality and decline that culminated with their fall by 1200 B.C.E. During this time, the Dravidic Great Goddess aspect (Durga, today) was known by the name Danu. She would give birth to her son, whom she wed upon maturation; he impregnated her with himself, died, and was reborn at Winter Solstice. This is the typical religious mystery of an agricultural society. Snakes and cows were associated with Danu and her son, Vritra, as they had been with their antecedents and successors, Shakti and Shiva.

The Vedic myth of the murder of Danu and Vritra by Indra (to gain supremacy—which lasted until Indra was deposed by Shiva) can be related to the Mesopotamian myth of Anu, the Indo-European sky god. The Mesopotamian myth dates to circa 1600–1400 B.C.E., and tells of the unsuccessful attempt to kill the Great Goddess and her son. When we see how Hindu mythology tends to be restated with different endings, we can see a merging of Danu and Anu with respect to the Sind deities. The God Anu may be associated with Shiva, then, and by examining the routes of Dravidic dispersion, reaching into Sri Lanka and Indonesia, and remembering that these Dravidians were noted sailors, we can be led to further associate these worshippers of Danu/Anu with the aborigines of Japan—the so-called "Hairy" Ainu. The Ainu were later displaced by the people now called the Japanese, who arrived from Manchuria and have pushed the Ainu onto isolated reservations, much as happened with the Native Americans.

In the wider panorama of archaeological studies, there is even a possibility of Dravidians sailing across the Pacific Ocean to settle on Easter Island, for the picto-writing of the people of Easter Island, who were dubbed the Long Ears, matches that of Mohenjo-daro. Shiva is usually depicted with long ears, and although his ears sometimes have rings or holes for earplugs, there are usually no ornaments present, or else flowers are indicated. The Dravidians may have progressed as far as Peru, based upon the connection made by Norwegian archaeologist Thor Heyerdahl between the Long Ears and the pre-Incan Peruvians, although he was initially working from the other direction. At that time he did not know of the matching picto-writing.

The masterful irrigation systems of Peru predate the Incas, and this is a technique first seen in the Indus Valley. The facility with irrigation techniques of the mysterious *Anasazi* of Mesa Verde in the southwestern tip of Colorado in North America, and their apparent differences from Native American tribes who refer to these people as *Ancient Ones* rather than as ancestors, could indicate a link with the Dravidians. The name itself is reminiscent of the people of Sind, locally called *Adivasi*, "first inhabitants," and possibly the most ancient surviving race of humankind. Again, irrigation is a feature of these unknown people, and when they disappeared, so did the technique in North America. The development of Native American tales about a *fairie people* could relate then to similar tales which appeared in Europe. If the Anasazi were indeed related to the people of the Indus, then they were colonists who eventually met with ill luck. The Long Ears were killed and eaten by the Short Ears, who were the local inhabitants of Easter Island; the pre-Incan Peruvians were driven out of Peru; and the Anasazi prospered for a time, then simply vanished, in a manner evocative of the Irish Faerie Folk.

The Dravidians had another route that historians now generally concede they took, and that was westward across Anatolia (modern Turkey) and into Eastern Europe, across the Mediterranean, and into Western Europe and the British Isles. They took their religion with them wherever they traveled.

Try to imagine the traveling bands of displaced persons in a time long ago. Transportation was by foot, wagon, horse, and oxen, with food herded and gathered along the way. And yet, once they settled into an area—Lydia, Etruria, Galicia, the British Isles—these were a cheerful, happy people. Just as the Aryan tribes invaded in waves, so the Dravidians migrated in a series of waves, starting in 2100 B.C.E. at the north and persisting until after 1250 B.C.E. at the south. Charles Picard, in his work *The Pre-Hellenic Religions*, mentions a substratum of foreign words in the Greek language whose origins relate to those of Dravidic Sind, and that the people of Minos, the center of the first Greek civilization, said of themselves that they were not Greek.

Later-arriving Dravidians brought with them some of the Vedic Hindu mythology that had already been incorporated into the myths of those Dravidians who dwelled in the perimeter areas controlled by the Aryans. In this way the myth of Daksha can be found in both Europe and India. This myth concerned the Aryan primal Father God whose daughter Sati wed Shiva against her father's permission. He gave a sacrifice for all the gods of Hinduism, but excluded Shiva. Sati threw herself into the fire to be the offering to her husband so he would not be dishonored. Shiva was naturally enraged, and beheaded the Aryan Father God. Some historians believe that this myth relates to an actual battle wherein the people of Sind defeated the Aryans and retook territory. The myth, however, does not end there. Shiva relented and restored Daksha to life, giving him the head of a goat to replace the one cut off. Daksha then became a devotee of Shiva.

While this myth may relate to a small reconquest by the Dravidians and the eventual blending of the two peoples and their faiths, it also shows that the Dravidians were made to set aside the worship of their Great Goddess, Shakti, in order to retain the veneration of their God, Shiva. Shakti is depicted as willingly stepping aside for the sake of her consort and her followers—throwing herself into her husband's sacrificial offering fire—because Shiva and Shakti are One, and to worship one is to worship the other.

The Vedic deity Daksha is frequently portrayed with a goat's head, and it is from this image that Baphomet, the enthroned goat-headed god of the Knights Templar, was derived. This was an attempt by these knights, who lived in the Near East and absorbed some knowledge of the past, to restore Aryanism during the Middle Ages. Baphomet was their Aryan image of God the Father. This would not be the first nor the last effort to purify Aryanism in Europe. The figure of Baphomet/Daksha has since evolved into the image of Satan, which is ironic since this is the same Aryan deity who became God the Creator in the Old Testament and God the Father in the new Testament. The cosmological injunction that the Devil is God inverted continues to be a theological problem in developing a purely upper level Aryanism. I find it especially interesting to see how at the Council of Toledo in 447 C.E. the appearance of the devil was decided upon, and the image is a merger of the typical Pagan Horned God and the Aryan Daksha.

The use of the horns to indicate evil is a relatively new idea. Moses was described as horned to show his wisdom gained from being in the presence of God, but when horns became associated totally with the devil after a few centuries, later translations of the Bible changed the description to indicate that a light shone from his forehead. There was some criticism of Michelangelo for his

Baphomet, the Aryan image of God the Father, which later evolved into the image of Satan. The horns that once signified wisdom now are considered a symbol of evil.

immortalization of the original version in stone with his monumental statue of Moses, complete with nubby goat horns. In Scandinavia there is a Bronze Age rock carving of a horned head and two hammers—predating belief in Thor—and there it is possible that wearing horned helmets evolved from an earlier custom of wearing the skin of an animal with the horns still attached as a means of gaining that animal's perceived power. Horns have been transferred in art and religion to normally nonhorned creatures, such as snakes, in places as far apart as Greece, China, and Mexico (although there are such things as horned vipers, but with a limited range). The Horned God of Sind is the oldest-known example of such a deity and has been for 30,000 years the god of a historically ancient merchant people who had extensive trade routes by sea.

The Biblical story of a dispute between Moses and Aaron is believed by some historians to represent a feud between two groups of bull and snake worshippers. Moses himself is said to have set up a bronze snake on a pole for the Hebrews to worship, and it is described as remaining in the temple for many generations. Since we know the golden bull was already a Hebrew worship object, insistence on the snake could be interpreted as an acceptance by the Aryan lawgiver of a tradition with a Dravidic influence. This could also be the foundation laid by the Levites writing the Old Testament in 650 B.C.E. to demand reforms.

Since Shiva was by 28,000 B.C.E. being depicted with the large, widespread horns of a bull, and the bull was sacred to him, it is possible that the symbolism spread to Europe during trade exchanges. As late as the tenth century C.E. the minotaur was being used in temple carvings at Khjuraho in India, expressing then the living tradition of Dravidic Shiva.

It is possible that the Green Witchcraft of the northern European peoples actually got its start from early contacts with the Indus people. The matter remains one of speculation until archaeology makes further discoveries, but the similarities are so marked as to be either an indication of contact between Europe and the Sind, or a normal evolution of human beliefs. The real divergence in customs only comes with the development of the ruling and warrior class system some 4,000 years ago, leading to a layering of religious traditions in Europe and a merging of them in the Indus. But the Dravidians also made their way to early Europe as permanent residents, reinvigorating the Green Level Paganism.

The Dravidians, migrating away from the Sind with the early invasions, have been identified by some historians as either related to or influenced by the Bronze Age Etruscans. Heroditus believed the Etruscans came from Lydia (in Anatolia) and arrived in Italy by sea. Mythic comparisons show Etruria populated by waves of migrations. The Etruscans appeared in Italy around 1200 B.C.E., during the Aryan push through Asia Minor into the Near East, and they established Etruria, a confederation of twelve cities. They survived there for seven centuries and were gradually diminished by wars against invaders, until falling under Roman domination in the third century B.C.E., during the Aryan push. The eastern influence was evident in the Etrurian fashions and decorative motifs, Asian in style and subject including lotuses and tigers, until being superceded by the newer Greek modes.

The Etruscans loved to dance and enjoyed life. Music was very important to them; flute players led their hunts. The contemporary writer, Elienus, said that the sounds of the flutes broke into the silence over the hills and in the woods, mesmerizing the animals, who then left their lairs. Indeed, much that has been written about the Etruscans is reminiscent of traditional Faerie legends. The women were equals with the men and participated in business and public life. Husbands and wives with their children are depicted in numerous paintings and sculptures as smiling, with arms linked or holding hands. Such displays of affection were unusual to the Greeks and the Romans who were, as described by Theopompus in the fourth century B.C.E., during the Aryan push, astonished by this and by the casual attitude of the Etruscans toward nudity and sexuality. Public sexual unions were not considered unusual. The women paid great attention to their grooming, engaged in gymnastics with the men while skimpily clad, enjoyed parties and drinking, and did not know or care who fathered their children. And while there may have been some exaggeration by the ancient author, who insisted that couples watched one another making love after banquets, the wall paintings of the Etruscans show a definite love of life and living well.

Like the Dravidians, these people honored the Horned God, depicted and interpreted now as Pan with his pipes, and images of the phallus were everywhere. The Etruscans were builders of fortified cities with sewer networks, drainage canals, and had a vast irrigation system in the Chiana valley. In fact, it was the Etruscans who built the great sewer of Rome. Again, these are characteristics of the Sind civilization. They were skilled with arches and bridges, and they usually decorated their archways with what has variously been called a human face, a Gorgon mask, or a foliate face. With the Roman conquest of the Etruscans, some survivors were assimilated into Roman society, but others fled into the mountains and beyond.

The Romans destroyed most of the Etruscan culture they did not themselves use, taking many symbols and ideas as their own while attempting with some success to blot out memory of the earlier people. The face commonly used by the Etruscans, however, became typical in Roman art and was known as the "Face of Truth." It is an image that is usually seen on walls or fountain plaques throughout Italy today, and there is a round tower shrine to the Face of Truth in Rome, which may be of Etruscan origin. The visage is fearsome, with a gaping mouth encircled by wavy hair and beard so as to look rather like a lion or a sunburst. The face does not actually relate to what is considered classical (Aryanized) mythology, and some historians shrug it off as having an origin lost in the mists of time. The origin is not lost, however, when we pursue the Indus connection and find the face once more in a myth about Shiva.

In the Shivan myth, a demon had created an army and attacked the Vedic gods. When Brahma and Vishnu realized they were about to be overwhelmed, they pleaded with Shiva to help them. The demon, hearing this, promptly mounted his attack against Shiva, but the Dravidic god simply opened his third eye and created a fiery, hungry creature who devoured the entire army. The demon leader saw this and begged Shiva for mercy. Since Shiva never turned away a petitioner, he spared the demon leader, who immediately became a devotee of Shiva. But now the monster prayed to Shiva, saying that since the god had created him hungry, and he had eaten all the demons save one, he must have something more to eat. Shiva told the creature to eat itself, and it faithfully complied, devouring himself from the feet up until all that remained was the maned face with its open mouth. Shiva was so pleased with the creature's devotion that he caused this image to be placed at the entry to all his temples, for the "Hungry Face" is testimony to the truth that all life feeds on life, and by the consumption of other life, life comes from death. Until one accepts this, one cannot know Shiva, and from this concept came both the Mediterranean symbol and its name—the "Face of Truth," or "Face of Glory."

The Etruscan image of the Face of Truth is still a popular figure in sculpture, commonly seen embellishing walls or archways. In the Shivan myth it was known as the Hungry Face.

Fortuna, Goddess of Abundance, is adorned with the horn, the snake, grain, and the Crescent Moon. Her image was a favorite in Roman art and public works.

In the early days of the Aryan expansions, the tribes moved south and east from the regions of northern and central Russia, but also northwest into Northern Europe. In Europe, the effect produced a compatible layering of the existing belief systems. The Pagans of Europe gained a multilevel system that reflected the class of the worshipper. The Chief (or King), priesthood, and Warriors have as their special deities a Father God, a Lawgiver, and a Warrior God, represented by the colors white, blue, and red. These deities had different names in Europe, depending on the location, but already we can see the same pattern as Brahma, Vishnu, and Indra (who was deposed in India by Shiva). The overall population of non-warrior/priesthood/rulers held onto their older deities—the God and the Goddess represented by the color green. Green Witchcraft was the worship of the God and the Goddess as equals/twins, and the practice of magic with herbs and natural substances, and shamanic union with the Universal Energy to effect magic and gain wisdom. When Dravidian refugees began to arrive in Europe, their practices and beliefs found them a place in this broad base of the

Teutonic pyramid of deities and their representative realms. Shiva and Shakti were easily equated with Frey and Freya (which translate as *Lord* and *Lady*). The assimilation of the religion of Sind into that of the European lower classes resulted in the Green level evolving into what is today called Wicca (the *Wise*) or Witchcraft (*Craft of the Wise*).

The people of Sind and their religious practices blended with the European nearly 3,000 years ago, creating a revitalized Wiccan tradition. This emphasis on the foundational level of religion—on the Lady and the Lord of Nature—was tolerated until as late as the fourteenth century C.E., when prosecution and persecution drove this layer of European practices underground until the early twentieth century C.E. It is not difficult to trace many modern Wiccan practices back to their origins in the religion of Shiva and Shakti. The idea of being sky-clad (nude) in the ritual gatherings of some traditions, for example, can be traced back to the worship of Shiva Digambara (*Skyclad,* or *Clothed in Space*).

The Craft has long been associated with fortune telling and with the tarot. The cards and suits of the tarot, from which modern playing cards evolved, are based on the accoutrements of Shakti as Durga—a short trident (wand/clubs), sword (spades/swords), finger drum (cup/hearts), and bowl (dish/pentacle/diamonds). The Major Arcan-um of the tarot was derived from the various aspects of Shiva and Shakti. While there are a number of suppositions as to the origins of the tarot, including a belief in some quarters that the cards came from Egypt, we do know that cards make their first appearance in India. We also know that the Romany Gypsies carried the cards into Northern Italy, and there is a possibility that the Gypsies who traveled across Egypt brought them into Europe through Spain. But what is particularly interesting is the derivation of the word "Gypsy." This name came from "Egyptian," when Europeans were of the mistaken impression that these people were Egyptians. Historians and anthropologists are pretty much agreed now that the Gypsies actually came from—you guessed it, India. They are, in fact, the direct descendants of the Dravidians who emigrated from the Indus, and carried the Old Religion back into medieval Europe with them. For this they were enslaved, murdered, and hunted at every opportunity. The life of the Gypsy was filled with terror and constant movement. They became clannish and isolated from the people among whom they lived—wanderers in the land they could not call home no matter how many generations passed. They were the harborers of the Old Religion, and were disdained as heretics and infidels. Needless to say, there are a number of Wiccans today who proudly trace their Gypsy heritage.

The use of a Craft name in Witchcraft comes from the same practice used by devotees of Shiva. This has been copied by the Roman Catholic Church with a new name being assigned to the devotee during the Confirmation ceremony, thus designating the individual as now eligible receive the sacraments. For the Shivaite, the new name is one that signifies the Supreme Deity, whereas most Catholic names are selected from a list of saints and angels. With the Solitary Witch, the Craft name may be any type and is the name by which the person is known among other practitioners. A Working name is one used in the performance of magic and kept secret. Often the Working name is one chosen by the Witch until such time as a dedication ritual when the deities reveal the Witch's name (see Moura, *Green Witchcraft,* St. Paul: Llewellyn, 1996). For coven settings, as in the case of the Shivaite and the Catholic, the Craft/Confirmation name is stated by the leader (priestess, guru, priest), and the initiate is welcomed into the coven or congregation by that name.

The Pagan concept of the cauldron of life producing the life of the Earth, referred to as the womb of the Goddess, is related to the Yoni of the Dravidic system. The life energy takes form through the cauldron; thus when life is over, the energy, or spirit, returns to the cauldron to be reborn, and there is no end to the bounty of that cauldron. The similarity of beliefs allowed for a merging of cultures into what would become modern Wicca. It is because of this that Wicca is likely to be much more true to the original religion of Sind than what can be distilled from modern Hinduism. The names of the deities may have been altered to reflect European culture, but the identity remains intact. The Triple Goddess is still Shakti, and the Horned God is still Shiva, who is specifically named in India as Shiva Tryambaka—*wed to the Triple Goddess.*

A living religion changes with time and evolves with the civilization it is centered in, and so the deities of Sind have also changed. Just as the Christianity of modern America is not the Christianity of the fourth century C.E. Stylites (people who sat atop high poles in the North African wilderness for decades as a testament of their faith, and who were made saints), the Wicca of today is not the same as that of the Middle Ages. Yet many of the elements remain.

The characteristics of Hecate and the Morrigu can be found in the Dravidian tradition to this day. Without Shiva, Shakti takes on the aspect of Dhumavati—*the crone,* representing the dark forces and black magic, and portrayed as a crow. From the Indus point of view, Shiva without Shakti is energy without expression, so it is only together that they function properly. They need each other for vibrant power, and this duality is implicit in their worship. As the

Hecate, the Triple Goddess of Roman mythology, is the equivalent of Shakti in her three aspects.

goddess of power, it was Shakti who dominated the religion carried to Ireland, and which evolved into that of the Celts. The name Morrigu, or Morrigan, the Celtic Goddess of War, turns up on Sri Lanka as Mururgan, the War God of the Dravidic-descended Tamils. Mururgan is worshipped with frenzied dance, and his weapon is the spear.

The Dravidic Tamils also venerate a war goddess, Korravai, whose name might have evolved in the British Isles to become Cerridwen. The Dravidic ancestors of the Tamils fled to Southern India and on to Sri Lanka, but the Dravidians also fled in the other direction, through Anatolia where they were Lydians, into Northern Italy where they were Etruscans, and across the Mediterranean to Spain where they were the Celtiberi of Galicia in the northwest of the Iberian Peninsula, and to Ireland. In Ireland, the first wave of refugees were the Fir Bolg, but they were themselves conquered by a later wave of the same people, circa 1500 B.C.E., who called themselves the Tuatha de Danu, Sanskrit for *People of the Goddess Danu*. Danu is described in Vedic texts as a Tree Goddess and is an aspect of Devi/Shakti that was popular in Sind between 1600 and 1200 B.C.E. The later arriving Celts formed another wave of the same people, conquering the Tuatha de Danu who had arrived earlier.

The influence of the religion of Sind upon the development of Wicca can be seen most clearly in the Celtic tradition. The Gaelic Celts who settled in the British Isles displaced earlier peoples but were most likely related to them. Some of the early legends of Pagan Ireland can be traced to Shiva. The tale of Cuchulainn and the killing of his son by the Gae Bolg mirrors the legend of the death of Andhaka, who was created when a drop of Parvati's perspiration fell into Shiva's third eye. Andhaka fell in love with his mother, and Shiva impaled his son with his trident—just as Cuchulainn impaled his son on the trident his Faerie father had given him. The Gae Bolg is the emblem of the god of a Dravidic, Tuatha de Danu father made as a gift to his Celtic son. Shiva then burned his son to ash with his third eye in order to purify and restore him. Today the scattered myths of Shiva retained in the Hindu religion refer to one another, so most historians believe that at one time there was a single connected mythology that was subsequently subdivided and repeatedly revised by the Vedics. The blending that occurred in Europe may actually provide a clearer view of the original religion of Sind than the contradictory progression of myths in Hinduism.

The veneration of the Sun and Moon, trees, animals, and snakes is characteristic of the Tamils and the Tuatha de Danu who defeated the Fir Bolg, and these elements are also part of the Celtic religion. All these peoples were related to the Dravidians of Sind, migrating toward Europe in waves over a period of 2,000 years. The color of mourning for Shivaites and Celts alike is saffron yellow, the burial techniques are the same, and red ochre, too, is the color signifying rebirth of life, used to cover the bodies of the dead.

What can be determined from the evidence is that Wicca in Europe developed from the merging of the Pagan Green layer with the religion of Sind. The Triple Goddess motif and the symbolism of the maiden, mother, and crone aspects of the Goddess; the Horned God; the Lord and Lady of Greenwood; the God and Goddess of Sun and Moon are all found in the worship of Shiva and Shakti. The difference between Wicca and Hinduism is that the Vedic influence is absent. Modern Wicca is practicing the worship of Shiva and Shakti merged with that of the Lord and the Lady of European Paganism in a way that is indicative of how the religion of Sind might have evolved if not disrupted by Aryan invasions and the subsequent imposition of Vedic orthodoxy and caste.

The Sacred Serpent inscribed on this Etruscan disk or amulet indicates that snakes were venerated from very early times.

The European tradition of Green Witchcraft continued to grow and evolve according to the surrounding influences. Despite the upper levels of the newer Aryan system, the Sind tradition continued to coexist. From Jutland in the first century B.C.E. comes the Gunderstrup Cauldron, an archaeological treasure and fascinating relic with its depiction of Cernunnos—*The Horned One*—Lord of the Animals. It is nearly an exact replica of the ancient Dravidic seal of Shiva, Lord of the Beasts. There is a flow of religious themes through time from Shiva to Dionysos, the god born in a cave, the sacred bull or ox nearby, his riding upon an ass for festivals, his death and resurrection, all laid out in the seasons in Sind, brought to Europe, renewed with subsequent immigrations, and finally adopted as a literal truth in Christian dogma.

The Vedic religion altered the religion of Sind. In the Near East the Levite influence worked to eliminate traces of the older religion,

The Sacrifice of a bull by Mithras. The themes of Moon Goddess and snakes continued in this Aryanized version of the resurrection myth, which was a strong rival to early Christianity.

but in Europe the evolution was such as to actually prepare the populace to initially accept a dual practice of Christianity and Paganism. The religious heritage of the common people was retained and even infused into the new system through the adoption of the older practices. Thus the Wiccan festival of Ostara, honoring Oestre, the goddess of spring, became the Christian Easter, just as with the earlier Judaism, Purim had been the celebration of Esther, who was actually the same as Oestre, Ishtar, Astarte, Ishtari Devi, Shakti. There may be a relationship between the story of Esther as the Jewish maiden who puts aside fancy clothes to win the love of a Persian king, and the story of Parvati winning Shiva's love by putting aside her finery and living as an ascetic. In the older myth, Parvati saved the Vedic gods from a demon by winning Shiva and bearing his son; in the newer myth, Esther saved the Levite Jews from a plot to destroy them by winning the trust of the Persian king.

The two major holidays of Christianity, Easter (the Spring Equinox) and Christmas (the Winter Solstice—Yule), were Pagan festivals that were incorporated into the new religion to make it more appealing to people. It was only after the Church had gained sufficient power and a large enough army to challenge the secular rulers that the practices of the common people became a heresy punishable by torture and death. The records and documentation is available to anyone who would take the trouble to read them, and the atmosphere was one of intrigues, murders, assassinations, anarchy (more than one pope claiming the title), chaos (yes, both a woman and a horse have been elected as pope), feuds, posionings, and debaucheries too vast to describe here. Yet the powerful position of Church leaders as rulers in both the spiritual and political arenas opened the door to such abuses.

The entire Church structure, from the pomp and ceremony surrounding the pope to the names of the priestly hierarchy and divisions of Church districts, was lifted from the Roman emperor who ruled before Constantine. Diocletian was a highly successful emperor who united the fragmenting empire through the force of his personality and his reorganization of the empire into a series of districts called dioceses, under the governing bodies of people he named ministers. After Diocletian retired to Yugoslavia to live in splendor and raise cabbages, he lost interest in the empire. Constantine arrived on a chaotic scene, and taking the structure created by Diocletian, filled the positions with the only people he could trust to not want to depose or assassinate him—Christians whose new power depended upon his survival.

Constantine could only delay the collapse of the Roman Empire for the duration of his life. In little more than a century, the empire was invaded multiple times, Rome was sacked periodically, and finally, only the Christian bureaucracy was left to take over the government. But this is not some altruistic matter—the empire failed because of the bitter and contentious policies introduced by Christian politicians. Once they were in a position to make and enforce laws under Constantine, the Christian senators passed a series of laws closing the schools, shutting down the oracles, closing the temples, and burning the libraries. They persecuted and killed educators, scholars, philosophers, and their students, and made it illegal to read and write unless the individual was a member of the clergy, and even then the selection was limited. Even the possession of a Bible by ordinary people was for centuries a criminal offense. It is not enough to say that the empire fell to barbarian invaders—the barbarians were Germanic Christians. If you proceed though history, you will see repeatedly the conflict between the German Christians and the Roman Christians, up to the very birth of Protestantism. The Reformation nearly destroyed Europe with bitter warfare, and the prelude to this was the destruction of the Roman Empire. The same themes play over and over, where groups attempted to assert their version of the Aryan heritage of political deities without the gentler influence of the deities of Nature.

The Roman Church held vast tracts of land throughout Europe, held serfs, owned manors, collected taxes, and governed within the realms of its subservient monarchs. The countryside Pagans were tolerated until the seventeenth century C.E., but the beliefs and practices merely went underground, into the privacy of the home, and under cover of darkness. While much has been written about the *Burning Times*, and there is a well-made video on the subject that has been broadcast periodically, there is a difference between the persecution of Pagans, or Witches, and the selective killing of people for their land and money, which is what the Inquisition came to do. Certainly, the pretext of destroying heretics, midwives, and herbalists, was strong, but so was the desire to seize property and wealth from widows and independent women. Slaughters of entire villages were the next level of terror as the frenzy of murders for the acquisition of valuables and territory spiraled out of control.

It took the power of independent civil law—separate from ecclesiastical law—under the firm grip of secular leaders with trained armies, to bring the situation to heel. What we are really looking at is not so much the persecution of a religious group, but a confrontation and battle for power between secular rulers and Church rulers, between civil law and Church law, between man's law and God's law as proscribed by the Church. And pulled back and forth between these forces, suffering the impact of being the spoils of war, are the ordinary people.

So horrific was the toll that the lessons learned were carried over into the New World. In writing the Constitution of the United States of America, the founding fathers determined to never allow the religious bigotry that had destroyed other nations to gain a foothold in their new government, and thus religion and government were mandated to be kept separate. One important safeguard is that in the election of leaders, religion may not be used as a test or requirement for political office—yet we see in modern times that when a religious interest group gains control of a political party with the intention of implementing a religious agenda, the conflict between religion and civil law once more comes into play, and the "test of religion" is essentially and unlawfully applied through campaign statements issued in the mass media.

Two-Five-Seven-Tower-Magician Spell

This is a spell in which conflict is faced and dispelled. If you are at a point where a lot of intense feelings may be generated over how badly things have gone in the past, and you may be wondering if there is any hope for change, or if things will simply keep going like this, repeating the same tragic battles for power, dominance, and control between secular and religious forces, freedom of spirit, and institutionalized orthodoxy.

You will need a black candle and a white candle, five card-size pieces of paper; a fireproof pot or cauldron, and a sprig of rosemary.

On the five pieces of paper, designate these cards: 2 of Swords, 5 of Wands, 7 of Wands, the Tower, and the Magician. You need not attempt to draw them, simply write the names on the papers to indicate the cards.

Representations

Look at the papers as though they are the tarot cards they represent, which are reproduced on page 128 to assist you in visualizing their symbolisms.

The two of swords in the tarot deck is a card that shows tension in the realm of ideas and thoughts between two opposites. There is conflict here, but due to matching strengths, there is no action or solution, only a standoff, truce, or maintenance of the status quo. As soon as the opportunity arises, however, the delicate balance will be lost and the disruption held at bay will be released.

The five of wands shows conflict and struggle in the realm of creative energies. There are obstacles in the way of attaining goals. The seven of wands shows a continuation of the struggle to bring new creative ideas to prevail against the stiff competition and outright hostility of others, yet there is an optimistic sense of the rightness and the power to overcome these obstacles.

The Tower card is one of upheaval where false values fall so enlightenment is attained. It is a card that shows a period of chaos that is quickly passed through to gain mental liberation and spiritual freedom. The Magician card shows new opportunities and the ability to control personal destiny by understanding the interconnection of the individual with the universe. An upsurge of creative energy is indicated in both the Tower and the Magician cards.

Light the black candle, take the 2 of Swords in your hand, and say:

> *Here is the conflict held at bay; the powerful forces holding*
> *on to their hatreds without solution or attempt at true peace,*
> *yet by their pressures, preventing creative new ideas from*
> *bringing a fresh approach to old problems.*

Take the 2 of Swords and light an edge of the paper in the candle flame, then quickly set it in the pot or cauldron to burn:

> *I burn away the stalemate of contentious rivalries; I burn*
> *away the power of fear generated by the tensions herein. Let*
> *Elemental Fire reclaim this energy and let Elemental Air free*
> *the mind. So Mote It Be.*

Hold the 5 of Wands in your hand and say:

> *Here are the obstacles blocking improvements and changes;*
> *the conflicts that work to stifle creative energies and new*
> *ideas.*

Take the 5 of Wands and light the edge of the paper in the candle flame, then quickly set it in the pot to burn:

> *I burn away the obstacles blocking the path of creative*
> *energy; I burn away the conflicts that make gaining this goal*
> *such a struggle. Let Elemental Earth reclaim this energy and*
> *turn it into creative strength. So Mote It Be.*

Light the white candle and take the 7 of Wands in your hand:

> *Here is the test that creative energy must undergo to succeed;*
> *the struggle against the hostility of others who would suppress*

*new ideas; and here is the knowing that change will prevail
and will be for the better.*

Light the paper from the white candle, drop into the pot, and as
it burns say:

*I burn into this spell the power brought out of two and
five. Let Elemental Water draw this power through the
subconscious mind, through the intuitive heart, that the
energy flows for creative ideas and new solutions to old
problems. So Mote It Be!*

2 of Swords   5 of Wands

7 of Wands   The Tower   The Magician

Take the rosemary sprig and wrap it with the Tower and Magician papers:

> *Rosemary, herb of protection and purity, invigorate this spell with your blessing, consecrate these symbols of enlightenment and new abilities that the energies gathered and released are redirected herein.*

Snuff the black candle and light the the rosemary sprig from the white candle, then drop it into the pot:

> *Gather together Fire, Air, Earth, and Water, be united as the force of change. Set free the mind and the spirit, that new ideas find new solutions. Release the grip of restrictions; let enlightenment flow that I may control my own destiny in union with thee. So Mote It Be!*

Put away the black candle, and let the white candle burn behind the pot for an hour. Then snuff the white candle. The contents of the pot should have burned down by now, leaving only ash. Take the contents of the pot and rinse out in flowing water if possible, or scatter on the soil. If there is a stiff breeze blowing, you could also cast the ashes to the wind. Any of these three methods of disposal releases the energies to do their work. The candles may be cleansed for reuse by passing through the running water, then drying and passing them through the incense smoke, and then sprinkling with salt.

Europe in Conflict

By the time the last refugees of Sind were arriving in Europe, their homeland was being devastated by religious warfare between Moslems and Hindus. Although these two religions share a common ancestry, through different Aryan tribes, they fought over interpretation and purity of presentation. The Gypsies, however, held onto the Sind influence that was not accepted by either group. When they arrived in Europe, their predecessors were already well assimilated into the Indo-European society, so that the newcomers were the outsiders. Many of their religious practices, even when mingled with Christianity, relate to those of India. The Gypsy fortuneteller was evocative in the European mind of the Sibyls of Greek and Roman tradition—uncouth, unkempt vagabond women who were compelled by the Sun God to prophecy, whether they wanted to or not. The Gypsies brought with them their tradition of river bathing and river veneration, reinvigorating the appeal of water shrines and holy springs.

While modern Wicca evolved from the merging of the Dravidic religion of Sind and the Green level of European Paganism, there is one more factor that inclined them to Wicca—the element of negative reaction to Christian intolerance. From this comes the popular misconception of all Witches celebrating a Black Mass and performing what were intended to be degrading acts with sacred objects like the consecrated host (presumably stolen from a Catholic Mass) and the crucifix (hung upside down). This is not Witchcraft, but an anti-Christian sentiment expressed by people deliberately displaying their contempt for a publicly endorsed religion. I see such people in the same light as children who in classrooms where the teacher has stepped out, draw an unflattering picture of the teacher on the chalkboard, then sit at their desks safely hidden among their giggling peers. These people needed a release of their tensions and a manner of expressing their hidden anger and despair.

The Black Mass and the Witch's Sabbat are not the same thing, although it has been convenient for mainstream religionists to treat them as though they were. The Sabbat of Witchcraft does not involve denouncing another religion, but is a celebration of human connection with the powers of the Earth and the Universe. Spellwork is generally not part of a Sabbat. The parodies of the Christian Mass, while irreverently burlesque, are also not the same as Satanism. This latter invention actually depends on the Christian religion for a reference point. The object of worship in Satanism is the God's alter-ego, the one who says meekness and fearfulness is not healthy for the mind or the spirit. The accusations of Satanic cults mutilating and torturing people, eating babies, and having sexual orgies have never been proven—although there are numerous Christian cults that have shocked the world with aberrant behavior; Jonestown and the Branch Davidians at Waco are examples of controlling Christian cults that readily come to mind.

Yet Christians are quick to link anti-Christian Satanists with Witches, while failing to recognize the older pre-Christian spirituality of Wicca. The Horned God is not the *Evil One* of Christianity— Wicca does not have an evil god—but he is the powerful and benevolent deity once universally venerated. Even Hell does not exist, save as Hel, the name of the Norse Goddess of the Underworld—a place where *all* go upon death for repose prior to rebirth.

In the fifth century C.E., the Byzantine Emperor Theodosus passed a law that permitted only one kind of Christianity to exist. Naturally wars and purgings of heretics and heretical ideas ensued until the Turks arrived with Islam and ended all debate on the Holy Trinity by saying there was none. There was only one God, named "God." The disputes over what was doctrine and what was heresy raged all over Europe, North Africa, Greece, and the Near East in the early centuries of Christianity. Theologians and religious philosophers argued over the meanings of Scripture passages, words, and even punctuation. One war erupted over dotting an "i"; since the first transcriber had neglected to do so, it could be heresy to so later. Correcting the error was heresy, and Edward Gibbon relates that after a death toll of over 100,000 people, the undotted "i"s won (*The Decline and Fall of the Roman Empire,* Vols. I-II. New York: Henry Holt & Co., 1985).

In the foundational years of Christianity in Rome, the highly popular religion of Cybele and Attis was celebrated with great pomp and pageantry. Attis was the beloved youth wed to the Goddess Cybele, and like the phases of the Moon, his death, three days of darkness, and resurrection was an annual event. There would be a procession through the streets of Rome, with his image transported on a platform carried on the shoulders of the devout. He would be hung on a tree in accordance with the mythology, buried in a tomb, and on the third day, his followers would run through the streets of Rome with lighted tapers shouting, "He is risen!" Sound familiar? This religious activity predates Jesus and Christianity, and was an ongoing faith at the time when Christians were just beginning to be identified as a group in 150 C.E.

There are no written records of the early years, the so-called "lost years," during the emergence of Christianity. John Dominic Crossan, a former Roman Catholic priest, scholar and DePaul University professor (now retired) has written a number of interesting books on the subject, including *The Birth of Christianity: Discovering What Happened in the Years Immediately After the Execution of Jesus* (San Francisco: HarperSan Francisco, 1998). With no letters or scriptures as guidelines, it is easy to see how this new religion, gaining a foothold among non-Jews, could develop from a number of popular, contemporary Pagan sources. By remembering that the religion never evolved from the desire of the general population, but through laws (passed by Christians placed in positions of political power through Constantine) that closed the temples and oracles, forbade the existence of a rival priesthood upon penalty of death, and closed the schools, you have a clearer picture of what actually happened. It took the deliberate destruction of education to prepare western civilization to accept a history reconstructed under Church authority, taught in Church-run institutions, and controlled by Church councils and boards who called dissident teachers, thinkers, scientists, and philosophers heretics—that was the basis for the European movement called *Scholasticism*, when education was reinvented in the thirteenth century under Church control to support the Bible and Church policies.

The confusing mixture of the traditions of Krishna, the practices associated with Cybele and Attis, the Green Witchcraft of European Paganism, and the missionary work of Buddhists and Shivaites in Rome make for a strange concoction called Christian tradition. Centuries later, in 1843 C.E., the Persian prophet Mirza Husayn Ali would see the connections and deify himself and his descendants for pointing it out to his disciples. He created the Baha'i faith out of Babism—*The Gate*—in which all faiths are related together in a pantheistic interpretation that includes abstinence from alcohol, begging, slavery, and polygamy. The curious thing about the term *pantheism* is that Christianity holds this notion as somehow primitive and inferior, yet the Bible speaks of God being in all things, and the Gospels state that God dwells within people. These are the same elements found in the ancient worship of Shiva and Shakti.

Throughout Christian history, there have been attempts at refining and reconstructing the basic tenets of the faith to make the religion more clearly defined. These efforts, replete with warfare, resulted in a plethora of denominations, each of which believed itself to be the only *true* religion of Jesus. The small number of faithful is encouraged by these sects because of the small number of those saved from the last days of Armageddon as indicated in the Book of Revelation.

With the practice of modern Wicca one should expect and welcome changes, otherwise Wicca and Neo-Paganism would be little more than archaic ritual with no real value in the modern world. Sympathetic magic is not needed for fertility in the fields (the Etruscans and others had ritual sexual relations in the freshly plowed furrows of the fields), no slain messengers to the gods are needed, and the same eucharist of the Christian is that of the Wiccan—as representational of the Goddess and the God. The flow of energy is constant throughout history, but the evocation should be naturally updated so as not to limit human growth to an anachronism.

Religion needs to be living and vital. Because persecutions have disrupted Pagan religious thought and coherent practices, we can only approximate how our beliefs have evolved, then select what is appropriate for this age. Thus may religion and ritual help people identify their place in the flow of the cosmic and natural forces around them, to be at peace internally and in harmony externally with one another and their world.

Chapter Five

Trademarks of European Paganism: Faerie and Asatru

Combine the following in a teaball
and place in a warmed teapot:
1 tsp. black tea, ½ tsp. chamomile,
½ tsp. dandelion root, ½ tsp. elder flower,
½ tsp. hops, ½ tsp. mugwort,
½ tsp. raspberry leaf, ½ tsp. rosehips.
Say as you pour the hot water into the teapot:
"Black for power, apple of night, root of the sun,
Lady's blessing, Lord's leap for joy,
then between the worlds,
to Fairy bramble, with token of love,
brewed to bring Fair Ones close to me!"
—Tea to Attract Fairies

*H*aving explored the path of Paganism from the Indus, through the Near East, into Greece, Lydia, Etruria, and Rome, we come to the special blend of attributes that give European Paganism its unique flavor. There are many Wiccan traditions that focus on ancient deities: Diane (or Diana, Artemis), Aradia, Dionysus, Pan, Cernunnos, Frey and Freya, Isis and Osiris, Shiva and Parvati, and triple goddesses such as Hecate, Bridget, and the triad of grain goddess archetypes found in Kore-Persephone-Demeter. But often these are names that have become disassociated in the European mind from their original spiritual focus and rituals. Indeed, there is one Tradition that warns against mixing pantheons, but uses deities from

Greek, Roman, Celtic, and Thracian heritage. I suspect they believe them to all be Roman. Many Witches prefer to simply use "Lady" and "Lord" as the titles for the Goddess and the God in Wicca, as this brings the Divine into close connection with the Seeker without the burden of reviving ancient and incomplete mythologies. Most names are really just qualities given as proper names in a non-English language, and even Frey and Freya, after all, translate simply as "Lord and Lady." So the groundwork is already laid for the Craft use of titles in the place of names.

I have found it fascinating to notice the appeal of foreign language in the practice of the Craft. To learn Gaelic, Greek, Egyptian, Hindi, Sanskrit, Romany and so forth is always a fine goal for expanding your education, but not if you believe this is the only way you can contact the Divine or that this makes your particular tradition or religion somehow superior to that of another. The language you study will not afford you the same depth of understanding as the one in which you are raised, and no matter how proficient you become in the new language, the nuances that come from living with that language all your life will elude you. There is also the possibility of misinterpreting the words, for not all meanings are literal. By all means, study and immerse yourself in other cultures for the sake of knowledge, but do not feel that your own culture lacks a path to the Divine. The people who live (or lived) the culture and language you study use different sounds to say the very same things you say in your own familiar language. Thus, you may call upon the Divine just as well in everyday language, and be confident that you are heard, and that your heritage is viable.

The ancient names of deities can be used to invoke the Divine, but so can the newer names, which is one of the three styles of Witchcraft. Thus, the Lady may be Artemis or Mary, depending on your approach. The Lady as crone may be Hecate, or Saint Anne, mother of Mary. The Lord may be Dionysus, or Jesus. The Lord of the Wildwood may be Cernunnos or Saint Francis, or Saint John the Baptist. The Power is vital and living, not lost in the dust of history, and so the Divine will hear and respond to you by any name bestowed upon them. "Great Mother" and "Great Father," "Lady" and "Lord," remain the same in any time or language. Your own words as you talk to them hold power and connection. I am reminded of the furor that arose when the Catholic Mass went from Latin to English in America. Many people felt there was a magic in the Latin words that was lost in English, yet the meanings were the same. The main difference was that in not understanding Latin, people ascribed greater power to the sounds than to the actual words. Psychologically, this was a last vestige of the mysticism of Roman Paganism. This idea of an older language form having more power than the familiar can be identified in ancient Babylon, where the language of religion was Sumerian, the culture that preceded the Babylonian and which had been a Dravidic colony. Even as a former colony of England, the long-standing traditions found in Europe did not reach into the United States of America, so that many Americans find themselves attempting to not only reclaim a Pagan past, but a European heritage as well.

The Pelasgian Demeter, Mother Goddess of the Grain.

The continuing heritage linking Europe and America takes us more directly to the style of Paganism and Pagan traditions of Europe and their influence on modern Wicca. One of the tenets of Wicca and old European practice is belief in Fairies or Faeries. The spelling differences are used to distinguish the ancient beliefs from the more modern deprecation of Otherworld and the inhabitants and powers thereof. The first word may be derived from the common perception of the Fair Folk being very pale in appearance. The second spelling of the word is more likely derived from the Old English word for "strange," although I have seen it related to the word *fey*. The term "Fey," however, stems from a tradition that sees the Fair Folk as dangerous and ominous to people who are not Wic (Wise). Fey implies unlucky and ill-omened, and is not recommended for use by Witches, for whom the Fairies are close associates. Fairy or Faerie Folk are often used interchangeably to describe the Other People, but I like the older method of distinguishing Fairy as a being and Faerie as their realm (W. Y. Evans-Wentz, *The Fairy Faith in Celtic Countries,* New York: Citadel, 1994, first published in 1911).

If anyone had said Fairies were real in the last century, as did the father of Sir Arthur Conan Doyle, of *Sherlock Holmes* fame, that person would have suffered the same fate—incarceration in an insane asylum. This might explain why Sir Arthur was easily fooled by faked photos of fairies—it would vindicate his father's obsession. Today, there are people in the Neo-Pagan movement who seriously approach the subject of the Fair Folk and offer explanations as to why mention is made of these mysterious persons in nearly every culture in one form or another, but usually as the *Shining Ones*.

Are Fairies a different species, living in a parallel world, connected to this world at the ley lines of magnetic pulses, and able to travel between dimensions? Are they a people so mysterious that the only description that suits them is to say that they are *Other*? Are they the Elementals in a visible form? Are they the remnants of ancient tribes like the Picts, for example? Or are they the diminished form of ancient deities? All these ideas have been discussed in varying degrees of seriousness, but the fact that figures in history—such as William the Conqueror—are said to have married someone of this race suggests that there is a more rational explanation for at least some aspects of the Sidhe (pronounced *Shee* or *Sheeth*, with the *th* very soft).

The Sidhe are the Fairie Folk of Ireland and the source of the term "Banshee," the ghostly figure of a wailing woman, sometimes washing bloody linen, that foretells a death. The nobility of the Sidhe is called the Daoine Sidhe (pronounced DEE-na SHEE), and the whole group has been linked to the Tuatha de Danu (pronounced TOO-a day DAN-nu), which is Sanskrit for "The People of the Goddess Danu." The Tuatha de Danu arrived by sea and took Ireland from the Fir bolgs, only to lose it centuries later (about 1000 B.C.E.) to the Gaelic Celts. These latter victors came by sea from the Near East by way of Spain (Galicia in northwestern Spain, the homeland of much of my mother's family, retains some very Celtic traditions to this day, including bagpipes and Celtic dances) at a time that corresponds to soon after the final Aryan push was being completed in the Indus Valley.

According to legend, the Sidhe put up such a good fight that the Celts were suitably impressed and offered to give the Sidhe kings the right to live under the grassy hills (sidhes) that are abundant in Ireland, or under the sea. Today, these fairy hills are believed to have been burial hills, but excavations are discouraged—just in case they aren't. The Irish have a special feeling for the "Little People," or "Good Neighbors," and do not like anyone, especially outsiders, disturbing them. There is also a great deal of superstition about the Other People, and the general tone is that avoidance is the best course. How much is mythology and how much is history? Perhaps more of the latter than modern people would like to admit.

The art work of the Celts and their customs show not only that there is a link between them and the Dravidians, but also between them and the Etruscans. The deities of the Celts included the Horned God and the Snake Goddess already seen in the Indus, the Near East, and Mediterranean, and among the statues of deities a male figure seated in a yoga position is described simply as an unknown deity. While the Celts settled into eastern and western Europe, having moved from Anatolia across Thracia and Romania and through Iberia and Gaul from 1200 to 700 B.C.E. (directly after the fall of Mohenjo-daro and the Mycenean Empire), their point of origin was beyond the Black Sea. The cult of the skull, so remarkably Celtic, echoes the skull traditions of Shiva as Destroyer, and Durga as Great Goddess—even to making vessels out of the skulls—and may be seen as further evidence of a relation between the Celts and the Dravidic people whose God by this time had been given the characteristics of the Aryan Rudra.

In Celtic lands, a hovering or moving light seen in a marshy place is still called a fairy fire or elf light, and said to be the soul of a dead warrior or a child (a corpse candle). These lights can be explained away as caused by atmospheric conditions and the igniting of gases, such as methane, emanating from decaying plant or animal matter, yet they have been associated with the Fairies for centuries, and not all sightings are so easily dismissed. W. Y. Evans-Wentz chronicles a vast array of encounters in his folklore study. In his writings, based on testimonies and oral accounts, framed within a scope of defining Otherworldly encounters, Faerie is a plausibly real place, where the inhabitants are Fairies or Fairy Folk, identified as a mixture of pre-Christian deities, deceased humans, and a separate race with special powers. Our world view is challenged to be expanded to accept the strange as normal, but humans are self-limited from this greater vision by the need to categorize and explain things to fit known patterns.

By reading through Evans-Wentz's book, you can distinguish the influence of the new religions debasing the elder legends into a

Christian-versus-Pagan motif, with the latter losing, of course. But there are still a sufficient number of experiences of daylight encounters to imply a different race or at least a people with developed abilities not utilized by most modern humans. The people of the Indus referred to the Elementals as Devas, or Shining Ones, and considered these manifestations to be generally neither harmful nor benevolent, but rather lesser deities or good spirits. For the Persians, who formulated the Zoroastrian religion with a distinctly good/evil dichotomy, the Devas were demons—the gods of one religion becoming the demons of the rival religion.

The Dravidian viewpoint having made its way to Ireland and into Celtic beliefs gives an indication as to the origins of the Sidhe, and the influences acting upon the early Gaels. The people of ancient times were far more mobile than most people realize today. They sailed and traveled in caravans to the far reaches of the world. The fact that burial traditions, such as the use of red ochre to cover the deceased, associated with indigenous Paleolithic European people can be found in pre-historic America is evidence to the interaction between the two places. The populations were not stagnant across the European and Asian continent: there was a movement of Aryans downward from northern Russia and the Ukraine into India, and a movement of Dravidians across Anatolia into eastern Europe, and into western Europe as they fled the Indus.

At the time of the Roman Emperors there was significant commerce between India and the Empire. People went to India for knowledge, and there were missionaries from India in Rome and the great cities of Rome's empire across North Africa and the Near East. In early Christian times, the Hindus in the Empire were initially scorned (Tertullian, near the end of the second century C.E., compared Christians as more industrious than the Hindus of Rome), and later praised (by Prosper of Aquitania several centuries later) as good examples of spirituality for Christians to emulate.

The Sidhe were described during early Christian times as the so-called fallen angels—too good for Hell, but not good enough for

Heaven because they did not choose sides in the war between God and Lucifer (the Prince of Light, from Roman times—the Morning Star; an androgyne Venus). The Sidhe were said to have been sent down to Earth before the creation of humans to be the first gods of the Earth. An intriguing message is hidden in this definition (recounted by Lady Wilde in her book, *Ancient Legends of Ireland*, n.p., n.d.) for it states clearly that these are the first gods of the Earth. And that is precisely who Shiva and Shakti are. What has happened in the case of the Fair Folk is that the followers of Danu and Her Consort—the Tree Goddess and the Earth God of Sind— have become intermingled with their deities. The Dravidians arrived in Ireland during the final stages of Aryan invasions in the Indus Valley, around 1200 B.C.E., displacing those who came before them. Today, the Sidhe provide a beacon to the true origins of religion and may be honored for giving mute testimony through legend, myth, and history to the travels of the people of Sind in the Western world. They dwell still among us, and any who practice the Craft may claim a spiritual kinship with them.

The very word "Sidhe" and the idea of such people being *of light* relates these people to Shiva. The word comes from the Sanskrit *siddha*, meaning "charged with energy." One becomes siddha by using words of power (mantras) of the God and the Goddess. In India, the word is used to describe the saints—people who are particularly adept in yoga, and have highly developed psychic powers and abilities such as clairvoyance and divination, as well as a sense of soul-knowledge or self-knowledge. In the case of the Tuatha de Danu, the power of the Goddess was naturally emphasized as the source of inspiration from her traditional aspect of instructor of occult knowledge. With Green Witchcraft, there is the understanding that by living this life in balance with Nature, we are connected to the whole of the life energy. Our Self is united with Mannuz— the Divine Self—and this brings us into union with the Divine. The Tuatha de Danu, Dravidians worshipping the aspect of Shakti as Danu, associated with snakes and trees, and becoming siddha during the recitation of mantras in religious worship, are one source for the Fairy People.

When the Celts arrived and defeated the Tuatha de Danu, they continued a sort of respectful deference to them. The worship customs of India can be found in the Celtic. The offering of flowers, grain, and honey to the Goddess and the God at hilltop sanctuaries is seen in both traditions. Shiva is worshipped with milk and flowers, and this custom may be related to the Celtic tradition of leaving milk for the Fair Folk. People let the elves know they were welcome visitors by growing rosemary by their doors, and the scent of lavender was known to attract the blessings of the Other People. The color green has long been associated with Faerie and was once a clue in Medieval stories as to the true nature of a character in song or story. Only people who were in kinship or affinity with elves wore green clothing. For the ordinary person, however, green was considered an unlucky color. There were strict rules in the making of green dyes in much of the Celtic world, and men were usually forbidden to take part in the process. The color itself is the descriptive used in the Teutonic system for the religion of the Witches, and for the level of practice that relates to the God and Goddess of Nature and the Elementals.

Saint Patrick escaped captivity from the Celts, then returned to Ireland to convert his former captors. The legend that he drove out the snakes was not a matter of sending away the reptiles of the land, but of forcing the Sidhe to leave, taking their religion of trees and snakes with them, or going "underground." Most Witches today can nod and say, "Been there, done that." The legends of early Christian Ireland tell us that the missionary of Christianity was greeted by the Sidhe, who offered him a ceremonial cup of drink for friendship so they would live in peaceful coexistence with the newcomer and his religion. The response of Saint Patrick was one of insolence and rudeness in which he cast aside the cup and stated that there could be no such agreement—that they would have to convert or suffer the consequences. The Sidhe King said that rather than do that, he would take all his people across the sea, and his curse would be upon the land he left so that it would always be a place of fighting and suffering until such time as Christian people learned courtesy toward his people. It is said that many of the Fairy Folk then sailed west, "over sea," to a new world, while others moved to Scotland and the Scottish Isles. Interestingly enough, the Pagans of Scotland held to their traditional ways longer than others of the British Isles, and today, Picta Wica is the modern tradition derived from Scottish Paganism. In North America, the development of Native American tales about a "fairie people" could relate then to similar tales that appeared in Europe.

The Fair Folk are also called the Other People, and this can be traced back to a name given to Shiva. He is called *Another* and *Other*; the Personal God; and his devotees are identified as his people. As so often happens, the worshippers become identified with what is worshipped. He is not affected by time or eternity, nor by the creative process in which he is involved. In one of the early Vedic writings of the Aryans, Shiva was depicted as the Divine Archer, reminiscent now of Herne the Hunter and the medieval depictions of Death as an archer. Shiva was said to shoot his arrows indiscriminately at people, causing them to suffer death or diseases, and this matches up with the "elf shot" of the Fairy Folk. Even the name, "elf" comes from the Mesopotamian root *El*, which is God. The white bull is Shiva's mount, and remained a sacred animal throughout the early civilizations of the Near East and the Mediterranean. The bull also retained a place in Celtic mythology as the form taken by two feuding deities whose heritage is Tuatha de Danu. This particular story is part of the legend of Cuchulainn and the war caused over the dun (pale) bull.

Then, too, remember that the very name of the *People of Danu* is Sanskrit. Danu is the Goddess of the Fairie Folk, and is in the Dravidic tradition both a Goddess of Plenty and a devourer of humans—the Parvati and Kali aspects of Shakti. Bridgit, Goddess of Knowledge, is an aspect of Danu, and is still venerated today as a "humanized" Catholic saint. In Sweden and Norway, the name of the sacred sites, *nysa*, is also the name of the Fairy Folk, the Elves or Nyssa. And Mount Nysa, of course, was where the Greek version of Shiva—Dionysus—created the festivals of the Bacchantes. The source for these names is the Indian word *Nisah*, which means "Supreme" and is an appellation of Shiva.

The traditional aversion of the Fairie Folk to iron, the metal first possessed by the Aryan tribes, would be natural for a Bronze Age people pushed from their homeland by the superior weaponry of their enemies. The magic of the Fairie Folk, illusion sometimes called *glamour*, is a characteristic found frequently in the Shiva mythology. He enjoys tricking the proud and the arrogant by appearing first as they want to see him, only to later show them that while he is the Supreme Deity, he is not lavish in dress nor opulent in taste. Only Parvati sees him as he is when others are deluded, and only the faithful recognize that his divinity surpasses the laws and regulations of the Vedas. Already one can see the direction this investigation is heading, and as the evidence piles up, the picture that emerges completes the circle.

The religion of the Sidhe is related to the religion of the Celts and other European Pagans by virtue of their having the same heritage of Sind. The Indo-Europeans are the stock of modern western cultures because the people of the Indus traveled and took their beliefs with them. Over the millennium, the ideas of Sind appeared in the Near East and Europe, developing along similar lines in these different locations, then evolved according to the needs of the people in the different regions. These beliefs came back to the source in Sind as a new form, Aryanism, only to return to the European region first as a revival of Green Wicca and then as a mixture of Aryanism and Sind in Christianity.

The Goddess of the Pagans has been embraced in Europe as Mary, Mother of God; her holy sites and sacred wells are cathedrals and places dedicated to various saints, such as Lucia and Bridgit. In many ways, the Goddess has been fully embraced by the Catholics and other religions closely related to them, such as the Anglican and Episcopal, but rejected by the later-developing fundamental Protestant versions of Christianity such as the Puritans, Methodists, and Baptists. Her major role in these latter religions is as a symbol of meekness and humility, a necessary vessel for the birth of the savior. Among the former religions, her holy springs, wells, blessed shrubs, and healing waters are still held in reverence, while her ancient shrines and temples now support churches, cathedrals, and house various religious orders. Yet for the Witch, she is the Lady of the Moon and the teacher of the spiritual mysteries.

The Horned God of European Pagans and the modern Witch descends from Shiva as Lord of Beasts—the protector of the wild animals and forests. His holy places are in nature; caves, springs, mountains, and quiet, lonely places. In modern usage, He is Herne the Hunter, Cernunnos, the Lord of Shadows, the Fairie King, Oberon. As Lord of Animals, Shiva reminds people to accept their animal nature and be brethren to the creatures of the wild. In doing so, his followers become his flock, and Shiva retains in Hinduism the title of the Good Shepherd.

The practice of Green Witchcraft varies with the practitioner. It tends to be utilized most often by the Solitary Witch, but includes the use of herbs in spells, Shamanic union with the Power, meditation, visualization, and even a variety of Tantric sexuality. This is not to say that all Green Witches utilize all these elements. Rather, they tend to favor one or more of these approaches. There are many Wiccans who practice *Natural Wicca*, relying on their intuitive, psychic connection with Nature and the Divine to guide them in their practice, and who do not even consider themselves to be Green Witches, yet they use many of the Green techniques. While the term is not seen as often, the components of Green Witchcraft are used frequently by those called *Traditional, Hereditary,* or *Family Heritage* Witches.

Otherworld Tarot Spell

The tarot cards that come to mind when thinking about the relationship between humans and the Sidhe are the Empress and the Emperor. These cards represent the Lady and the Lord of Nature, with abundance and creative power. They encourage self-expression and attainment, but with the awareness of responsibility, and as deities of Nature, they afford you passage between the worlds. The Fair Folk revere Nature and where they dwell, the land is fertile, lush, and attractive to wildlife. They enjoy the company of people of like mind, and if you want to attract elves to be near you, here is a spell for making contact and creating a gateway to Otherworld within a fairy crystal—a multi-colored flourite of green, gray, and purple.

This spell is best done on a Wednesday, a day that enhances divination, communication, and self-improvement. The herb of this day is lavender, which is conducive to connecting with the Other People. Mercury is the planetary sign for Wednesday, and again, this emphasizes communication skills. The colors of the day are yellow, violet, or gray, and since we are doing a spell with an Otherworld (Faerie) focus, I prefer to use gray. The timing should be the third hour after sunset—again, the emphasis is on Mercury/communication, but you can alter this to suit your needs and personal perception. You might want to select one of the hours of the moon, for example, which on a Wednesday fall on the second and ninth hours after sunrise, and the fourth and eleventh hours after sunset. Choose a Wednesday in a waxing or full Moon.

Have ready for your spellwork: the cards of the Empress and Emperor, a designator card signifying yourself, lavender or jasmine incense, a light gray candle (votive is fine), your wand and athame, a cauldron or fireproof container for the candle, a flourite crystal, mugwort tea cooled and in a bowl to use as a wash for the crystal, dandelion or burdock root, rosemary, a bowl of flower petals (lavender, rose, lilac, heather, or wildflower), a bowl of milk, a biscuit with honey or a sweet muffin, and a cup of tea. You might want to make a pot of Fairy Tea as described at the start of this chapter, or use Earl Grey (which is flavored with bergamot, an herb for success). Light gray or light purple candles are a good choice for your altar or spellwork area. Have a libation bowl on the altar as well for Cakes and Wine.

When you cast your Circle, use the bowl of mugwort tea in place of water, and use the burdock or dandelion root (ground or diced) in place of salt. Call upon the Elementals to aid you in your work, invoke the Divine, conduct the following spell, then use cakes and the Fairy Tea (or other beverage such as the wine or juice) as part of the process, give your farewells, and open the Circle as described in chapter one. Use the tarot cards to designate the Lady and the Lord, with the Empress at the left and the Emperor at the right, and use your designator card at the center. Set the votive candle in front of your card. You will have already lit the incense and altar candies during the casting of the Circle and invocations.

Take your wand in both hands and raise it over your head:

> *Hail to the Elementals at the Four Quarters! Welcome Lady and Lord to this Me! I stand between the worlds with love and power all around! I call upon my Lady and my Lord as Empress and Emperor of all of Nature in every land to bless my communion with the Other People. I affirm my Joy of union with the Divine in all realms and worlds, and I acknowledge your blessings upon me. What I send returns to me, and I conduct my Craft accordingly.*

Set down the wand and pick up the knife. Hold it over your cup of tea.

> *Great Lady, bless this creature of Water and Earth to your service. May I always remember the cauldron waters of rebirth and the many forms of being. Of Water and Earth am I.*

Set down the knife and hold up the cup of tea:

I honor you, Great Lady!

Return the cup to the table (or altar top) and now hold the wand over the incense:

Great Lord, bless this creature of Fire and Air to your service. May I always remember the sacred fire that dances within all life and hear the voices of the Divine. Of Fire and Air am I.

Set down the wand and hold up the incense:

I honor you, Great Lord!

Set down the incense and hold up the bowl of flower petals in one hand, and the bowl of milk in the other:

I call upon thee and greet thee, People of the Undying Lands of Otherworld! Hear my call and let the gateway be opened between our worlds. In the names of the Lady and the Lord, Empress and Emperor of Nature, do I call upon the Fair Ones in peace and love.

Set down the bowls on either side of the votive candle. Light the votive candle and hold it up in its container:

As this light shines before me, let the light of Otherworld reach into this place.

Set the candle down and add rosemary to the candle:

Let the power of rosemary attract to me the Folk I seek in company.

Take the flourite crystal and rinse it in the mugwort water:

Let the power of mugwort cleanse this crystal, purifying it to be a gateway between the worlds.

Set the crystal on the altar by the votive candle and raise your ritual knife in both hands:

> *I call upon the power of the Elementals and the Divine to*
> *this place which is not a place, in this time which is not*
> *a time, as I stand between the worlds at the gateway to*
> *Otherworld within the temple of my Circle, to empower*
> *this crystal of earth and light, focused as a gateway.*

Feel the power of the Lady and the Lord course into the blade, then lower the knife to touch the crystal with the tip of the blade. See the energy run through the knife into the crystal. Set down the knife and hold the crystal up to your forehead. Concentrate on the purpose to which this crystal is dedicated and feel the energy enter into the crystal to unite with the matrix so the stone recognizes your energy:

> *With me and through me do you work to allow passage*
> *between the worlds for Fair Ones of like mind, for we are*
> *connected one to the other through the Elementals and*
> *the Lady and the Lord of Nature, that we are kith and kin.*
> *So Mote It Be!*

The Empress　　　　　　Your Designator　　　　The Emperor

Now lay the crystal on the altar on top of your designator card, and touch it with the tip of the athame:

> *In the names of the Empress and the Emperor of Nature*
> *do I consecrate this crystal to be used in my practice of the*
> *Craft for passage between the worlds for Fair Ones of like*
> *mind. I charge this be so and empower this crystal through*
> *Elemental Earth and Elemental water . . .*

Sprinkle the crystal with the water and pass it through the candle flame of the votive, then through the smoke of the incense:

> *. . . and through Elemental Fire and Elemental Air. By the*
> *power of the Elementals is this crystal focused to aid me in*
> *my work. So Mote It Be!*

Hold the crystal up in your right hand, place your left against your heart:

> *I work with the powers of the Goddess and the God with*
> *perfect love and perfect trust. By your power, Great Lady*
> *and Great Lord is this crystal charged, imbued, and*
> *dedicated to my Craft.*

Envision the light energy coming from your heart, passing into the left palm, traveling through the left arm, across the shoulders, into the right arm and into the right hand to fill the upraised crystal. Set the crystal on your designator card, then kneel to touch both your palms to the ground:

> *As what is sent returns, so I return to my Lady and my Lord*
> *the power so graciously sent to me. My crystal is sanctified*
> *through thy power and grace, attuned to me by passage*
> *through my flesh and my blood, and is ready for my use. So*
> *Mote It Be!*

Stand and hold the crystal up to the votive flame:

> *With milk and flowers, with rosemary and lavender (or*
> *jasmine if using jasmine incense) do I call upon and invite*

the Fair Ones to be close to me that we may live in peace
and joy together. Here is the gateway through which you
may pass to visit and counsel me, that there may be commu-
nion between us. So Mote It Be.

Now gaze into the crystal, looking for the forms of your visitors
and the site of the portal between the worlds. Seeing this, now
wrap the crystal in a soft dark cloth or keep it in a special pouch.
This is your passport and connection with Otherworld and the Fair
Ones. If you did not see a portal or visitors, don't worry about it.
The crystal is attuned to your mind and will reveal itself when you
are ready. In the meantime, it is an active channel.

Set the crystal near the votive. Snuff the votive candle:

The energies borrowed are returned, yet remain as part of
the continuing cycle of life essence. The path between the
worlds is closed, yet remains open to my heart and to my
Craft as I have need.

The Simple Feast

Here is a simple Cakes and Wine ceremony or, in this case, a biscuit
and tea ceremony, that helps wrap up the spellwork and ritual:

Raise your arms to the Divine:

I acknowledge my needs and offer my appreciation to that
which sustains me. May I ever remember the blessings of my
Lady and my Lord.

Hold the teacup in your left hand and with the right, lower the
athame into the cup:

As the Lord and the Lady unite for the benefit of the universe
and the Earth, may their union promote the promise of life
that the Earth be fruitful and her wealth spread throughout
all lands.

Set the knife on the altar and pour a little tea into the libation bowl—this is the offering of the first draught to the Divine. Then touch the biscuit with the tip of the knife:

> *This food is the blessing of the Lady and the Lord, given*
> *freely and freely received. May I also give as is needed of me.*

Drop a portion of the biscuit into the libation bowl, then eat the rest and drink the tea. This gives you the opportunity to refresh yourself and ground your energies. When you are finished, proceed with opening the Circle as shown in chapter one. After you conclude the ritual and clean up the altar, take the milk and flower petals outside and set them in a place where you want to honor the Other People. I have a piece of natural driftwood with a branch that arcs on one side like the antlers of a deer, and I use the flat center portion to hold a bowl for offerings. You may want to make a decorative place in a garden or beneath a tree or shrub for your Otherworld shrine.

Teutonic Connections

The relationship between Wicca and the Teutonic system is another hallmark of European Paganism in one form or another. There has sometimes been a misconception about the Northern Teutonic (Asatru) Tradition. Margot Adler's 1986 revision of her 1979 book, *Drawing Down the Moon*, places it apart from other Pagan roots, yet links together Wicca, Druidism, and ceremonial magic. There have been charges of Nazi ties to the the Odinist version of Paganism, not all of which are unfounded, but this tends to draw attention away from the importance of this system in rediscovering our Pagan heritage. Adler falls into the pattern of dwelling in the main upon racial, ancestral, and conservative elements of the Teutonic religion in relation to how it functions on the level of a practiced faith. But more intriguing is the Teutonic connection with Wicca.

The roots of Teutonic Paganism are firmly entangled with those of Wicca, and the unraveling leads to a likely explanation of how that system developed. It is possible to determine where it turned from the earlier form of religious beliefs that had demonstrated either a greater equality between the sexes with a God and Goddess as Lord and Lady, or a matriarchal tendency with a Great Goddess and Her Consort. Nevertheless, in order to understand the progression from these beliefs to a dominant Father God and resulting societal class distinctions, it is necessary to consider the current format of Teutonic Paganism.

The Teutonic magical system has been influential in Europe since the seventeenth century C.E., and when one looks at the Tree of Yggdrasill pattern, the comparison to the earlier Jewish Kabbalah is readily apparent. Although there are nine rather than ten segments to the Tree, and the names vary, one system shows the influence of the other. Teutonic magic is not ceremonial magic however; the timing and the historical interest in ceremonialism by German practitioners tends to blur the distinctions to some degree in modern application. During the long history of Teutonic Magic, it was also applied to the Hermetic and Rosicrucian practices.

In the early centuries of the current era, Northern magic practices in general were spread throughout Western Europe by the Teutonic tribes of Vandals, Goths, Lombards, and Visigoths, so that even the Mediterranean areas of Spain, Portugal, and Italy were affected, particularly after the Roman Empire had collapsed about 476 C.E. One must remember that the Northern Tradition is itself composed of four branches—Gothic, Scandinavian, Anglo-Saxon, and German. There are various kinds of Teutonic magic and practitioners, the main two being *galster* (which is Runic) and *seidhr* (which is basicly traditional Witchcraft), but both are called *vitki* (wise one), from which, some people contend, comes the Anglo-Saxon term "Wicca" or "Witch." This is a matter of debate since it can also mean "to bend or twist," as with sorcery, or "viable and alive," as with plant life. The Teutons are usually solitary practitioners, and this in itself adds to the validity of the lone practitioner of the Craft, as has occasionally been questioned by covens following traditions of initiations and degrees.

In Teutonic mythology, the World Tree, called Yggdrasill, consists of nine worlds, realms, or homes, only two of which need be discussed here—those forming the two homes of the Northern deities. There is the realm called Asgard, which is the home of the Aesir, in particular Odin (Woden), who rules the gods and goddesses of all the realms, and the realm called Wane-Home, home of the Vanir, in particular Freya and Frey. In between these two structures of the deities lie the Warrior Class—under the direction of Thor, known for his hammer and called the Thunderer. The Goddess Freya and Odin may travel to each other's realms, and each is renowned for magical skill. The Aesir Gods, Odin and Tyr, represent Runic magic and law respectively, and are associated with the colors blue and white accordingly. Thor represents strength and is associated with the color Red (as is Mars). Frey and Freya are twins who represent reproduction, fertility, Nature, wealth, love, and peace, and are associated with the color green.

Green Witchcraft, then, represents the primal force of the Northern religion with its emphasis on the Lord and the Lady (Frey and Freya translated) and the use of herbs and oils in magical spells, potions, and ointments. This comprises the third, or base, level of the three-tiered pantheon of the Asatru in both symbolism and reality, for it is the foundational structure for what has come to be known as the Northern Tradition. Even the mythology makes it clear that it is the Lady who teaches *natural magic* to Odin, while the Runic magic of Odin, obtained through self-sacrifice on the World-Tree, is shared with Freya: a kind of early melding of Wiccan and Ceremonial styles of magical practice. In the Tantric form of Vedic Hinduism, it is also the Goddess who teaches the gestures, symbolic markings, and lore that does not exist in the purely Vedic practice. The Green Wicca of today is more like the Anglo-Saxon version of the base level of the Northern Tradition, the *Hedge Witch* (an itinerant Witch who practices along the roadways next to the hedgerows) of Great Britain as it were, with the deities derived from the Celtic, Gaelic, Pictish, and Anglo-Saxon heritage.

The interconnectedness of religions is never so clear as when one considers the context of the Aryan religion merged with the first religion of humankind—that of the Goddess and the God. This took place in Northern Europe as a result of the natural evolution of human society, and in the Near East as the result of conquest, but the religion of the Indus was not erasable simply because it was the same as the old religion of the pre-Aryan northern Pagans. To find out where the connections occurred, we only have to look at the rise of the Aryan social structure and its effect on the religious practices of the northern people. This is where it becomes obvious that the people of the South were not all that different from the people of the North—the Sun people, the Ice people—the Fire and Ice of the Teutonic tradition seen not as metaphor of the interaction of the cosmic forces that brings the universe into being, but as descriptive of the two sides of the same religion.

The main Teutonic deities may be categorized as Aesir and Vanir. The Aesir represent the deities of social consciousness, law, and social order. This is the home realm of Odin (Woden), who is chief among the gods and goddesses of the Teutonic pantheon. His wife Frigga is a hearth deity concerned with things related to domesticity and the home—a woman's deity in a male dominant hierarchy. But this is not the total picture. The Vanir are powerful deities, with the chief among them being the twins, Frey and Freya—the God and the Goddess of prehistoric and pre-Aryan times—and of the two, it is the Lady whose power allows her to travel to Aesir at will.

It is the Goddess who controls the cycles of Nature and has the power of magic, called *seidh*, or *seith*, which shows the same relationship to the Dravidians as we saw with the Fairies and Shining Ones. Freya uses natural substances in the practice of magic, including sexual activity, as is done in the Eastern Tantric practice. Here then, in the Vanir, is where East meets West, where Fire and Ice created the religious basis for both worlds in pre-Aryan times. But now there must be one more realm added to the hierarchy, and that is represented in Thor—the Thunderer—who is the god of the warrior Class. In Hinduism, he may be recognized as Indra, the great warrior of the Vedic rulers.

At the earliest stage of development, the Northern tradition was the same as the Southern tradition, but something happened to change that. In the South—in the Indus of 30,000 B.C.E.—a communal civilization arose, with no temples, no organized clergy, and no central authority. The practice of religion was a solitary tradition, with the community gathering for celebrations of fertility, solstices, equinoxes, moon phases, and agricultural stages. The Northern Tradition also began in this same manner, but the Northern climate and the land did not lend itself to the communal lifestyle of the Indus, and as society developed, villages grew with an expanding population. Leaders arose among the communities to guide and direct the life of the people.

These chiefs needed to have others to aid in the protection of the community and to ensure their own rulership, and thus a warrior class developed to serve the rulers. The common people worshipped the God and the Goddess and knew the rituals and the magics of Nature—they were Green Witches—and if the rulers kept to the same egalitarian deities, there would be nothing to sanctify their authority or set them apart from those they ruled. This could lead to

Shiva, the Destroyer. The circle of flame identifies Shiva as the Shining One, perhaps the origin of the halos seen later in Christian art.

challenges of authority and prevent a ruler from unifying his forces. With the advent of superior weaponry and battle skills came the birth of the Aryan conqueror. Frey, as a fertility deity, was considered too gentle a God for a tribal chief in a time when authority and strength of arms meant survival. Freya, another fertility and magic deity, was not seen as representative of fighting prowess. In time, Frey would become the archetype for the gentle aspect of the Jesus of neighborly love, and Freya for the Mother of God, with both being submissive to the all-powerful, domineering Father God.

Initially, the chiefs were nothing like the kings of Christian European history. Their warriors were farmers and herders of cattle who carried weapons for their chief when defense of the community was needed, or when expansion of territory was required. Durant states that the very word for war in the Aryan language simply translates into a desire for more cattle. Able-bodied women were often part of the warrior class until marriage, then they were restricted by the duties of hearth and family. It would be centuries before this system would be altered into a divine right of kings to govern with a warrior class who ruled serfs tied to the land they farmed for their overlord. Yet it was from the need for legitimacy in rulership that the need for a new god came—Odin, the god of social order; the god of a new magic called Runes, practiced by a select group—a nobility of rulers and warriors.

The warriors who defended the community also needed a deity to bless them and set them apart from the farmers who were the Green Witches of the Vanir, and they received Thor, the Warrior God. It was in the religious practices that the change from equality between the sexes, and possibly a matriarchal power structure, shifted into male dominance, involving a male clergy, usually derived from the relatives of the warriors, who alone knew and transmitted the specialized rites of sacrifice to the deities associated with that particular class of people who now governed society.

It must have been a shock for the migrating Aryan conquerors to run into the expression and practice of Vanir religion again and again as they moved southward during their expansions, for this extolling of the way of the wise by southern peoples was equally a glorification of the individualistic farmer/defender and a threat to the new gods and powers of the ruler/warrior classes. The one crucial difference between the fighting skill of the Aryans and that of the Indus people was in the forging of superior weapons, first of hardened bronze, then of iron. The Aryans had learned to use horse-drawn chariots in a way that gave the warrior strength, speed, and agility unmatched by the southern peoples.

Iron was itself a secret kept by the Aryans for several centuries and the primary source of their power. Durant shows that the Hittite Aryans used iron and their chariots to conquer the land between the Tigris and Euphrates Rivers, circa 1925–1800 B.C.E., and it was not until four centuries later that their contemporaries gained the knowledge of ironworking, a family tradition passed down from father to son for generations. Soon after that, the Hittites disappeared from history. It is no coincidence that the Fairies have a natural aversion to iron, for it was iron that destroyed their idyllic world.

The notion of civilization coming from the Aryans is a myth that still affects modern research. The Dravidic language is related to the Finnish, Hungarian, Turkish, Mongolian, and Eskimo languages, which is further evidence of the widespread nature of Dravidic contacts. It is their view that the Dravidians spread their culture to these areas long before the Aryan invasions—during the Paleolithic Age prior to 20,000 B.C.E. when the first cave paintings were appearing in Europe. But aside from language and cultural similarities, no hard archaeological evidence has yet been uncovered to make the connection a stated historical fact. At the present, this is still theory, but theory that has wide acceptability.

The survivors of the Indus invasions, beginning around 2150 B.C.E. and continuing in stages until the destruction of Mohenjo-daro in 1200 B.C.E., moved across the lands now known as Afghanistan, Iran, Iraq, Arabia, Palestine, Turkey, and through eastern Europe into western Europe. Their migrations are known to have gone as far as Indonesia, and, as previously considered, possibly into Japan, Polynesia, and as far as the Americas. They knew about boats, were active traders, and so they migrated away from the Aryan invaders and took their religion with them. For those moving into Europe, their religion was easily merged with that of the local population, where the veneration of the God and the Goddess, the celebration of the cycles of nature and fertility, and solitary practice were already local Pagan features.

Along with their language the people of Sind were assimilated in Europe. Continuing waves of invasions in the Indus Valley resulted in waves of migrations, so that in time, the Dravidians were battling Indo-Europeans—a people of their own heritage—for possession of places like Ireland, winning for a time, and then being displaced by later waves. This is the history of the Fir Bolgs, the Tuatha de Danu, and the Celts in Ireland, Wales, and Scotland. These are the Picts and these are the Fairy Folk. All represent the varying degrees of integration between the indigenous European population and the successive migrations of Dravidians.

Even in looking to Crete for vestiges of early European heritage, historians see a Dravidic influence, agreeing that the people of Crete were most likely Dravidians. They note that the Cretan family name "Pandion," which is connected with the Sun and the Moon in festivals, relates to a tribe in Attica (the region of Athens) named Pandionis, and they are connected to the Dravidian dynasty Pandia. This last people are recorded in the Indian epic poem, *Shilappadikaram,* as fighting against the Vedic Aryan in the Mahabharata War circa 1400 B.C.E. The Dravidic Pandia tribal myth alleges that they descend from the Moon, and the name Pandu, whose sons fought the Vedic invaders, translates as "White."

Moving further westward were the Celts, whose origins are accepted by many experts as coming from the Indus Valley people. They traveled from the Iberian Peninsula northward, and by the seventh century B.C.E. their ithyphallic deity could be found carved in rock in Sweden and represented in wood in Denmark.

This new influx of Indus people served to renew the Green traditions and preserve the Old Religion operating parallel to the Aryan system in a subordinate position, which later resurfaced as Teutonic Paganism.

The original primacy of the Old Religion, Witchcraft, over that of the patriarchal system of Odin and Thor is still evident in the mythology of the Northern Tradition. Freya, like Hecate, is the Goddess of eroticism, natural magic, and controller of the cycles of nature, and it is she who teaches Odin her magic, to which is added his Runic magic. Yet she also knows this magic, and Runes are

Shiva Mahayogi, the Great Teacher.

commonly used by Witches today. The consort of Freya is her twin brother Frey—from these two come the Sun God and Moon Goddess. This structure is similar to many other Pagan pantheons, such as the twins Apollo and Diana, for example. This was easily accepted by Dravidian immigrants as manifestations of the united (twinned) Shiva/Shakti—the Horned God (since the God of the Northern tradition also represented eroticism, well-being, and Nature) and the Goddess of Power.

The roots of the Wiccan and Pagan interchangeability of the aspects of the God and the Goddess come from the integration of the traditions of Europe and Sind in the Androgyne aspect of the Divine. Earth God, Earth Goddess; Sky God, Sky Goddess; Sea God, Sea Goddess; Lord of Beasts, Lady of Beasts; God of Fertility, Goddess of Fertility—these are all cross-identifications of Europe and Sind occurring over a period of a thousand years, from 2150 B.C.E. to 1200 B.C.E. But this practice of the ancient and familiar tradition was relegated to the non-ruling classes for the most part—it became the religion of the common people, the *paganus*, or "peasants." The elevation of the god-form of a ruling, father deity was politically created, primarily to sanctify the earthly reality. Thus it is that the Vanir are the true foundation of the Northern Tradition upon which was built that of the Aesir in the early days of Aryan migration and conquest. It is the pyramid of tradition, from Vanir to Aesir, with the younger, narrower tradition seated upon the base of the elder religion, but it is also the pyramid inverted to its point in terms of importance by the historical development of a few powerful rulers controlling the larger population.

Today, Northern Paganism is a vital mixture of the whole belief system. Although sometimes accused of racism and ties to Nazism, the tradition does not really encompass either of these. While a nationalistic interpretation was perverted by Hitler into a policy of racism, it was his aim to subvert Teutonic Paganism to serve his own ends. His archaeological efforts, however, did not lend support to his thesis of the Aryans being the conveyors of civilization. This line of investigation not only failed to support his claims of Aryan superiority, but went so far as to undermine it by showing that the Aryans had destroyed superior cultures. By then Hitler himself, seeing defeat in war coming, evoked this destructive image of the Aryans as a reflection of his own activities. The modern Northern Tradition, however, claims to speak to a sense of association by heritage. In America, in particular, the usual norm of common language means that anyone who speaks English is a candidate for the Anglo-Saxon branch of Northern practice—which could then be a person of Italian, German, Polish, Scandanavian, Oriental, or African heritage. By the second and third generation, most of these ethnic groups are brought up speaking English. If this is accepted, then the power of amalgamation in America could be one factor in making a revitalization of Neo-Paganism, even a Northern Tradition, without the racism remembered from the corruption initiated in Nazi Germany.

Artemis (left), a Moon Goddess, and Helios, the Sun God, were the Roman Moon and Sun deities.

Wicca and the primal Vanir aspect of Teutonic Paganism are two versions of the same religious/magical system, with the only major differences being the names for the Goddess and the God, and the development of Runic magic. Yet even in these two areas, the Divine names are the same descriptives used in Wicca—Lady and Lord—and Runes are popularly used by Wiccans today for divination, meditation, and often for inscriptions and spell work.

The cross-fertilization of the earlier, universal beliefs and deities with those of the far-ranging Aryan conquerors resulted in a kind of deja vu sensation as the Teutonic Pagan motifs were carried into what would develop into the modern mainstream religions of the western world via the Near East. The tree from Eden, the sexuality of Eve, the crucifixion of God (as Son) as a sacrifice to himself (as Father)—all these elements were Northern Tradition carried into the Near East, assimilated, and brought back to Europe as a "new" religion. Part of the reason why the Germanic tribes could accept the new religion so quickly was because it mirrored their own Pagan beliefs—indeed, it *was* their faith. The strange personality changes found in the Biblical Old Testament God are more rationally understood if you consider that this one God (Jehovah, or Yahweh), is really the assimilation of the three powers as seen in the Teutonic system: Father/Ruler, Lawgiver, and the aggressive, "no mercy/no quarter" Warrior. With Christianity, you add the Son and Holy Spirit, along with the Mother.

The incorporation of the Father God, Odin; Lawgiver, Tyr; and Warrior God, Thor are indicative of the rise of rulership, civil and religious law, and class distinctions in an early fighting society spreading out into the civilized lands of Bronze Age cultures. Since modern societies rely on laws and rulers, elected or otherwise, to govern the populace and direct the nations of the world, there is relevance in the Asatru tradition. The fact that Americans and many other national peoples prefer a separation of church and state means that the expression of the Northern Tradition is no longer reserved for those who rule, and can no longer be used as a means of authorizing that rule. For that reason, the Father God and Warrior God may be seen as superfluous by Witches who follow the Green Path of Nature, but nevertheless acceptable as secular deities who embody the ideals of state and citizenship.

Chapter Six

The Interwoven Roots of Ceremonialism and Wicca

Cast your Circle and call the Quarters.
—Standard Ritual Instruction

I n the Neo-Pagan community there are sometimes disagreements and controversies over which path is the most appropriate and valid. There is a traditional (and generally friendly) rivalry between Wiccans and ceremonial magicians (or mages) concerning magic in the terms of "High" and "Low." Yet both groups recognize that Low Magic refers to material things. Ceremonialists divide Low Magic into creative white magic and destructive black magic. High Magic is accepted by both groups as applying to the unifying of spirit and matter apart from either creative or destructive magic, and therefore, transcendant rather than a practice of white or black magic. With Wicca the term "Low Magic" applies to the actual magical workings, as it does to ceremonialists, and High Magic is the internal process affecting an individual at Esbats and Sabbats—celebrations usually ignored by ceremonialists.

The controversy, then, stems from methodology and purpose, or attitude. Most witches also do not distinguish white or black magic, since the dichotomy of white being equated with "good" and black with "bad" is a product of mainstream religious outlook. Magic is magic, whether the energy is of light or shadow—it is the intent of the practitioner of the Craft that distinguishes the ethical or moral form of the magic. Creative and destructive magic can both be applied to the same goal, as well. For example, if you want to cast a spell for wealth, and the Moon is waxing, you focus on gain, and the magic is white. If the Moon is waning, you focus on banishing poverty or want, and the magic is black, but the goals are the same, and the magic is created for the same purpose. Since it is so easy to confuse good and evil with white and black, these terms are potentially counterproductive. And why distinguish between creative and destructive when these are only processes for approaching a goal? Again, the association of these words with good and evil is the norm in contemporary society, and misleading. The ceremonialists got their most recent impetus when three Masons formed the Hermetic Order of the Golden Dawn in 1877 London. These men were influenced by medievalist magical practices as well as by the Enochian system created by Dr. John Dee, who was Queen Elizabeth's court astrologer in the sixteenth century, C.E. Twentieth-century members of the Golden Dawn later included Aleister Crowley (who left to form his own order, Silver Star) and Dion Fortune. These two people did much to popularize the Order. Crowley (1875–1947) was a prolific writer, and much of his work continues to influence mages. His practices and teachings, those of the Golden Dawn, and the widely used tarot of the Golden Dawn Order (Rider-Waite) incorporate the Jewish kabbalah and letter symbology, along with pre-Hebraic symbols of the Tree of Life, Elements, Moon/Sun phases, Egyptian aspects (Book of Thoth), and even a touch of Hinduism (only the names of the Chakras and Kundalini are changed). Many witches feel free to disregard the kabbalah aspects in their use of the tarot for divination, and there are several tarot decks available that are specifically designed for Wiccans.

It was Gerald B. Gardner (1884–1964) who, after spending many years of his life in the Shivan area of Sri Lanka and the Far East (which I find both rarely mentioned and highly significant), popularized Wicca in the twentieth century. He wrote a number of books after going public when England's laws against Witchcraft were repealed in 1951. He claimed to have been initiated in 1939 and encouraged covens to meet "skyclad" (nude). The aspect of nudity can be traced to Charles Leland's book, *Aradia* (1897), in which the practitioner was enjoined (in the "Charge of the Goddess," which was added to by Doreen Valiente and Gerald Gardner) to be skyclad as a sign of being "really free," which indicates a lack of continuity in the understanding of the meaning of being clad in the sky. However, the Charge could also be a reference to the use of nakedness in India among devotees of Shiva as a sign of holiness and truth through virtue and freedom. Ritual nakedness, too, was symbolic among the Celts. Some Gardnerian covens tend to feel that solitary practitioners are not true Witches in that the solitaries do not use degrees (from one of initiation to that of high priest/priestess). This is merely a point of artificial elitism against a solitary tradition that has its roots in an earlier matriarchal descent—the "Grandmother" heritage that is sometimes disputed by organized coven traditions (such as the Seax-Wica denomination of Gardnerian Wicca created by Raymond Buckland in 1973, which recognizes solitaries as authentic, but hereditary Witches as unlikely), although acknowledged by Gardner.

Solitary Witches tend to be female and have a tradition of intuitive powers and the ability to function as "Natural Witches" passed down from mother to daughter, but often the present generation can recall little more than two or three generations, and from this comes the "Grandmother Heritage" expression. Yet the tendency of organized covens toward an orthodoxy and subsequent diminishing of the maternal inheritance has caused many female solitary Wiccans to either remain silent to avoid debate or to begin to doubt their heritage. It is worth looking at the context of Gardner and Leland for an understanding of this question of recognized validity, although today, fortunately, there are few Wiccans who do not accept the reality of practicing solitary Witches.

The Golden Dawn, Crowley, Leland, and later, to some degree, Gardner, who appears to have borrowed rituals from Leland and the Golden Dawn, in which order he was once an initiate, according to Aidan A. Kelly in his work, *Crafting the Art of Magic* (St. Paul:

Llewellyn, 1992) all came from a time when the social atmosphere of the Victorian Age (which did not end until 1901) was suffocating and impossibly strict. The industrial revolution (Burns, Lerner, and Meacham's books *World Civilizations* Volumes B and C offer some insights and further reading on the position of women during this time) had made a shambles of country life and family life; women were reduced in status even more than ever before in England— becoming pretty props for the male-dominated society, producing children and demurely running the household as icons of morality and virtue, but incapable of serious thought. The dark and depressing aspects of life in the Victorian Age almost never seem to make it to the pretty films about that time period. The ugly side of balls and flouncy dresses, big houses, elegant living, and lots of servants is carefully ignored, even in modern movies and stories, unless it is a film dealing specifically with the downside of the period. The whole vision rarely appears, and instead, people grow up today remembering Shirley Temple as the "Little Princess," the lavish classic films of life in the Victorian Era, and costume affairs loosely based on Charles Dickens novels.

The horrible fact is that females were often forced to undergo clitorectomies at an early age (twelve through fourteen being most common) so that they would not be able to enjoy sexual relations. If they became rebellious due to the lack of purpose in their confined lives, they were sent to hospitals for hysterectomies to remove their uteruses. Anesthetic in the form of ether had just been discovered, and it would appear that doctors were eager to use it as often as possible. Nevertheless, this use of cruel and unnecessary, debilitating surgery is reminiscent of Nazi surgeries on concentration camp prisoners. It is hard to imagine the trauma and fear that would be instilled in a young girl who has been so brutally maimed or in an adult woman so casually violated.

Women went from the "protection" of their fathers or brothers to the "protection" of their husbands. They could not legally own property, they could not buy or sell anything without a man's approval, and they were certainly not expected to take part in any intelligent conversation with males—obedience and submission was their lot in life. For the lower classes of workers and domestics, the rules were the same, but impossible to uphold due to the working status of many women. Thus the lower class women were frequently exploited shamefully by the men of all classes, with nowhere to turn for relief, and they often ended up as prostitutes or wet nurses in order to support their fatherless children.

If any woman became too difficult to control (in the subjective opinion of her male guardian), she could be medically sedated and tranquilized, locked in a room for days, weeks, or months until her protector decided she had regained self-control; forced into a surgery promoted by the male-dominated medical profession as a means of controlling hysteria (root of the word hysterectomy); or she could be declared insane by a male protector (either a male family member or someone arbitrarily assigned by the legal system) and sent to an insane asylum, where male doctors in the tradition of Freud expounded upon the sexually based psychological problems of women. This then was the social environment in the era of modern ceremonial magic and Leland's Wicca.

The quaint displays of sexual freedom in an inhibited time came from a restricted and naive people who were titillated by coven gatherings where a man might actually touch a female's private parts, as when the priest (even the covens were male-dominated, with the priestess taking her cues from the priest) anointed women on their breasts and genitals, and then had the satisfaction of being anointed in turn by a woman. The advent of secret societies, occultism, and seances popular at this time was a reaction against the Victorian social strictures, and included some rather childish antics designed to be "outrageous." Crowley was a master showman who enjoyed shocking polite society with his flamboyant displays of iconoclastic abandon, as when he painted the numbers 666 on his forehead and named himself "The Beast." Modern Fundamentalist Christians would today be as horrified as were the religious people of the nineteenth century.

All this really shows, superficially, is a desire to throw off the bonds of convention. Yet underneath was something much more enduring and ancient, something that was finally and properly released when two world wars turned the artificial social order upside down. The Old Religion was not dead, and in the wake of new freedoms and an increasing equality of the sexes brought about by the need of men and women to fight in unison for their mutual survival, the suppressed Old Ways—the Vanir traditions of the common people—were brought out into the light.

Thus, while initially the modern advent of occultism, magic, and skyclad covens may have been an attempt to renounce the stifling effects of the Victorian Age, and doubtless this feature did lure a number of people to learn about Wicca, the fact remains that there is historical evidence that some ancient peoples did perform rituals naked, and included sexual intercourse as part of the process. This is especially easy to see in Etruscan funeral cave paintings where men and women are depicted copulating between the furrows of freshly plowed fields. Yet, this same act is depicted in Christian inspired art work as naked female Witches copulating with demons from hell and eating children. It is all a matter of context in the historical sense, and a blending in the Christian mind of Pagan rites with anti-Christian rites. The two do not belong together as the first is religious expression, and the second is a protest against a particular religion.

It took a little while for the people experimenting with a revival of Pagan practices to realize that what they were doing was not "exciting" so much as it was energizing—channeling the Universal Energy focused through the Elementals and the God and the Goddess directly into their bodies to be used for whatever purpose they desired. People were finally able to cast aside the artificial inhibitions of the Judeo-Christian tradition and recognize that their sexuality was nothing to be ashamed of; that the human body was not ugly or evil; that sexual behavior was not a sin. Although humankind may no longer feel it necessary to perform sexual rites in the fields to ensure a good crop, people may now enjoy the energy and joy of sexual pleasure without fear or guilt. Education and knowledge make all the difference.

To the Witch, magic is a natural phenomenon involving the cosmic energy of the Elementals of Nature. Focusing may be achieved through rituals that vary from elaborate to simple to effect the tuning in with natural forces to accomplish a desired result. To the ceremonialist, magic is achieved by the mage controlling the forces of nature by controlling what he *perceives* as the Divine. Both methods work because both simply provide a means for aligning one's own energies with existing external energies for redirection. The reason a person chooses to be a Witch or a mage is based upon personal preference, personality, and sometimes simply what was readily available when first starting out to work magic. Mages sometimes even state as their reason the desire to display their power to subvert the Divine to their own will. This is different from the Wiccan concept of joining with the Divine without a surrendering of the self, to work to an end. Ceremonialism is instead an attempt to dominate the forces in order to redirect them through internalizing the force of energy and then sending it back out.

Whereas the Witch unites with the energy, the ceremonialist attempts to be superior to it, and therefore, can never aspire to complete satisfaction simply because of the impossibility of the task he or she set for themselves. The mage tries to absorb the All into the Self, but the Self cannot contain the All—this would be self-destructive—and yet this is the ceremonialist's ideal. Not even an Adept can hope to conquer the Divine, for that would mean to replace the Divine in power, and therein lies egotism that would surely make Shiva smile. One can be god, but not "The God"; one can be divine, but not "The Divine," and this inbuilt restriction can pose a problem for the ceremonialist in conducting effective magic.

The main difficulty with ceremonial magic comes from its basis in the kabbalah. The Judaic religion is itself the product of Aryan Levites attempting to eradicate an older religious system, and only dates back to around 621 B.C.E. as the start of an orthodox form, while the Hebrew people themselves can only be placed at circa 1250 B.C.E. The kabbalah can be traced to the Renaissance with German magicians and to Dr. Dee in England. The current ceremonial tradition most widely recognized, the Golden Dawn, incorporates both Dee's Enochian system and the kabbalah. Gershom Scholem, in his *Origins of the Kabbalah*, shows that some aspects of the kabbalah system were known in Provence, France around 1130 C.E., but these may have been based on earlier, non-Jewish sources. The oldest-known manuscript, however, is dated to 1298 C.E. and was translated into Latin for Flavius Mithridates, and used by Mirandola in 1486 C.E. Basically, despite allegations of the ancient origins of the kabbalah, the historic reality is in the Jewish community of medieval Europe.

Scholem admits that there are elements in the kabbalah that do not reflect the traditions of medieval Jews. Instead, he alludes to unknown influences stemming from an earlier time in Italy and from the Orient, which is not surprising, since the Hindu missionaries were well-established in Rome and throughout the Empire. The kabbalic use of Hebrew letters to perform magic can be traced to the mysticism of Hinduism and the Buddhist interpretation originally intended to regain the power of the priest class. The fifty letters of the Hindu alphabet are said to constitute the body of the Goddess in the Tantric tradition, and by placing the letters on different parts of a person's body, the mortal body can be transformed into a divine one, limb by limb. Constant chanting of mantras accompanies the writing process, which is considered to work because Shakti is Matter (while Shiva is Spirit). The use of circles with sacred letters and symbols used by the ceremonialist is easily related to the Hindu Mandala (Circle).

In addition, it is now accepted that the Hebrews were never an outside people who entered into Canaan with a different ethnic and religious background, but were themselves pastoral Canaanites who wandered as they tended flocks, while urban Canaanites dwelled in

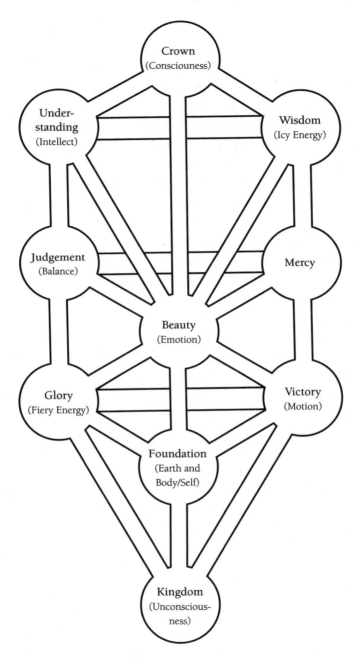

The Kabbalah and the Nine Realms of Yggdrasill arranged to show the matching between the two: Beauty and Mercy are combined as emotion in the Teutonic system, hence nine rather than ten realms.

cities where they made goods and raised crops in nearby fields that would in turn support the herders. The distinctions between the herders and the farmers were based on occupation and dwelling place, not ethnic or religious background. Here was a society of one people interacting for mutual benefit in a division of labor. It is known that after 1250 B.C.E. there was a combination of political, climatic, and economic factors in the Mycenean kingdoms of the Aegean that affected the entire Mediterranean world. This correlates with the final conquest of the cities of the Indus Valley as well, and so it becomes clear that the Aryans were again pushing southward in a wave of conquest and destruction.

The disruption of trade and political upsets resulted in the Canaanite cities being abandoned decades before the supposed conquest of the Canaanites by Joshua in the Bible stories. Instead, there was a slow change whereby the wandering herders began to settle on hilltops to make up for the absence of support from the cities in the valley. Thus, with refugees from the cities, the hilltops were turned into more defendable settlements where land would be cleared and crops planted, while the herders now had community goods available closer to their flocks. Some archaeologists have concluded that the stories of Exodus and Joshua were created by court poets eager to flatter the later Israelite and Judean kings. They believe the slavery of the Jews in Egypt and the "Passover" never happened, but are merely the contrivance of the Aryan Levites, with borrowings from Assyrian myths, to explain the Pagan celebration of the Spring Equinox in a way that made it acceptable to the Aryan religion.

This type of writing wherein history is used to promote a cause while distorting reality has been used many times, and Livy's *History* can be used as an example. Livy's diatribes against the Dionysian cults (an attempt at discrediting them by claiming they were guilty of heinous crimes) were not based on the actual practices but upon a campaign of slander. It has taken archaeology to point the way to the truth. The allegations of Livy are echoed in the

Christian allegations of Witchcraft activities and are equally false. Indeed, these charges have been leveled against a designated opposition, uniting people against an enemy throughout European and American history. The latest examples include World Wars I and II, where the English and the Germans made accusations against each other, and the 1992 American Presidential campaign where a spokesman of one party blamed the Equal Rights Amendment for abortions, divorces, and acceptance of Paganism and homosexuality. In these ways are the distortions in the past transferred to modern times.

The true history of the Israelites shows that the population in Canaan was local, and the Israelites were not nomads so much as they were pastoralists. It would compare to there being two types of people in Europe at the collapse of the Roman Empire in circa 476 C.E.: herders living in the open, and farmers, traders, and craftsmen living in cities, tending nearby fields and plying their crafts. Trade collapses when the Empire falls, the cities are deserted, and the population gravitates outward. The herders eventually make more permanent settlements to grow food and create shelter, and soon there are castles with a warrior class for protection and fiefs with serfs to maintain the system. The serfs, then, are the Hebrews, and the Aryan Levites are the overlords, and from these later people come the rabbis, princes, and kings of Israel (Jerusalem and outskirts) and Judea. The Israelites were the refugees of Canaan, and the Aryan Levites were the conquerors.

I mention this element of history because it has an impact on a person's perspective. What does this do to ceremonial magic and its reliance on the kabbalah? If the Bible is not taken literally, then it is useless to believe that there was a Key of Solomon. Everything in the Bible, besides being relatively recent, is borrowed from a variety of older non-Judaic sources and altered to promote Judaism and the domination of the Hebrew people by their Levite overlords.

This need for acceptance of Judaism as an authoritative distillation of what predates it rather than as the new religion of its time, attempting to obliterate all that had come before, requires one to put aside knowledge in order to work within the system. The ceremonialist, then, becomes an inadvertent supporter of Judaism and all the religions that have sprung from that source, rather than a representative of an older historic pagan tradition. The Wiccan does not have to deal with this problem since invocations do not involve a lengthy appeal to Jewish ethereal spirits who are not reliably what they are supposed to be, anyway. Renaissance mages were floundering in a sea of misinformation, but they could put it together in a way that worked for them because they did not know that they were ignorant. Today this system is made harder to work with because you have to deliberately suspend your understanding of the historical truths of the Hebrew people and Judaism to make it function. In Wicca, no Names of Power are needed; no letters of power (not to be confused with Runes) are necessary.

Let us suppose the kabbalah is not the Renaissance invention (based, as it were, on scraps of Medieval Jewish Gnostic material) many historians believe it to be, and let us say that its tradition reverts to an older Hebrew source; it is still a compromised attempt to hold onto the pre-Judaic traditions of magic in nature. That effort is flawed because it was accomplished in a manner that would emphasize an invented new-found uniqueness through renaming and altering beings to be identified with the forces of divinity and the Key of Solomon.

This is not to deny that the sources may go back into antiquity, but historians and archaeologists know today that, relatively speaking, Judaism does not. One effect of Jewish monotheism was to distance the people from the more ancient cosmological traditions, so it is very likely that some Jews sought to preserve this information in a socially and politically acceptable manner. Unfortunately, the side effect was to lose the purity of natural magical practices and to infuse a taint of racism, intolerance, and egotism (having the only true God and being chosen) that has persisted to this day in Jewish orthodox faith and in many of the denominations of its Christian

An ancient woodcut depicts
a Runic Calendar (right).

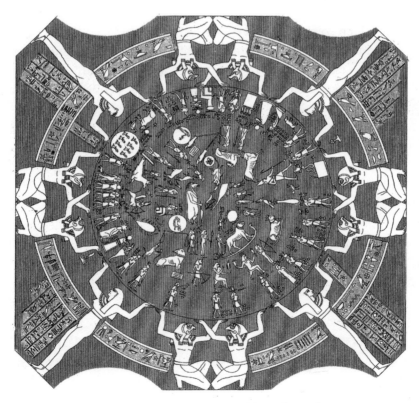

This Egyptian Zodiac was very likely scribed on a sheet of papyrus.

and Islamic descendants. Prior to this, the gods and goddesses of other cultures were accepted and were even incorporated into the local pantheons.

Return to a time before the Hebraic rituals, or the overworked intricacies of the Egyptian priesthood, and the original basis of both ceremonial magic and Craft magic is clear—all rests upon the flow of the Eternal Energy, that spark of life that exists in all living things and cannot be destroyed, but is immortal and thus makes life itself immortal—the unity and the separateness of male and female; the Elementals, Sun phases, Moon phases, seasonal changes, and the natural schedules for planting and harvesting. Bulls and snakes are the ancient symbols of strength, fertility, wisdom, rebirth, and trees the symbols of knowledge and truth (and the source of the word) from which comes the understanding of life.

The point that is frequently repeated in Neo-Pagan gatherings and conversations between traditions is that there really is no right way, only paths that have worked for different people in different times—ways that others adopt for themselves in order to find direction, or at least a starting point. Today there are many books openly available that deal with spells, rituals, magic techniques, and divination methods. Practitioners of the Craft may be skyclad, robed, or dressed in any way that feels right to the individual, whether as a group (coven) decision or as a solitary. One may draw the symbols and call upon the spirits of ceremonial magic and still feel contact with the power of the natural energies, just as the mainstream religionists may tap into that same energy when in fervent prayer. But the problem with the kind of diversity prevalent in Neo-Paganism is the inherent loss of direction and isolation due to an approach that is often restricted through lack of knowledge and reduced to an almost continuous improvisation. This is a view that leads some Neo-Pagans to suggest an orthodoxy might be in order to concentrate the efforts of the Seeker. Most Neo-Pagans, however, are sufficiently independent to reject this or any other type of regimentation. The Seeker must therefore be sincere and persistent in order to gain understanding, yet alert and cautious to avoid being victimized by popular crazes and baseless initiations.

The principle of Karma remains in effect no matter what path is taken, and this is why even Christians are cautioned not to judge others lest they be judged, and to remember that vengeance is not to be meted out by the individual, but by God (as Karmic energy). If the negative aspects of the subconscious are dredged up to focus on dark powers to effect harm to another, the unpleasant results actually rebound upon the user, and this makes the use of black magic hazardous not to the object of the magic, but to the practitioner. Gardner's Wiccan Rede of, "An' it harm none, do as thou wilt," is matched in Christianity with, "Do unto others as you would have them do unto you," and in the ancient Witchcraft injunction that what is sent out comes back (threefold, according to some traditions). The thrust of these redes is that people are discouraged from projecting negativity for their own sake. Yet the dark powers can be effectively used for positive results. The dark is simply the balance of the light, and the whole brings one unity. Dark is not the same as evil, any more than light is the same as good. Instead, one reflects more of the raw energy of chaos while the other reflects more of the gentler energy of order.

The Hierophant and the Greenman Meditation

This is a good time to think about your own needs in spiritual and religious practice. Take out the Hierophant card and Fool card from your favorite tarot deck. Arrange them propped up so you can see them both easily, the Hierophant on the right, the Fool on the left. On the right side of the cards, light a purple candle. On the left side, light a dark green candle. Tapers are best for this purpose, but you can also use votives. If you like, you can have your cauldron in front of the cards, with a charcoal disk upon which you might want to smolder some mugwort leaves or a resin incense such as copal or frankincense. Cast your Meditation Circle, invoke the Elementals and the Divine, then sit comfortably to begin the meditation.

Look at the two cards. They represent two approaches to spirituality. Do you enjoy a lot of ceremony in an area set aside as your temple? Do you feel a need to adhere to the use of special words and gestures in your rituals? Then you are expressing the structuring influence of the Hierophant card.

Do you enjoy casting your Circle outdoors? Do you find yourself voicing impromptu spells or celebrating the God and the Goddess in a moment of exhilaration at the sight of the Moon, the Sun, or beauties of Nature? Then you are expressing the wild freedom of the Fool, or Greenman card.

Do you find there are times when you prefer a familiar ritual, such as at Yule, and other times prefer to express your unity with Nature with uninhibited abandon, such as running through the grass barefoot at Beltane? Then you are like most people who have moments when they find comfort in a familiar structure, and find joy in the thrill of a new expression of connection with the Divine. Look at the Hierophant card. There is usually a ritually dressed man sitting on a throne, with supplicants kneeling before him, beseeching his spiritual guidance. This is the card of organization of spiritual forms, of celebrating the seasonal rites and observances, of

The Fool/Green Man   The Hierophant

codifying spiritual insights. Do you feel that you are close to this card? This is the card that signifies the writing of your own Book of Shadows, for example, so every witch has at least a little of the Hierophant within. This is also the card of the ceremonialist, for whom ritual is the primary method of honoring the Divine.

Now look at the Fool card. This is a card whose name relates to the European image of the Wildman and the Greenman. Here is untamed Nature, raw enthusiasm, and joyous energy. The Fool signifies both an open mind and the vitality of eager creativity. This is a card signifying the power of fertility, originality, and spontaneity. Do you feel that you are close to this card? This is the card that signifies the harmony between the worlds at Midsummer—a connection between the witch and the Fairy Folk, and hence between the Witch and Nature. This is the card of the Witch walking fearlessly in union with Nature.

Both cards and both archetypes exist in us all. There are times when the security of ritual is desired, and there are times when we like to experiment, turning loose our imaginations to sing to the Moon or compose new invocations to the Divine. There is both the Hierophant and the Fool within us; both the ceremonial trappings and the witch's wilderness; both order and chaos; structure and creativity. We feel comfortable with this when we have achieved a balance of the two forms of spirituality. Too much rigidity leads to a suppression of the spontaneity of Nature and creative energy. Too much primal chaos and we loose track of our goals and destiny. As in all things, a balance needs to be maintained.

As you gaze at the two cards, open your mind to the images inspired by each. See if you can find the positive and the negative in each card. How do they relate to you? Are there areas of your life you want to address with them and perhaps alter?

Take a deep breath, hold it a moment, and release it. Repeat. Close your eyes, let the stillness enter into you as you find the quiet place within. Now let the images invoked through these cards come to you. Open yourself to the Universe and feel yourself in balance with the powers of the Universe, with form and chaos, with structure and freedom. Take another deep breath, hold it a moment, then release it, bringing this balance into your presence. Take another deep breath, hold it a moment, release it, and open your eyes. You are back in normal awareness. Have something to eat and drink, snuff out the candles, and let the incense burn out as you put away your cards and tidy up, then return to your normal routine.

Witchcraft Today

The advantage of Neo-Paganism is the absence of the baggage of guilt and unworthiness so often heaped upon mainstream believers. Humans as individuals need to relate to the environment and to that spark of Divinity that dances in all life as well as in each person. There are many paths to choose from to achieve this goal. The acceptance of this one fact is what prevents orthodoxy from gaining a grip on Pagan practices. The validity of one system or another is moot, as all are as valid as their practitioner's ability to use them— whether they have a history centuries old, or are relatively new— because humans are not a stagnant species. As long as the mind and spirit function, progress can be made, and no religious system (not even the Judeo-Christian-Islamic systems as evidenced by the variety of denominations in each) can expect to freeze the human heart in mid-beat to adhere to one set of rituals or beliefs. The energy of the Neo-Pagan/Wiccan movement is in its flexibility and open acceptance of its continuing evolution. There will never be a "Mother Church" nor an orthodoxy for Pagans, as it is the spirit of individuality that distinguishes modern Paganism from mainstream religions.

It is significant, however, that some of the structural formats of the ceremonialist system have been adopted into the Craft through the establishment of Wiccan "traditions" created by people with former associations with ceremonial orders like the Golden Dawn. This has led to a Wicca that does not genuinely reflect the *Old Reli-*

gion of Witchcraft, but since so much of those practices has been lost, the use of these formats may be helpful in conducting a satisfying ritual or spiritual communication. It is a matter of selecting that which appeals to the individual. The Green Witch does not need to follow prescribed rituals, perform specific motions, or possess the accouterments so often associated with Witchcraft, yet by developing a *Book of Rituals* the individual witch gains a viable and amendable record of personal growth. Marian Green, in her book, *A Witch Alone* (London: Aquarian Press, 1991), allows that while Witchcraft is a religion without dogma, there are still those whose practice of the Craft projects a patriarchal and rigid, ritualistic point of view. For some Seekers, such a tradition may be useful as a starting place, but for others, it could be inhibiting or a drain on their personal power. Because of varying views of how the Craft should be practiced, it becomes important to chose your coven associates with care, both for your own level of comfort, and theirs.

There are in fact people who are Witches who have never attended a coven, never followed a prescribed ritual, and have had such great success at their practice that they have been sought out for advice, spells, divinations, and healings. One does not become a Witch by following another's path, but by making the connection with the Lord and the Lady individually. This can be (and has been) done in the context of accepted religions. The Craftwise have worked through the centuries within the system, in some cases even as members of a nature tradition such as the Lay Order of Saint Francis, in the nations where the Catholic system has overlapped the Pagan. This is particularly evident in Central and South America, and in the Caribbean Islands, but this can also be said of the Mediterranean nations and Eastern Europe. There has never been an Inquisition in Romania, for example, where Witches have never been consistently persecuted.

The Alexandrian tradition created by Alex and Maxine Sanders is based on the rituals of the Gardnerian tradition, and Gardner's own rituals have been traced to the Golden Dawn (although many Gardnerians may argue the point). So whereas it can be supposed that the Neo-Pagan coven movement in Wiccan traditions has ties to ceremonial magic, the magical, herbal, and connective practices of the solitary (Green) Witch harken to Sind. The Seax (Saxon) Wicca tradition recently created by Raymond Buckland evolved from his Gardnerian background. Over and over, the roots of these traditions revert to Gardner and the morass of ceremonialism. Such roots do not reflect the Old Religion of Nature, but rather the relatively simplistic western Judaic-based theological concepts whose dogma and tyranny does not provide the answers people are seeking.

It was this lack of satisfaction in religion that caused a veritable eruption of alternative religious styles in what has been labeled the New Age. The Seeker, however, must always continue to learn and grow. The Aryan influence of form over content has permeated religious expression in the West for so long that it is difficult for people to recognize the Sind elements and return to the source of humanity's first religion. You can take as a clue, however, that when a ritual or ceremony becomes annoying or boring, you have moved away from the source.

When leaders of Wiccan traditions announce that theirs is the only true path, that initiations and degrees are required, and that ritual formulae and attire (or lack thereof) must be followed, they are inadvertently expressing a connection to ceremonialism. When the kabbalah is incorporated into the Wiccan structure, the ancient Craft is compromised. Most writers on the subject will admit that many elements from ceremonial magic have entered into Witchcraft, but you only have to remember that the magic comes from within, and that the trappings are incidental. The Seeker must first identify what needs require filling, and search for the path that best meets those needs. Fear of questioning has no place in Neo-Paganism, and structures that deny this are self-serving and not much different from the mainstream religions.

"Perfect love and perfect trust" and going naked before the Divine does not necessarily refer to nudity, but rather to internal soul-baring, for there are no secrets from the God and the Goddess. The concept of using sexual energy to accomplish a goal is one fraught with dangers and may not be as successful as raising earth energy through dancing and chanting, simply because sex is a normal activity—one to be celebrated and enjoyed, but with equality between the participants. It is this sense of equality that is missing from much of the Buddhist Tantric tradition. Buddhism, having begun as an Aryan reform movement in Hinduism, speaks to the dominant male aspect of the religion, and thus historians such as Danielou can write of Tibetan Buddhists using prostitutes in certain rituals and of the male-oriented nature of the Vedic-Shivan sects, while yet acknowledging that the original Shivan people were matriarchal. The very practice of this type of sexual magic, then, is degrading to the women who make up half of the process. This is a flawed perspective of the union of Shiva and Shakti. The Goddess is not a prostitute; she is not to be used, then discarded. To do so with a woman is demeaning to the perfect union of the God and the Goddess, and demonstrates the influence of the Aryan, male-dominant, political deities.

The sexual aspect in a coven setting could devolve into a way of controlling people and giving them a sense of participation without actually providing any real information on how to work magic, and should disagreements take place among the members, the potential for trouble is greater. The Seeker must always remain alert to the possible abuse of power in coven traditions. Magic comes from within, and is not a matter of initiation or pronouncement. Only the practitioner knows what he/she feels when working magic, and when one feels it work, someone else's initiation is irrelevant. The evolution of a priesthood came from one group of people keeping secrets from the rest of the people so as to generate and hold power over them. Some consider the written word invalid in magic, believing the formulas need to be passed along orally. In Wicca, there are some who believe that power shared is power lost, and so they encourage secrecy. Then what about the numerous spell books available in bookstores? These are also not complete. For one to practice magic effectively, one must put part of oneself into the process. Scott Cunningham was been most clear about this in his writings when he advised people to alter the spells and to add their own words.

There is more to Witchcraft than form and ritual. It is a craft—an art—and will therefore vary with the person practicing it. To say that one must be initiated by someone else who has been initiated and thus establish a lineage to Gardner is to ignore the fact that Witches come from all over the world, not just Great Britain. The source of Witchcraft travels with the Green Witch, the Celts, the Etruscans, the Gypsies, and the Indus Dravidians, back to Sind. In order to work magic effectively, one need only turn to the source, for the God and the Goddess will provide. Accepting this unconditionally is the true meaning of "perfect love and perfect trust."

Wicca needs to be more than the ceremony of the Sabbats and Esbats. It is not reasonable to put aside knowledge (the very thing the God and Goddess want humanity to possess) in order to perform seasonal rites mourning the death of the God, honoring his rebirth at Winter Solstice, cheering him on in his pursuit of the Goddess, acting as voyeurs at their union, and honoring his entering the soil for the harvest, her pregnancy, and so on through the cycle anew. People today should be aware that the seasons will change and the seeds will sprout whether people are here or not— that is the order of Nature. Then what are Witches supposed to be doing at the Sabbats? Are they practicing the rituals of a newly entrenched clergy to dominate others, or mimicking rituals once believed essential? The first is manipulative and the second is shallow. Over time, with education improving and becoming more commonplace, the old Judeo-Christian images become more quaint than realistic; the rituals are a form of social conduct; the extremism is blunted—that is why education is the bane of those organized religions that have maintained power through control of education. To fall into this same trap would be the end of Wicca.

Witchcraft can be little more than a variation of that same mainstream form unless it is allowed to evolve as humanity evolves. To be effective, Wicca can not remain fixated on a dimly remembered past. It is not a protest statement, but an intuitive understanding and union with Nature. This cannot be legislated by ritual formats and by sculpted words. Intuition must be felt by anyone who would be called a Witch, and it is because of the personal nature of this intuition that a rigid tradition based upon a hierarchy of degrees of initiation is impossible. This is essentially a manifestation of an element of natural Chaos disrupting the human-created Law of the sect.

Play is the word often used to describe how a Witch makes contact with the All, but as with children, even play must be rational on its own level and abide by its own rules of engagement. Thus the value of the solitary tradition lies in the fact that no energy need be lost or wasted trying to align a number of people's rules of engagement. In the practice of ceremonial magic, the use of terms and forms that were once the Pagan gods and goddesses, revised into demons and angels under an Aryan rulership, may seem more like offering an insult to the Lord and Lady. This in itself may be one reason some people report bizarre and self-injurious results from their attempts. Their subconscious is offended and directs the subsequent anger upon the conscious for the outrage of imposed ignorance. It is only after the subconscious is beaten into submission that ceremonialism can begin to appear effective. The inner awareness was trying to chastise the outer, not destroy it, so it becomes a weak voice where it could have been a strong one.

The rigid forms of some Wiccan traditions require the same sort of willful ignorance, and that is also an affront to the Tree of Knowledge. So what do the Sabbats and Esbats mean to the modern Witch? The Sabbats are calls to the Elementals, who are the kin of humanity and live within each person, and to the Divine Substance and Divine Energy that forms and animates the individual. It is a homecoming or reunion between the conscious mind and awareness with the transcendental forces united through the subconscious. When the witch invokes (not summons) the Elementals and the Deities, the Self is opened to flow freely with the larger aspect of what forms the individual. The God and the Goddess may be described in Tantric cosmological terms as Shiva being the primal explosive force that created the Universe, pushing the particles and energy away from the source, and Shakti being the force that brings the energy and practicies together to form the stars and solar systems, These opposites are found in all of existence, and just as it is the aim of the Shivaite to bring about the union of the opposites within the individual, so it is the goal of the Witch, whose religion can be traced back to Sind, to do the same.

With four of the Sabbats (Yule, Ostara, Litha, and Mabon, called the Green Sabbats) one may find that the Solstices and Equinoxes generate a natural desire within to join with the ebb and flow of energy and particles—like a planet drawn to the sun, the spirit yearns for union with the larger mass of cosmic energy at those times when the energies are at their greatest, equal, or weakest force. Perhaps there is a subconscious feeling that by opening the Self to the flow, one may draw the energy tides back and forth, as the sea tides are pulled by the Moon. Hence, people worldwide, expressing this sensation through different forms and different religions, become the moons for the Elementals and the Deities, who participate in the unions as much as the celebrants.

Marking the Esbats brings you into alignment with your Moon essence and intuitive abilities, and thus affords the best results when doing magic. The Moon unites with your personal tides, both internal and external. For the other four Sabbats (called the White Sabbats), internal restoration and alignment are the focus. Imbolc is the time for cleansing, for purifying the inner temple of the Self; a time for restoring balance, for rededication, or for performing an internal housecleaning. Beltane is a time for feeling renewal and the joy of life in alignment with the Earth's springtime. Lughnassadh brings a feeling of comfort and plenty that can be appropriately celebrated with a

Wiccan altar set for a Full Moon Esbat celebration incorporating images of Sind. The disk in the center has a pentagram carved on its surface.

Bread Festival to acknowledge the Earth's bounty with gratitude and respect. Samhain is the time when one's spirit reaches out to unembodied souls with the instinctive recognition that all are of the same essence, no matter the outer form or place in the corporeal world.

The sepulcher of Jesus is no more than another interpretation of the similar theme from Dionysos, whose temples contained a representation of the empty tomb, just as did the temples of Horus in Egypt. The God of life has traditionally been associated with the harvest and with death, to be like Hades, the god of the Underworld, or like Shiva, the King of Shadows. The aspect of the God as Time and Destroyer has its place in the darkness of the turning of the seasons. Now the Goddess moves alone as the crone, devoid of Her Shiva, until the Winter Solstice renews her as Mother with the rebirth of the

God. But it is with Samhain that the Witch finds a quiet, somber mood in which to reflect upon the gentle union all beings hold together as spirits, flowing from life to life through the passage called death, and to know that all are an integral and personal part of this great fluctuation of energy through matter.

There are those who see a trend emerging in the western world toward a return to the concepts of Shiva, but often this return to a respect for Nature is linked with the particularly male-focused practice of the sex magics of the Tantras. This is still a reflection of the Aryanization of the religion of Sind, for the Vedic Shivan practice still does not demonstrate the balance of the Lord and the Lady—Ardhanari. There are Tantric Shakti practices as well, but it is the legacy of Aryanism that has left this union split asunder.

With the Tantrics, evolved from the Puranas texts written between 900 and 1000 C.E., the message remains essentially the same as with the modern fundamentalists of Judaic-Christian-Islamic traditions, namely that only those followers of the God will survive an apocalypse to create a new human race. Dravidic Shiva puts his hand to his forehead and shakes his head. This is not the message of Sind, this is not the message of the first world-wide religion of humanity, but the Aryan message of exclusivity and intolerance that has sullied human affairs in the Near East and Western worlds for 3,000 years.

If you can accept that you are part of the universal flow of energy through matter, then there is no apocalypse—for there is no "ending," only the continual ebb and flow of all life in energy. The tides of electrons and neutrons, of Moon, Sun, Earth, and practitioners of any number of faiths, are but a microcosm of the tides of the Universe itself. Many religion theorists make much of the comparisons of ancient texts, but the link of one set of Aryan documents with another is not sufficiently made to show that the similarity found in these doctrines should be anticipated, and that they differ from what predated them in Sind. It is the message of Shakti as the Tree of Life—denied by the Aryan politicized religion— that all people are immortal, that is missing. Not only may the East be able to help the West to recover its lost traditions, as Rene Guenon suggests in *The Crisis of the Modern World* (Ghent: Sophia Perrennis, 1996), but the West may be able to help the East in return by reminding it that it has the politically exclusive elements of western Aryanism inter-mixed in its ancient Dravidic-associated religions. Together, Orient and Occident may find a spiritual unity in the application of a purer Sind tradition.

Chapter Seven

Challenges to Neo-Paganism and Wicca in the Twentieth Century

Lady of Shadows, Lord of the Night,
Open my vision to thy inner sight.
Vast is the time and vast is the way,
Guide me in passage, to you this I pray.
—Crystal meditation invocation

Much has already been written about the six million Jews who were killed in the Nazi Holocaust during World War II, but what identifies the other six million people who were exterminated? What motivation did Hitler have for all of these deaths, and what led him in the selection of his victims? Although people have known for many years that Hitler was very interested in the occult and sought a revival of Germanic Paganism to support his regime, this has generally been dismissed as only further evidence of his insanity. But as one studies the subject of religion, noting the spread and subsequent *pollution* of the Aryan ideals, one can see the method to Hitler's madness.

Neo-Pagans of the early twentieth century were also targets for Nazi prosecution, and many prominent Pagans were incarcerated in the concentration camps. We need to keep in mind that there were numerous Pagan groups in Europe active as secret societies and such since the nineteenth century, with practices that included aspects of Celtic influence, and thus the heritage of Sind. There was also a Jewish influence evident in the German magic tradition dating from the fifteenth century. The Pagan connection leads us to ask "Why the Holocaust?" and "What does the new millennium hold?"

The other six million, as briefly delineated by Martin Gilbert in *The Holocaust: A History of the Jews of Europe During the Second World War* (New York: Henry Holt & Co., 1985) are the real clue as to the purpose of the Holocaust. The Jews were not the first people to be targeted by the Nazi regime as a people who had to be erased in order to return to the Paganism of the Aryans. The "cleansing" first consisted of the mentally ill, Gypsies, Slavs, and homosexuals because of what they represented from the historical, occult, and religious points of view. It was through Romania and Hungary that the early Celts had arrived in Eastern Europe and spread across what is modern Austria, Switzerland, and France. The Slavs, and the Gypsies who wandered across Europe taking with them the early beliefs and customs of their ancient forebears, posed a threat to the new mythology of Aryan superiority being created by Hitler.

By tracing the history of religion, language, and civilization in an unbiased fashion, one discovers that the Near East was not the place of origin for the great ideas of humankind, but the later area that preserved these concepts for historical record. Much of the Hebrew written account and mythology in the Pentateuch revolves around the denial of the earlier systems of belief and the ostracism of those who retained any aspect of those beliefs. Because the record is available for anyone who reads, the Jewish people were targeted for extermination—as were Christians, but for them the extermination would progress after the other deaths had been accomplished. In time, the Catholic Church would have been a target, and so would have any Protestant religious group. A successful Holocaust would have instituted an upper level Aryan Paganism *in its pure form*, without the lower (Green) level from which it had evolved, and without any trace of the ceremonial magic practices of the fifteenth and sixteenth centuries.

The source of the "contamination" of Aryan Paganism (and subsequently of Judaism and its family offshoots) was the religion of the

Indus Valley—the indestructible God and Goddess, Shiva and Shakti; AUM and UMA. The Jews had to be killed to destroy the record they so faithfully kept without realizing the implications of what they were keeping, The Gypsies had to be killed because they were the original wanderers from India who kept the ancient faith in their own way. The Slavs had to be killed because they were the closest to the ancient people who migrated from India and retained many of the Indus traditions. The homosexuals had to be killed because they were the evidence of the Androgyne Deity and had been respected as such in ancient cultures, and the mentally ill had to be killed because of the ancient tradition that considered insanity to be indicative of being touched by God, so that even today, the enraptured devotee of Shiva may act in the manner of one who is insane, since closeness to divinity results in the realization that nothing in this life really matters.

The Aryan religious system, devoid of the Green aspect, was dedicated to a God of fire who dwelled on a mountain; was a patriarchal system with the males being in touch with the supreme deity through fire worship and sacrifices, and was patrilineal with inheritance by males and, subsequently, male dominance over females (no matter how benevolent or equitable) maintained through the necessity of monogamy solely for the females and female exclusion from performing the rite of the sacrifice.

Hitler had an ambitious plan to literally reverse the flow of history by taking his race back to what he considered to be its pure form. He recognized that people had been conditioned by centuries of religious instruction and religious wars to faithfully believe in what he knew was an "impure" religion. His fascination with archaeology and the occult point to his determination to find the proof that the pure form of Aryanism was superior, but all his experts actually discovered was that Aryanism was the religion of a people becoming organized to fight for expansion. This led Hitler toward the end of his power to declare that he would then take the world out in a conflagration with no regard to any race, not even his own.

His efforts at purification did not meet with great resistance simply because he was careful about the order in which his purges took place. Not very many people complained about the destruction of the mentally ill—they were expensive to maintain in asylums during the Depression. Not many others complained about the labeling of homosexuals—they were denounced by all mainstream religions already. Not many complained about the treatment of the Gypsies— they were alien and suspect in their mysterious living habits, and besides, it was the popular belief that most were probably thieves anyway. When the Jews were labeled and then rounded up, it was just another unwanted group. People had been reduced to "types", and this lack of identity as individuals made it easier for the Nazis to isolate and launch attacks against large segments of the population in stages that were acceptable to the general population. The fact that modern religionists have since pointed to the Bible as predicting the rise of a Hitler is not realistic—the Bible was written for its own self-preservation, and the rebellion against its tenets was expected because there was always the chance that someone would try to revert to the original Sind-based religions at the very time of the writings. This was a case of contemporary injunctions against the current religious situation and denouncements in advance, warning the devotees of the impure Aryan system to fight for their religion. It was not expected, however, (and this in itself disproves the "prophetic" nature of Scripture) that the rebellion would come from Aryan purists.

The problem with what are generally accepted in modern times as mainstream religions is that they are basically a corruption of the older systems. All are based in pantheism, as Arnold Toynbee saw it, and any attempt to return to a purer form of the Nature Religions is seen by mainstream religions both as threatening and heretical. The truth is, however, that the mainstream religions are the heretical aspects of the older religious forms and exist by threatening revivals of their antecedents, be it by burning witches at the stake or by utilizing the vast tax-free resources of modern religions for widespread use of the media to revile Neo-Paganism and instill in people a fear for non-mainstream religions and their practices. Name-calling used blatantly to induce hysteria, and false claims about doctrinal differences are symptoms of the fear brought on by the resurgence of the old beliefs. There are those who have a vested interest in maintaining a general ignorance of the origins of mainstream religions in those older beliefs.

The scapegoating of Pagans and Wiccans by fundamentalist groups serves solely as a means of uniting people in a manufactured cause against changing awareness and education. By providing something relatively harmless, like the general term of Paganism, as a focus for rage and hatred, all the ills of society can appear to stem from religious nonconformists rather than from mainstream religious views, the individuals themselves, or their outmoded social structure. In this way, the children who commit horrendous crimes, as with the Columbine High School killings in Colorado in 1999, are isolated as somehow involved with the "occult," but their being raised in Christianity is ignored. One prominent televangelist went so far as to call the two boys in the above-cited case "evil from birth." Yet they grew up attending church. Nevertheless, the deaths were used as an opportunity to cast suspicion and fear on Neo-Paganism, Wicca, and anything considered linked with the occult, so that for a time, students in various schools across the nation were forbidden to wear black clothing—a color associated with Witches and used to ward negative energies. Months later, without the same widespread news coverage, officials admitted to other motivations for the rage and sense of helplessness of these two youths—related not to Paganism, but to a culturally endorsed favoritism in the treatment of school athletes, whose arrogant and sometimes violent behavior was tolerated, whose trophies were more valued than the artistic and intellectual achievements of other students, and who were allowed to openly flaunt gifts of expensive vehicles and violate rules that the rest of the students were expected to obey.

Wiccans and other Neo-Pagans are labeled by many mainstream religionists as Satanists, Nazis, evil, and perverse, when in truth, all these Pagans are doing is accepting the oneness humankind shares with the Earth and the Universe; accepting the duality of Divinity and the equality of all humans, male and female, of all races and ethnic backgrounds. They can see how, as genetic people living on and integrated with, the Earth (which is itself seen to be a living organism, Gaia), humans can be expected to evolve and experience changes in spiritual, physical, and mental development.

Variations in human expression are not seen as threatening by Pagans. Unlike many mainstream religions, the need for conformity is not a prerequisite for acceptance. Life forms are as different as the interplay of basic genetic harmonics permits, and this gives rise to the various expressions of human sexuality, creativity, intelligence, and physical characteristics. There are infinite possibilities to human adaptation and change, which does not alarm Neo-Pagans or Wiccans because of their sense of being in balance with all nature, but typically it does alarm the mainstream religionists because their sense of being depends on the power they can claim based on the amount of community conformity to their faith. Thus, while one never hears a Pagan telling someone that he/she will go to hell (because the Pagan knows that the only hell that exists is the one a person creates for him/herself) that threat is used to keep mainstream participants cohesive.

The connection between the occult (hidden knowledge), Paganism, and Nazism is not what has traditionally been presented. The matter is much more complex. The Gypsy tradition, along with those of witchcraft and ceremonial magic, and the religions that developed from the Indus were the enemy to Hitler. What modern religionists do not want to face is that Hitler placed them in the same category as Wiccans and Pagan Gypsies—the very people that Christians and Jews had themselves discriminated against and persecuted. Such religionists do not want to accept that they are themselves the products of these repudiated belief systems. Hitler may well have seen that connection and wanted to correct what he perceived as the mistake made by the Aryans. They were the minority who conquered civilized people by means of their superior Aryan weapons and techniques of war. But once in a position of power, the Aryans were literally surrounded by their foes. In order to rule, they had to integrate those they had conquered into a workable power structure—and religion was the perfect tool. Their only failure was that the integration worked both ways, and elements of the local religions became incorporated into the Aryan systems.

Judaism represents the first remarkable attempt to purge the Aryan system of pre-Aryan, Vanir-level beliefs, but this was not truly successful until after the Christian adaptation of Judaism occurred and lent support to the relevancy of the Jewish faith through the active Christian destruction of Pagan sources. It was the unequivocal acceptance of the Old Testament as literal truth by the Christians that reinforced the maintenance of Judaism, even to the extent of forcibly giving the land of Palestine to the Jews for a homeland called Israel, and continuing the support of that nation through financial and technical aid in current times (over $3 billion dollars yearly from the United States government, and this does not include private fund-raising in America).

Fundamentalist Christian support of Israel reflects a desperation to have Bible prophecy fulfilled. The end result of fulfillment is interpreted as bringing the Christian faithful into a position of world domination after the annihilation of billions of hapless nonbelievers, in a variety of horrors from which the faithful will be blissfully absent (the *Rapture* concept of Christianity in which the believer is taken bodily into Heaven before the wars leading to Armageddon commence). It is this notion of nonparticipation in the results of their violent activities that makes the fundamentalist movements of any sect dangerous. They feel that they have nothing to lose and will not have to face the consequences of their actions.

When it becomes apparent that all the Jews will not return to Israel, whether it be because they are at home in their adopted land or simply do not want to live in the Near East, the next event might be a persecution of recalcitrant Jews in order to force history into the misunderstood mold of the New Testament Revelation. It is this kind of ignorance of ancient cosmologies that has twisted the making of history for nearly two thousand years. Thus it was that, from Hitler's point of view, the Christian religions were as much a pollution to the Aryan faith as the Jewish religion.

The earliest failure of Aryan religious purity occurred in India; from this land came the Gypsies who left their indelible imprint on the Slavs. When the Vedic Aryans invaded India and displaced Shiva, they must have been surprised to see how this deity retained his power over the hearts and minds of the local people. Even when insulted and degraded in early Vedic mythology, Shiva endured. His calm, unperturbed demeanor captivated his conquerors until Shiva displaced the Vedic mountain deity, Indra, as one part of the Aryan Trinity. His status was then upgraded in a succession of myths that now stand in perplexing contrast to one another. Yet even this is seen as a positive aspect of the power of Shiva—one cannot destroy the Destroyer—and in time one must recognize that he is also the Creator who dances the Eternal Dance of life and death and life again.

If the Vedic Aryans had been successful in eradicating all belief in Shiva at the outset, they might have altered the history of India and that of the world. There might have been no impetus for the creation of Judaism, Christianity, or Islam, and it is quite likely that Hitler realized this, and thus included these three religions in his ultimate plan for religious reform. These historically recent religions only came about because the influence of Shiva and Shakti continued to threaten the power of the Aryan priesthood by infiltrating the Aryan religion.

The revival by Hitler of Teutonic Paganism in German society was gradual, but deliberate. His concept of genetic purity of the race is consistent with the Teutonic Paganism, but taken to the extreme. Ancestry and genetics both are in play in the Teutonic belief of the soul passing down a family line, so that the belief in reincarnation is not just that of rebirth, but rebirth into the specific family, tribe, and race. One could argue that the Jungian idea of archetypes shows this same transmission through genetic inheritance rather than simply through cultural heritage.

In Neo-Paganism today, there is an element of heritage emphasis among the Odinist (or Asatru) Pagans. They do not consider themselves part of the general Neo-Pagan movement, do not incorporate

Shiva Nataraja (Lord of the Dance), in his dual role as the Destroyer and the Creator who dances the Eternal Dance of life and death and life again.

the ideas of Witchcraft or Eastern beliefs, and do not seek racial integration in their system. For many of them, following the Odinist system means that reincarnation will occur in the genetic family unit, and this makes it necessary to prevent dilution of the blood with outsiders, while also making propagation and sons (to carry on the family name) an obligation. The religion itself is insulated from non-Odinist deities and concepts. Hence, it does not incorporate astrology, tarot, kabbalah, or chakras into its practices. Instead, Odinists turn to the Scandinavian, Norse, and Germanic deities (of which Odin is a predominant figure). These Pagans today sometimes find themselves compared to Nazis, or attracting people who have Nazi leanings, because of their emphasis on ancestral roots. Yet Teutonic Paganism can not be blamed as the culprit or cause of Nazism, any more than Christianity can be blamed or seen as the cause of the Inquisition. What people in power DO with religion is what causes atrocities.

Modern Odinists tend to believe in "live and let live," and over the decades there has been some adoption of Wiccan practices, as evidenced by Norse and German-style tarot decks becoming recently available. While still maintaining some degree of exclusivity, Odinists seem to wonder why anyone not of Norse, Scandinavian, or Germanic heritage would even consider the Asatru path, and feel such people should seek their own roots. But racial awareness can become very sticky when one considers the possibilities for intermarriages and unions over the past few millennia and even in recent centuries in America. That was why Hitler created his farms for racially pure *human stock*—his ideal blond-haired, blue-eyed children created from genetic matings of pairs deemed suitable by his geneticists—to start over with what would become a *purebred* race of people.

It is dangerous for Neo-Pagans to proudly point out their heritage today and make this a factor for isolation in their own religious path when they cannot be certain that one of their own offspring might not betray a genetic mixture from their buried past or create through natural genetic mutation a new characteristic that does not fall within accepted parameters. The idea of racial exclusivity in Aryan Paganism most likely did not even exist in the original practice of religion until their warlike migrations brought the Aryan tribes into contact with a diversity of peoples and beliefs, and so the true bloodlines prior to expansionist campaigns are as subject to infiltration as anywhere else.

Here is a meditation using a black mirror to look into your own ancestral past. The mother has long been the recognized link throughout time that determines one's heritage, and in ancient times this lent power to the concept of matriarchy. The Aryan idea of ownership, extending to wives and children, fueled the attempt to trace lineage through the paternal line-father to son, but the sinister nagging suspicion that went with this new heritage was that in the birthing of children, only the mother was certain. Even in patriarchal Judaism, the child is considered Jewish only if the mother is Jewish. This is a vestige of the matrilineal heritage of our ancestors who were well aware of the powerful connection of mother to child. The Etruscans never had this worry or concern, for they cared not who fathered their children. In the old Pagan traditions of Europe, the special sanctions of May Day allowed for procreation to be a gift of the Divine through fertility rituals permitting unrestrained sexual liaisons. Today, the Pagan celebration of Beltane tends to be more restrictive, with the sexual energy of spring being channeled to couples united through marriage or acknowledged partnership. The following meditation lets you look into the mirror to see the faces of your ancestresses. I like to use this one during Samhain as a part of a ritual honoring the ancestors.

Mothers of Time:
A Black Mirror Meditation

For this meditation, you will need a table and chair, black mirror, black candle, mugwort incense, libation bowl, and a chalice containing a dark beverage such as blackberry wine, grape juice, or cranberry juice.

Arrange the table with the mirror at the center, the black candle in front of it, the libation bowl in front of the candle, the incense to the right, and the chalice to the left. Cast your Meditation Circle around the table and chair. With the room dark, light the candle and the incense, then sit so you can look comfortably into the mirror.

> *Mothers of eternity, passing thy light through me; Mother love thru time; mother love from past to future generations flows; our genetic bonds tie our love through the ages. Mothers of my ancestry, mothers of my heritage, we are connected be.*

> *All the mothers of my line, pass our love thru all time. Past, present, future family, mother love is blessed be, blessed be, blessed be, now as then to eternity. So mote it be.*

Let the incense smolder, adding more of the mugwort herb as needed. Gaze into the mirror and see your own reflection. Keep watching your reflection, and now see how it changes first into that of your mother, then your grandmother, and then in more rapid progression, the images of your maternal ancestresses will appear. Notice how they differ? Sometimes the features show similarities to yourself or other family members, other times the face will seem strange, but all are your mothers in time. Greet them with love and remembrance.

> *Mothers of mine in time, I honor thee. You who have passed the gift of life unto me, I honor thee. Mothers of my line and my blood, I honor thee.*

Take your chalice of dark beverage, lift it up before the mirror in a salute, then pour a libation from the cup into the bowl. Now take a sip from the chalice. You may want to reflect on the many faces that pass into view in the mirror, perhaps asking one or two to pause and show you something of their lives. Remember that these are the faces of your own family, and you may feel at ease and comfortable with them. They live in your blood, your very cells and DNA. Now offer more of the mugwort herb to smolder and waft the incense to the faces in the mirror.

> *Mirror of time and love, I offer the scent of remembrance unto my mother heritage. Blessed be the mothers of my family now and through all time. Without them, without their sacrifices, love, and nurture, I would not be. Blessed be the wombs that have carried the children of my line. Blessed be the hearts that have loved the children of my line. Blessed be the eyes that see and the hands that heal. Blessed be my family.*

This meditation can also be used as part of a spell for fertility, simply by adding a request to your mothers of time to help you to pass on the blood of your line:

> *Mothers of mine, mothers in time, you who have passed the blood of my line: hear me in my call to thee, aid me now to emulate thee. You have had your child and now I seek mine. Help me to carry on our family line. Give unto me thy support for our family, guide new into me, that I as thee may blessed be. This is my call unto thee maternally, that as I will so mote it be.*

When you have completed your visit with and honoring of your ancestry, snuff out the candle. Waft the incense to your mirror:

> *Mirror mine I clear thee now. Images gone, memories linger, thy purpose has been fulfilled and you are sent to your rest.*

Cover the mirror with a black cloth, open your Circle, and put away your tools.

The Goal: A Purer Race

It is the element of exclusivity that distinguishes the Teutonic Paganism of Hitler and the religion of the Aryan invaders of India and the Near East from the regional beliefs of the people they conquered. It was this concept of exclusiveness that created the Brahmins of Hinduism and the Levites of Judaism, and encouraged the schism in Islam over whether the religion must be run by descendants and relatives of Mohammed or by anyone of Islamic belief. The Shiites are the ones who accept rulership only from the family of Mohammed (in true Aryan tradition), while the Sunnites accept the rulership of any man who has studied the faith and advanced in religious degrees to a point where he has gained the respect of his fellow devotees (in the Sind tradition except for the subjugation of women, which is not Sind, but Aryan). From these two views of Aryanism the world now sees the results in the wars between Shiite Iran (ancient Persia) and Sunnite Iraq (ancient Sumeria and Babylonia), along with other such polarizations between Islamic nations with populations heavily one tradition or the other—Afghanistan, Pakistan, and Turkey come readily to mind.

The Jews can be seen as following the Aryan tradition of exclusivity by their acceptance of the hereditary rulership of the Levites, while Christians may be seen as "living in Sind" for allowing themselves to be ruled in religious matters by anyone who holds the position of church elder, pastor, reverend, and so forth. The closest that Christianity comes to emulating the exclusivity of the Aryans is in the denominational rivalries that cause different sects to claim salvation as belonging only to their particular members. In the Roman Catholic Church the title of Pope is held in the same authority as a hereditary Aryan ruler, for the Pope is the infallible ruler of that branch of Christianity—but Popes themselves are elected and not genetically related. Mormons have reinstated the Aryan element of exclusivity into their corporate form of Christianity through their system of rulership by the twelve patriarchs who are the descendants of the original followers of Joseph Smith. They also advocate the use of family genealogical studies of the membership for the purpose of baptizing relatives into the faith, alive or dead, willing or unwilling—all for a price.

It was because of the predominance of Italian leadership in the Catholic Church, and its incorporation of many Goddess elements into its liturgy, that Hitler planned to strike them next, and he doubtless felt that he would have the support of anti-Catholic Protestants in this persecution. Next would come the turn of the Christian Protestants to be eradicated. Only then could the Aryan Paganism be fully restored with the new race specially created for him.

The Christianized version of Aryan exclusivity (warring over doctrinal differences with each sect claiming to be the only sect that is faithful to Scripture and therefore *saved*) was what allowed the German people and others of Europe to passively accept the Holocaust. The fact that the people most visible in the persecutions were themselves exclusive because of Aryan influence is an ironic contrast to the plight of the non-Aryan Gypsies.

The real battle between Aryan and non-Aryan Pagan belief systems should have been a moot point in a modern world, yet the battles of 2000–1250 B.C.E. were resurrected in the early years of the twentieth century C.E. What Hitler was attempting to do was go back in time and correct the mistakes of the earlier Aryan conquerors, to eliminate the infusion of non-Aryan beliefs into the Teutonic system. The results, had he succeeded, would have been staggering. Imagine then, the religious systems, one linked with a political system, degenerating into two basic fronts—the purely Aryan, political religion of the mountain, patriarchal Father God, against the non-Aryan, nature religion of earth-fertility, matriarchal Mother Goddess and her Consort, the gentle, loving Horned God. Yet this is exactly the scenario that is anticipated in biblical prophecies. This is not prophecy, but the recognition of Levite priests by 621 B.C.E. of the potential power of the oppressed victims of Aryan conquest. You need to remember that the Bible is an Aryan tool, after all, created by conferences of rabbis and then by consuls of priests, to present a particular point of view, prosecute heresy and nonorthodoxy, and legitimize spiritual dominance in the material world.

From the Judeo-Christian perspective, Hitler then becomes the hero of the Aryan (and therefore, Levite) cause, by supporting the Father God and Aryan patriarchal system of the Old Testament. He becomes the champion of Christian Revelation in his fight against the worship of the Mother Goddess in her guise of Mary the Mother of God, in the Catholic Church, and in his restoring to purity the Aryan faith that had been "sullied" by the Hebrew Semites who dared to name themselves as the Chosen People, while excluding the Germanic Aryans from this honorific title. It is all a matter of interpretation, and Hitler was able to use this fact to accomplish the horrors of genocidal extermination.

There were many people who closed their minds to the murder of innocents because they felt that they were caught up in a holy cause; a predestined and God-ordained holy wrath. This absurdity continues to this day as fundamentalists in America cheered the war in Kuwait and Iraq as evidence of the end of the world—they were willing to allow millions of people to die so that their own Rapture could be accomplished. But there was no Armageddon, just loss of life and despoiling of the waterways. The cheer died out, but the sad part is that cruelty, violence, death, and earthly destruction are eagerly desired for others by these people in the hope that this will lead to the world-wide warfare of Armegeddon and their being carried up into heaven.

After Desert Storm dissipated, the bombings in Serbia over the ethnic cleansing directed against Albanian Moslems received huge support from televangelists—many of whom own and operate their own television networks. There was almost no mention of the previous centuries of hostility between the Christian and Moslem populations, nor of the historical tradition of eastern Europe fighting the Moslem invaders from the Ottoman Empire to give a sense of understanding to the events taking place. Because the Moslems were halted in Eastern Europe, Western Europe was left secure to evolve its own culture without the imposition of the Turkish Empire. Only in Spain, where the last great foothold on Europe was lost to the Moors during the reign of Isabella and Ferdinand, does the memory of Moslem invasions and occupation linger.

Western Europe moved on, as it were, but eastern Europe spent decades in a veritable time capsule enforced by Communism. When the Communist rulership was overthrown, the door was opened not to the twentieth century, but to the fifteenth through nineteenth centuries. Great Britain and Russia had already fought the Ottoman Turks, and to the rest of western Europe, the matter was closed. But to the eastern European, the fact that Moslems had lived for centuries in Christian lands was nothing less than an overly long-endured foreign occupation ignored by the rest of Europe.

It was the perverse pessimism engendered by the Christian need for a huge war that allowed Hitler to pursue his objectives. It was only after they stopped and surveyed the damage that people realized the enormity of their error. The Germans were not alone in this for there were many people worldwide who supported or condoned these exterminations and felt empathy for this intolerance because they saw it as predicted in the Bible. People could be manipulated because they had been conditioned by religion to anticipate righteous mayhem through a garbled interpretation of the Bible, and when they were confronted with the reality of what they had done, they turned away in shame. Today, one would be hard-pressed to find anyone in Germany, for example, who will admit to ever supporting Hitler—yet the throngs of his followers can be seen to number in the hundreds of thousands in old film footage. Hitler could present himself as a biblical hero to his supporters throughout the western world. When mythology is taken as history and as a genuine prophecy from a divine source, reason is shut down, and intolerance is given sway. During World War II the Bible was used to popularize anti-Semitism; today it is used to promote homophobia, anti-feminism, and hysteria against Neo-Pagan spirituality. If Wiccans stood before television cameras and said, "Suffer not a Christian to live," the uproar would be immense, but not a sound of protest is heard when televangelists say, "Suffer not a Witch to live," without even realizing that this is a sentence invented by the Bible editors of King James at a time when the horrendous British persecutions (which, incidentally, were greater than those of the Spanish Inquisition) needed Divine sanction. The word "Witch" is not even Hebraic, but Anglo-Saxon, and never existed in the original text. Yet in 1999, a Representative in Congress had the audacity to write to a commanding officer of a military base where there are practicing Wiccans, telling him to "stop this nonsense now." (Rep. Robert Barr, Jr., R-Georgia), and threatened hearings and legislation against Wicca. For as much as I hear the expression, "Never again the Burning Times," I have to wonder. Can we hold onto freedom of religion in the face of continual challenges? Perhaps I will feel a little more secure when there are Pagan or Wiccan television networks, or open temples in neighborhoods for Pagan gatherings.

In Neo-Paganism, we can see a more peaceful recognition of the interaction of the two ancient religious traditions of Sind and the Aryans. Why should one branch be more prone to exclusiveness while the other is more open to the integration of human kind? The clue lies in the geographic location of their development. Here then is the heritage of the Sun People and the Ice People as recently expounded upon in university settings. Whichever path one follows depends upon individual preference and heritage. People with Nordic, Scandinavian, and Germanic heritage *might* be inclined to a Celtic tradition, but it is more likely that, being familiar with the gods and goddesses of the Vikings, they would gravitate to the Asatru. People from areas of Europe that were influenced by the Celts and Indus travelers might tend to gravitate toward the deities of their ancestors—the Mother Goddess and the Horned God. People from the more southern regions of Africa could gravitate toward their own ancestral deities, some of which have distinctly Indus touches brought through contacts in pre-historic times and from the integrated southern societies of those days. People of the Far East have a different heritage that contains aspects of the Indus tradition in the Yin and Yang, as well as localized beliefs that are similar to Aryan ancestor worship, although such a tendency is problematical due to the nonorganizational aspect of Neo-Paganism. Today we might easily find shrines in Pagan-Wiccan households dedicated to the Chinese goddess, Kwan Yin or to the Santerían god, Chango. Thus there is always the possibility for the formation of a group of Black Odinists.

As long as the ugly spectre of *superiority* does not get a foothold in Neo-Paganism, all the Pagan systems, be they Aryan, Shamantic, Kabbalic, or Wiccan, should thrive together. The primary key to the modern success of the Pagan revival is the unifying belief that each person is free to follow his or her own path, and that all paths are equally valid. The need for a concept of superiority came from the political aspirations of a leader intent on regressing history in order to change it. Racial and ethnic superiority were the enabling tools of a dictatorship that hoped to eventually destroy the very people being deluded with praise of their greatness, in order to replace them with genetically screened children.

The reason Hitler was doomed to failure from the start was because in the end, he could not create quickly enough, nor maintain, a segregated system and win in a war against a homogenized nation such as the United States of America. The ancient Northern and Southern cultures were too integrated in America for the Aryan cause to be palatable. There were too many people of Italian, German, Irish, Hispanic, French, and Native American descent, many with a mixture of these cultural heritages, in its armed forces for America to be divided into Aryan and non-Aryan regions.

Orientals and Negroes were not factored into the equation, for the baffle lines were based primarily on a conflict of European worship systems, and thus Hitler tended to view these people as not important, even when aligning himself with the Japanese Empire. Also, in Hitler's time, the armed forces of the United States were still not fully integrated, and African-Americans were the subject of seg-regation in many facets of daily life in America. This also explains the reason why Neo-Nazis see a need for a separate region set aside for white supremicists. They want to retain the Aryan past and the Aryan Pagan system of genetic reincarnation and patriarchal inheri-tance, but in the face of modern trends toward the empowerment of African-Americans and women, interracial unions, the acceptability of women retaining their surnames and having matrilineal descent through non-marriage (single mothers), and the need for multicul-tural studies in schools because of the shrinking of the world through mass communications, the Aryan supremicist is foundering in an eroding social structure that used to support the Aryan ideals of male dominance and racial segregation. These same factors are what Fundamentalist Christians and Orthodox Jews have focused on in order to identify religious nonconformity as the scapegoat for the modern social changes that threaten to erode their power base. Hence, the tragedy of children driven to extreme measures based on their sense of alienation in their school is dismissed by virtue of their having been "born evil."

The Neo-Pagan and Wiccan trend toward eclecticism can be traced to the interactions and intermarriages of various ethnic peo-ples. Most Americans are a combination of cultural backgrounds rather than purely Irish, or German, or Italian, etc., and thus can easily assimilate a variety of deity concepts into one workable path. The tendency toward eclectic traditions in Europe stems from the same intercultural unions, as well as awareness brought about through mass media and migrations of peoples from former (or cur-rent) colonial possessions.

It may well be that the reason the Neo-Pagan/Wiccan movement has become so popular in recent years is because the authority of mainstream religions has been undermined by a combination of more readily available education, greater discoveries in the fields of history and archaeology, and the ability to spread the associated ideas through the media of printed matter, television, movies, and the computer-linked internet. Mainstream religions cannot maintain their suffocating grip on the minds of the populace once college-level education is available to the masses, and the ideas inherent in Paganism and the New Age are no longer kept out of bookstores, the press, and television. Thus, people are exposed to programs such as Shirley McLaine's film, *Out On A Limb*, and various talk shows wherein guests speak positively about Neo-Paganism and Wicca. Public Broadcasting Systems (PBS) and cable networks like Discovery Channel and The Learning Channel present quality educational shows such as "Testament" and the "Myth" series of Joseph Campbell.

J. R. R. Tolkien and other writers are able to strike a chord by presenting an alternative reality that works in its own framework and meshes with the tenuous fibers of human history, thus demonstrating how one person can create a myth that will appeal to millions. Joseph Campbell's intriguing series of books and lectures on human mythological systems forced people to realize that the themes of modern Judeo-Christian religions were not exclusive and not the word of any one god, but a collective and unifying mythological experience of all peoples, worshipping many deities in different ways. Campbell saw science fiction and science fantasy as the rising new mythologies replacing the old. Sir James George Frazier, detailing his search for the lost history of magic and religion in *The Golden Bough* (1890), suggested that the past religious concepts have simply been transmuted into those of the present, so now we can speculate on how those of the present will be transmuted into those of the future. The monopoly on western thought held by Christian churches is being broken, and as time goes on, the likely path is one of further divergence from mainstream religions.

In trying to avert this loss of power and control, the churches are already either adapting to include the ideals of the Neo-Pagans in their own liturgy, or attempting to terrify their followers and insulate them from knowledge and public education. Both paths are in evidence in varying degrees in a number of churches. The only other option, erupting sporadically but not truly viable, is warfare against the nonconformists, and this is evidenced by bombings and killings at various Women's Clinics that have been renamed and targeted by Fundamentalist Christians as "Abortion Clinics." People are harassed, video-taped entering and leaving, their license tags written down, and abusive literature sent to their homes because of this notion that Women's Clinics, although offering a myriad of services oriented to the specific problems and concerns of women, only serve to support abortions. Thus one woman was murdered in a bombing who was there for a followup on hip surgery, and a man was murdered in a bombing while waiting for his wife during her prenatal maternity visit. These attempts at warfare and righteous insurrection have instead taken on the appearance of terrorism of the worst sort, linking inflamed, misguided erstwhile Christians with all other modern terrorists and airplane bombers. Here is the same dehumanizing method of Hitler at work, and this is not spirituality in any religion.

The advent of mass migrations and the influx of population with a variety of ethnic backgrounds represented in many countries like France, England, the Netherlands, and the United States make warfare against the nonconformists an unwieldy course, one that would result in civil wars of religion all over the world, with ultimate power going to whichever country had the most ethnically insulated group—perhaps Japan or China—and without the need for effort to be expended in conquest. Even a victory for orthodoxy would be a defeat because of the high cost of such a war with today's weapons. Everyone would be affected, and everyone would know that the cause was based on intolerance, in direct violation of western democratic and constitutional traditions, let alone the biblical injunction of Jesus to "Love thy neighbor."

Today there are wars of religion in various locations around the world. Irish Catholics against Protestants, Indian Moslems against Hindus, Hindus against Buddhists, Sunnite Moslems against Shiite Moslems, Shiite Moslems against anyone not Shiite, Moslems

Phidias' statue of Athena or Pallas (right) once graced the Parthenon on the Acropolis at Athens, Greece. In 1994, a copy of this statue was placed in the replica of the Parthenon in Nashville, Tennessee.

A statue of the Hindu snake goddess is displayed in a ritual setting in the author's home (below).

217

against Jews and vice versa, and Christians against Moslems in Eastern Europe. Already, world opinion decries these senseless massacres of innocent people who are the pawns of political leaders divorced from the suffering they inflict upon others or driven by fanaticism to not care. With education and the spread of knowledge concerning the roots of these conflicts, people may come to realize that religion is only a cover for the real cause for wars—that wars are political and economic, involving power and control, not spiritual salvation. When taken in that context, people can see that wars come from greed, and that invoking the name of a deity is no excuse for killing because there is nothing sacred about human avarice. Perhaps then people will be less likely to be swayed by bigotry disguised as righteousness, and the result would be a shaking of faith in any religion that deliberately demands such destructiveness. This, in turn, might well generate appreciation for a more tolerant, Earth-centered path of duality. The better aspects of the old Paganism could receive a worldwide revival.

I would like to think that the advent of mass education will help to forestall further civil wars of religion and give nations an opportunity to recognize that conflicts rooted in ethnic differences come from not understanding the oneness of humanity. These conflicts, then, are most likely to occur in regions where intercultural education has either been neglected or perverted to add support for a regime that would otherwise fail or be forced into accepting changes. A culturally insular nation such as Japan offers an example of the types of strategies used to control information that might affect the powerbase of the ruling class. Japanese education, for example, traditionally ends high school history courses with the late nineteenth century rather than cover the events of World War II.

So what can be the future of religion in the world? Can a personal mythology be the answer? Perhaps, but only with the general recognition that no one path is superior to another. It is likely that most Neo-Pagans and Wiccans already accept this tenet, and an orthodox path will never be established. Each individual must seek to find the Divine within—individually—soul to *Soul*. With the Neo-Pagan movement gaining momentum, opposition will increase, but the powerbase of the Church is eroded in America by design in the mandated separation of state and church. This is what gives America the edge in exploring new spiritual ground. The Founding Fathers (and Mothers) knew what they were doing; knew that it was wrong to legislate another's soul or conscience. It would seem that ultimately the Neo-Pagan movement must be successful because it will work inside people and cause them to be more loving and accepting of each other. People cannot preach against that without exposing a base of self-hatred and irrational fear of others. That is what makes Neo-Paganism the better alternative.

Let us look forward with hope for justice and a gathering in of a fruitful harvest as designated in the tarot cards of Justice, The Star, and Judgement. Here is a tarot spell to focus on the activation of these influences.

Justice, Hope, and Harvest Spell

Set on your altar the tarot cards for Justice, the Star, and Judgement. Altar candles may be light blue or white. Have a blue votive candle in a cauldron, a little St. John's Wort, anise (star anise), oats (from oatmeal is fine), and hyssop.

Begin the spell after you have cast your Circle and invoked the Elementals and the Divine. Light the candle in the cauldron, and hold up the card for Justice.

> *Here is the symbol for balance in thought, word, and deed.*
> *This is the card of impartiality, Let me remember that fair-*
> *ness is not easily given, but comes through demand. May I*
> *have the courage to define my principles with objectivity and*
> *careful assessment, that I am able to defend those ideals.*

Place the card in front of the votive in the cauldron and add some of the St. John's Wort to the flame.

Here stands the Law of Returns, for what is sent comes back.

Hold up the card of The Star.

I hold in my hand the symbol of hope and opportunity. Let me remember to have faith in my self and my destiny. I know that difficulties will be overcome, and I hold the light of the Star to guide the way with optimism. May opportunities arise to open the way to free acceptance of the variety of spiritual expressions in this land.

Set The Star card behind the cauldron and add some of the anise to the flame.

Let this light of Justice shine with Hope and Opportunity behind it.

Look at the flame for a moment. Visualize a world where people are not oppressed or persecuted for their beliefs and spirituality. See people living in peace and harmony, with malice towards none and love towards all. Feel balance and optimism emanate to make all things possible. Now take the card of Judgement and hold it up.

Justice   The Star   Judgement

> *Here is the reward for our actions. Here is a harvest of what*
> *we sow. May we sow with care that we reap with joy, for we*
> *are accountable for what we do. Let there be a new beginning*
> *from our past, and a new focus for our future.*

Add a little of the oats to the flame, then add a little hyssop. Set the Judgement card on top of the Justice card, then place the Star on top of them. Motion your wand over the candle three times, saying:

> *St. John's Wort for balance of Justice; anise for the hope of*
> *The Star, oats of our past tempered with the purification of*
> *hyssop for Judgement; Release thy powers unto this spell! Let*
> *thy energies be directed to the freedom of spiritual expression*
> *in this land!*

Then when you feel the power has built up, raise your arms with the wand in your power hand so as to gather the energy together, and quickly direct the flow into the votive candle.

> *The spell is cast for Justice, bound in Judgement, and sealed*
> *with Hope, So Mote It Be.*

You may now conclude with Cakes and Wine, then open your Circle. Let the candle burn for an hour, then snuff it out and put away your tools. You may want to look for images of divination relating to your spell in the cooling candle wax. Bury the candle in the ground out of doors to release the energies to spread their work.

Chapter Eight

Reviewing the Past to Uncover the Future

Hold up thy torch, Dark Goddess of the Underworld,
that thy Light may lead us
through the passage of thy domain
and into the promise of spiritual rebirth.
—Samhain black mirror invocation

When I think about the past, I view it from a historian's perspective that compresses our miniscule recorded time against
the vast millions of years of life on Earth. The notion of a
short-term lifespan for humanity as a whole has never had an appeal
for me, and so the apocalyptic mainstream religions of western society have never satisfied my rational mind. I cannot ignore the
archaeological evidence of human existence that transcends 400,000
years and several ice ages, nor can I accept the unsubstantiated suggestions that everything prior to two thousand years ago was evil
and wrapped in darkness. I have seen the beauty of the past in the
surviving archaeological structures and the recovered artifacts during my travels in Europe, so I know there is evidence of people living joyful lives in cultures where art and music thrived. By looking
at these reminders of our heritage, and keeping the embers of my
family tradition alive, I deeply feel the connection of now with then,
and I want to share this sensation as much as I can. To determine
who we are and where we are going, we must first find our past and
where we have been.

There are several lessons from history that have had a subtle effect on the resurgence of the Old Religion and Neo-Paganism in the modern world. Why are people looking to their ancient roots for a new spirituality? What are the lessons of the past that shape the new approach to this ancient spirituality? How did the political-ization of religion interfere with individual spirituality? The ruined remains of pre-Christian western heritage show vibrant, artistically alive and beautiful societies spread across the Mediterranean and Europe. The artifacts of human adornment, the clothing and needlework skills, the dwellings, the ships, the utensils, all point to a full integration of art, beauty, and refinement in every aspect of life. Oh yes, there were invasions, there were wars, resulting mainly from rising population and avarice, and wars are still with us. But the cultures of the time show a sophistication, intelligence, and cre-ativity rarely recognized by our contemporaries. Instead, society expects us to accept the idea that technological progress makes us somehow superior to our ancestors. Yet we are genetically one with them, and they too had their technologies that now amaze us and leave us in wonderment when we gaze upon Stonehenge, the Pyra-mids, Knossos, or the Parthenon.

But why the spiritual change then from joyful love of life to self-loathing and hatred of the beauty of Nature? Why the redirection of material pleasures from the hands of the populace into the hands of the priesthood and the selected and protective aristocracy from which it drew its membership? Why did people accept the dour misery imposed upon them by a ministry that enjoyed the opulent decadence they condemned emperors for? Why the revulsion of over half the society in an artificial denouncement of the female sex as a sub-human creature whose very nature is supposedly evil? Why fear and loathing for people's love for one another? Why the reviling of the bountiful earth and sea? Why the alienation of the people from their world, their art, their knowledge, and their enjoyment of life? WHY? Who are we spiritually? Where did we come from? And why in the name of the goddess Hel did we let ourselves get into this horrible condition where in so many of the world's wars people slaughter one another over religious practices that serve only to glorify the priesthood and instill ignorance in the populace?

Today, the ogham symbol straif, the *blackthorn—strife*, that has for so long represented the lot of the Craft and the practitioners of the Craft, is being turned around to be the *whitethorn—overcoming coercion*. Political forces are now being turned around to grant legal and judicial support to the followers of this most ancient of spiritual paths. Today, networking among Pagans is resulting in positive support and genuine fellowship. The following spell may be used to help you focus on turning around adversity, or overcoming almost any kind of strife faced in daily life. Do not rush the spell—give the candles time to burn as you go along.

Blackthorn-Wheel-Lovers-Chariot-Whitethorn Overcoming Adversity Spell

Along with your regular altar items, you will need juniper oil (for cleansing), rosemary oil (for releasing negativity), benzoin oil (for changes), the tarot cards of The Lovers, The Chariot, and The Wheel of Fortune, three candles that may be votives or small pillar styles—one black, one white, and one amber; bayberry incense (for transitions); a bloodstone (heliotrope) for removing obstacles, bringing balance and integrity, and enhancing talents; and the following herbs: hawthorn berries (to enhance Witchcraft skills), hyssop (for removing malevolence and negativity), mullein (for deflection and return-to-sender influence), purple heather (for cleansing, spiritual attainment, and prosperity), vervain (for purification and opening psychic centers), and woodruff (to overcome obstacles, clear barriers, and encourage changes).

Place the candles on the altar with the black to the left, the amber in the center, and the white to the right. Light the bayberry incense, and think about the significance of this herbal scent for transitions. Lay out the tarot cards with The Wheel of Fortune card in front of the black candle, The Lovers card in front of the amber candle, and The Chariot card in front of the white candle. As you set these cards in place, think about the Wheel as change, the Lovers as partnership and making choices, and the Chariot as overcoming obstacles and merit recognized.

Inscribe on the black candle
the symbol for the blackthorn:

Inscribe on the white candle
the symbol for the whitethorn:

Inscribe on the amber candle a pentagram
with the symbol for the ash (awakening/
rebirth) in the center portion:

and the symbol for the elder (change/
evolution) at the upper point:

Inside the two equal-arm points,
draw the symbols for the Goddess in
the left and the God in the right:

Inside the lower two points, draw on
the left side the symbol for the aspen
(overcoming obstacles):

and on the right side, the alder
(strong foundation):

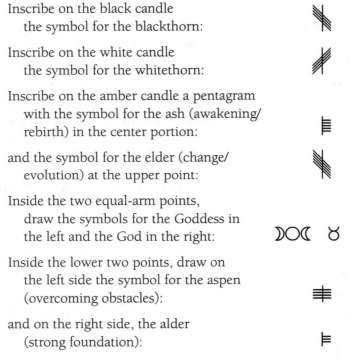

Rub the amber candle with juniper oil and set it back on the altar:

This is the candle of the Craft; with juniper I cleanse and purify this candle, preparing it for fresh changes and new beginnings.

Rub the black candle with rosemary oil and set it back on the altar:

This is the candle of the past; with rosemary I prepare this candle for the releasing of negative energies.

Rub the white candle with the benzoin oil and set it back on the altar:

> *This is the candle of the future; with benzoin I prepare this candle to direct the changes to come.*

Hold up the bloodstone:

> *Here is the remover of obstacles—blood and stone, the life essence of the Earth, steady through time, yet ever changing and evolving.*

Place the bloodstone on top of the card of The Lovers. Light the black candle, then drop a bit of the hyssop into the candle flame:

> *From the past there has been adversity, obstruction and strife toward the practice and practitioners of the Old Religion. By the energies of the hyssop I remove this obstructive and malevolent influence from the past.*

Drop in some of the mullein:

> *Through the energies of the mullein I deflect any ill-will back to the sender that there be evolving changes and progress for the revival of the Old Religion.*

Hold up The Wheel of Fortune card over the black candle (not close enough to be singed!):

> *Turn about, turn about, reversing the flow. Turn about, turn about, the wheel must go. Look once to the future; Look once to the past, changes made now, are now made to last.*

Then set the card down again. Light the amber candle and drop a bit of the heather into the flame:

> *The present awaits, with choices to be made, with the energies of heather I cleanse and prepare the present for the good fortunes to come.*

Now drop three hawthorn berries into the amber candle:

*One for the skills of the past, one for the skills of the present,
and one for the skills yet to come. May the energies of the
hawthorn berries aid in the renewal of the witchery skills of
the Old Religion and encourage their growth.*

Hold up The Lovers card over the amber candle:

*Partnership of influences, partnership of beneficence!
By heather and hawthorn is the old brought together with
the new that this present move brightly into the future
unimpaired by the past.*

Set the card in front of the amber candle. Light the white candle
and drop a bit of the woodruff into the flame:

*With the energies of the woodruff I overcome obstacles!
The barriers disappear that change may take root.*

Drop in some of the vervain:

*Through the energies of the vervain I open the psychic
centers, clearing the pathways, bringing a cleansed and
purified evolvement of the renewed Old Religion.*

The Wheel · · · · · · · · The Lovers · · · · · · · · The Chariot

Hold up The Chariot card over the white candle:

Victory and recognition of merit await at the gate! The
psychic paths are open for renewal of ancient faith. May
we build with nobility of spirit and generosity of heart; May
we graciously finish what we joyfully start.

Set the card down again. Take the bloodstone and set it on The Chariot card.

With balance and integrity is the future now sought. With
talents enhanced is the old Craft renewed.

Open your arms and say:

With three cards, three candles, three oils, and six herbs,
this spell is cast three times three, with six to mix well. Past,
present, and future move now in harmony, for as this do I
will, So Mote It Be!

Let the candles burn for eighteen minutes, then extinguish the black one. If your piece of bloodstone is large, you can use it to snuff the candle (later, cleanse the stone in spring water and let it rest on amethyst or wrapped in a black cloth to renew its energies). In another eighteen minutes, extinguish the amber. After another eighteen minutes, extinguish the white candle. You may want to have a simple feast during this period, then open your Circle and put away your tools. Bury the black candle in the backyard, the amber in the side yard, and the white in the front yard, or bury them in flower pots you place at these locations, or create your own symbolism that distinguishes the past, present, and future aspects of these candles.

Religion and Worship

European Witchcraft hearkens back to the worship familiar to the people of the Indus some 30,000 years ago, while the Teutonic variety, differing from this by minimalizing the female aspect of the Deity, dates to a little over 4,000 years and represents a different evolution of worship in which the new politicalization of religion blended with the older style. Expansionist warfare, and the subsequent development of an authoritarian hierarchy for social control and warfare, resulted in a specialized Teutonic clergy whose duty was to validate this system by standing between the ruled and their deities. The limitations of the Northern environment may also have resulted in an emphasis on the value of brute strength needed for the protection of females and young in the harsh life at the edge of the Ice Age. Yet, the new system brought about a man-centeredness and signaled the end of living with respect toward Nature and the environment.

Religion everywhere had been based in nature and ecstasy, but the new version was based in ritual and a newly defined morality that served as a means of controlling people. No longer was humanity part of the Divine process of Nature, but separate, and given the injunction to dominate without thought for the future, since there was only final judgment and eternal bliss or eternal damnation. Because of this attitude, enforced by civil law, dogmas stifled individual self-realization and destroyed the intrinsic joy of being part of the Divine through living the creation. The attacks on sexuality were defined through lack of any other suitable teaching; these provided a scapegoat focus for people who were by law and clergy no longer allowed to participate in the sacred firsthand. Through the power of the clergy the individually experienced magic of the past was reduced into mere public ritual.

Western religion today reflects an amalgamation created by the intersection of Aryan practices and beliefs with those of ancient Sind. The Aryan aspects can be traced by reverting and retrogressing to the themes constant in Christ, Buddha, Krishna, Indra, Thor, and Odin. The themes of Sind are found by taking what is left. If negative, this reflects an Aryan rebuke of a Sind practice or belief. If incorporated into the overall system, this reflects a Sind aspect absorbed and tolerated, if not always accepted by the Aryans to form the conglomerate of modern religions. Thus, there are three components in modern western religious beliefs: Sind, Aryan, and the Aryan rejection of Sind. Since parts of Sind were accepted, these aspects were aligned with the religion of the Aryans, and have effectively become identified as Aryan. From that point, whatever was rejected was labeled Sind, to become modern sin.

Included in the accepted Sind practices are ritual bathing, water baptism; an all-powerful, yet personal God; a nurturing consort/ Mother; a Holy Spirit; accessibility of the God and the Mother of God by the individual through personal prayer and gifts (be it lighting candles, presenting flowers, or burning incense); and the concepts or practices centered around the idea of God being within the individual; rebirth through the union with the Holy Spirit; and unity with God. These are features that are absent from pure Aryanism.

Aspects of pure Aryanism include the use of an altar and fire sacrifices (be it animal or human) to appease God; a God of wrath and vengeance approachable only by a selected priesthood; ritual words, motions, and adornments; temple artifacts, priesthood duties, ritual attonements, and rewards codified into a holy law; holy laws as the sum of mundane existence, with penalties for disobedience placed in the hands of the administering priesthood; a Savior to redeem a people considered naturally evil; a Heaven where the saved labor for God and praise God continuously; and a Hell where the *unsaved* are eternally tortured. Good women are not offered an afterlife reward, but they are admonished to be meek and submissive to the power of men.

Aspects of Sind rejected by Aryanism and labeled as *sin* (derived from *Sind* as previously explained) involve the power of the Goddess, who was generally designated as male and a demon or devil; snakes as symbols of immortality and wisdom, being made evil in the Bible version of Creation; the ready availability of eternal life symbolized by a tree, of whose fruit Adam and Eve were forbidden to partake; manifestations of the energies inhabiting plants, animals, and minerals, with devas becoming demons and evil spirits; independent women, who are personified as a variety of contemptible, threatening, or homicidal demonesses like Jezebel, the succubus, and Lilith; freedom of the individual to approach God on a level of daily life without a special holy day each week or prescribed rituals involving an ordained clergy, such individuals being labeled as heretics and eliminated through war, torture, and execution; the inherent goodness of people and sexuality being considered normal, this being specifically repudiated in doctrine that is enforced through religious and/or civil law; and the right to enjoy life without fear of a hell (or even a heaven) for the law of Karma lays the responsibility and repayment for one's actions on oneself, rejected by dogma in the Judeo-Christian-Islamic, but accepted in Buddhist systems.

Hinduism, as a closer combination of Aryanism and Sind, is more erratic in the acceptance of Sind traditions, and any of these aspects entering into the Aryanized faith becomes a component for one of the various denominations of Hinduism. Even so, the early mythology of the Vedics stresses the superiority of the Aryan race (the Ramayan frequently emphasizes this), and describes the original inhabitants, who are followers of Shiva, as Demons. These Dravidic peoples are recognized as having occasionally defeated the Aryan deities, but one of the purposes of the mythologies is to integrate Shiva into the Vedic pantheon, so the original peoples are defeated by a combination of Vedic and Dravidic beings (the "ape-men" and "bears") and deities. Here is where Shiva's title of "Lord of Demons" makes sense—he is the Lord for the native population, whose still fighting hold-outs to Aryan conquest were labeled as Demons.

Thus, sin comes from following the religion of Sind—the religion of Shiva and Shakti. Even the Goddess Ishtar's father was named Sin in Babylonian mythology. Archaeological evidence shows that there was abundant trade between the advanced region of India and the less well-developed regions of Arabia, Iran, and Iraq around 2900 B.C.E., and it is considered likely that the earlier Sumerians of 3600 B.C.E. were colonists from Sind. It would therefore have been natural for Sind to be a major influence on the religious development of these regions.

Shiva, as the oldest continuously worshipped deity known to human society, was the basis for widespread natural religious beliefs—beliefs which over time incorporated veneration of the phallus, vaginal womb, horns, bulls, snakes, trees, wheat, and wild horned beasts, dating from the Paleolithic period until around 4,000 years ago with the development of a political religious system.

In contemporary Hinduism, just as in pre-Vedic times, Shiva has been depicted as both male and female combined (Ardhanari) or separated into two aspects as Shiva (male) and Shakti (female). The name for God traditionally is AUM or UMA, depending upon which aspect is being addressed and, in a way later echoed by the Hebraic kabbalah tradition, each letter has meaning. Tantric Hinduism has it that the A equates to *Grace* (male), U is *Power* (female), and M is the *All* (androgyne). The term AUM (also written in modern Hinduism as OM and used as a powerful mantra with a pronunciation that incorporates all the vowel sounds) is identified as male Shiva, with the emphasis on the aescetic Grace.

The female aspect of UMA, seen in modern India as well as ancient Sind and early Sumer and Babylon, is the name of the Goddess with the aspect of power being emphasized. Nevertheless, Shiva is Shakti, and Shakti is Shiva, and They are both united in either name by the All, which is Shiva and Shakti as androgyne. The mantra should run continuously in recitation so the Lord and the Lady blend into one Divine Sound as "AUMAUMAUMAUMA . . ." Who can determine where AUM ends and UMA begins? Perhaps cats were honored by ancient cultures because they seem to say the sacred sound of the Divine Names repeatedly.

The ancient term "Dravidic" is generally applied to the Indus people who lived in the Sind region before the advent of Aryan invaders. Today there is still a distinct regional people in Southern India known as Dravidic, and they are considered to be descended from the refugees who fled the Indus during the Vedic invasions. These people today still worship the Goddess as primary, with Shiva as Her consort being secondary to Her Power. Both the Dravidic Shiva of the Indus and the Shiva of modern Vedic Hinduism are still often portrayed as hermaphrodites, and this image was carried by migrating Dravidians to various parts of the western world by at least 6000 B.C.E., as evidenced by Neolithic Eastern European and Mediterranean European artifacts and burial customs.

In both ancient and modern works of art in India, Shiva is sometimes depicted as split down the middle, head to toe, with the right side being male and the left side being female. That is why modern Wiccan altars generally will place the God on the viewer's right and the Goddess on the viewer's left—to make the positioning accurate from the viewer's perspective. This veneration of a dual deity is one of the basic differences between the practices of Witches and those of the Teutonic Pagans.

In post-Dravidic Hindu tradition, OM is the Supreme Being in the form of sound and comes at the start and end (alpha and omega) of all hymns, religious actions, and recitations of sacred text (as is similar to *Amen*). It is the most powerful of all mantras, spelled AUM in the Tantric tradition of Hinduism, which is believed to be based on the tradition of Sind. This relates to the mainstream Christian view of the power of the Word of God; Judaic inhibition against speaking or writing the Name of God; and the use of *words of power* by ancient Pagans and the Neo-Pagans of today. Mantras were adopted into use by kabbalah and subsequent ceremonial magic traditions in the sense that people tried to use these ancient sounds (mantras or words of power) to make the gods subject to the will of the practitioners.

The Vedic tradition, with its attempt to suppress the Dravidic, changes the meanings of the letters of AUM into *Wakefulness, Dreaming,* and *Deep Sleep,* with the whole being *Transcendence.* The fact that the more ancient tradition was not lost speaks to the resiliency of the Old Religion. The powerful concept of male and female in union as equals, as Shiva/Shakti, was too appealing an image to be swept aside by the Vedic deities of Brahma, Vishnu, and Indra. Instead, Indra was diminished, and the male Shiva was given a place in the Triad, with Shakti relegated to the position of his spouse in the male-oriented religion.

In Sind, the Vedics worked hard to discourage the worship of the Horned God, the Lord of the Beasts, the God of Fertility, the Lord of the Dance, by aligning Shiva with one of their own negative tribal war deities, Rudra, and giving him new aspects in their mythology—Lord of Vampires, Terror, and Destroyer. Yet the Destroyer aspect of Shiva has always been in reference to the ebb and flow of the Universe. Over the centuries, the mythologies changed in acceptance of Shiva's endurance and the deity advanced in the religion of the people who conquered the Dravidians. Today, Shiva devotees see him as the embodiment of Love (the modern metaphor of "God is Love" came from the Hindu statement, "Shiva is Love" some two hundred years earlier), and affirm that Brahma and Vishnu are merely aspects of Shiva, who is All. Some Tantric versions emphasize Power over Grace, call Shakti the primary deity, and revere her as Devi, the Mother Goddess, Great Goddess, and many other forms still seen today in modern India.

The origins of religious tradition in Mesopotamia can be traced to the Indus River Valley with the worship of Shiva and Devi (male and female, grace and power) in one aspect or another. It was to refute the God and the Goddess that the Judaic system was devised, thus does Judaism owe its beginnings to Shiva/Shakti. The very word God comes from the German *Gott,* which is derived from the Sanskrit root, *Go,* meaning "the bull," while the French and Latin version of *Dieu* is derived from the word *Div,* meaning "radiant," the same as Deva ("shining one"), and in description, the same as the term applied to the Fairy Folk, Sidhe (Siddha—"charged with energy"). In these ways it becomes clear that the popular deity image of the Old Religion is still retained in the vocabulary of modern mainstream religions.

The devil, then, is merely an antagonistic view of the Goddess, or Devi, of Dravidian belief. The name of David applied to the House of God can be traced to the far more ancient name of the Dravidic people and their religion. As their beliefs formed the basis for the most ancient religion known in Mesopotamia, the Dravidians were themselves the *House of God*—the people from whom the concepts of the dual deity originated. By 2000 B.C.E., the Dravidians worshipped Shiva in the aspect of a god of the wildwood, and Devi was a tree goddess, which reflects the influence of the heavy forestation of the Indus region and the importance of woodcarving skills among the inhabitants. Devi was also identified with snakes (the venom being most likely used by priestesses for oracles and divination purposes). Saul, Israel's alleged first king, is a name for a durable and prized tree of India, and David succeeds this *Tree* (of the Goddess) as Dravidic Shiva (male aspect assuming Aryan Power).

The writers of the Bible frequently turned female deities into males (the goddess Ashtoreth becoming the male demon Astaroth, for example) and distortions in names were deliberately used to prevent the Aryan Yahweh from being compared to a female. Thus Saul actually represents the female tree of the Goddess Devi, while she then became a male devil. This is all a metaphor expressing the transition of the Semite Hebrews through stages into a Judaic religion. David weds Bathsheba (*daughter of Shiva*) to fully subordinate the female aspect of Shiva. Their son Solomon is, in mythical terms, the first Aryan king of the Hebrews, and is called peaceful and wise. Why was David's dancing into Jerusalem before the Arc of the Covenant deemed wrong in the Bible story? Because it showed that Dravidic Shiva, Lord of the Dance, entered the region before a Levitic Aryan deity could be established.

Why did the Queen of Sheba (*Shiva's Queen*) come to Solomon? So the Aryan king could demonstrate the superiority of Judaism by sending Shiva's wife (Power) to wed an obscure mortal king and be submissive to him. Shiva's aspect of wisdom is fully integrated into Solomon and the Aryan religion here, and Shakti is depicted as mortal and vanquished in the light of Aryan supremacy. These were not historic events, and archaeologists and historians today recognize this, present this in professional journals and books, and show this on cable and public television programs, but make little or no headway in public education because our textbooks fear to treat modern Aryan-based religions the same as any other mythology. Thus in school books, the religions of India are treated with a cool analysis that belies any spiritual value in them, contrasting significantly with the deference offered in discussions of Judaism and the Christian religions of post-Pagan Europe.

The Old Testament stories are myths used to bolster the importance of a new religion in the minds of Semitic Hebrews, simply because these people were in reality very eclectic in their religious practices. The main thrust of the Bible is the difficulties of the Levite priesthood in keeping their subjects from reverting to the religious customs that pre-dated Levitic Judaism. One must also keep in mind that the Old Testament was not even begun until 621 B.C.E., that the New Testament was not pieced together and edited until circa 400 C.E., and that major tenets of Christian orthodoxy were still being formulated after the Second Council of Constantinople in 553 C.E. It is no coincidence that the equating of evil with money, possessions, and social stature is emphasized in the Bible—this is the religion of people who had very little in a world where the practitioners of far older religions had plenty—the *have-nots* raging against the *haves*. Karl Marx would have seen them as the disenfranchised, the potential Communists, and indeed the early religious communities of Christianity followed many Communist precepts.

This phenomenon is seen in the various Christian cults that arise from time to time and demand that all the followers' earthly possessions be turned over to the cult leader. This mentality of turning over one's wealth to a church or religious leader has been instilled by centuries of religious programming so that for many people of former Christian heritage, turning to another spiritual path is often signified by turning over their possessions to a person or institution as an act of cleansing, contrition, or submission to a new law. One of the lasting conflicts in Judaism is control of wealth among the membership—the Levites are no longer as powerful as they once were, and thus those advocating a return to strict orthodoxy are seeking to return power to the elite priesthood of the rabbis.

Once Christianity became established through civil laws, beginning with the reign of Constantine, the problem of what to do with prosperity was handled by encouraging the dying rich to will their material gains not to their heirs but to the Church. The Church, then, became the very repository of the immense wealth previously decried as evil. Meanwhile, the Pagan traditions of the Old Religion still were being practiced, the Pagan holidays were being observed, and the Pagan deities were being honored by the vast majority of the population.

Why does Christian tradition say that God is *Three In One*? Possibly because Shiva is traditionally called *Trimurti* (three-embodied). Why does Satan have a pitchfork? Because Shiva's symbol (painted on the foreheads of devotees at ceremonies) is the trident, which shows the Trimurti aspect by having three points joined into one weapon. This is also the significance of the *Gae Bulga*, the Fairy weapon given to the Irish hero of Ulster, Cuchulainn, whose father was supposed to be of the Fairy people. It was a weapon a Dravidic father would give to his half-Celtic son; the trident symbol of his Dravidic God.

Why was the widespread Hebrew veneration of cows and the Exodus story of worship of the golden calf a practice denounced by Levite priests? Because the cow is sacred to the Goddess as Shakti in her aspect of Danu just as in her Egyptian form of Hathor, and the bull (the root for the word God) is sacred to Shiva as his mount,

Trimurti bas relief from the temple of Elephanta, showing the three aspects or bodies of the god Shiva.

Nandi, who is still accorded great reverence in India today. Why did sexual relations become a sin (something from Sind)? Because Shiva's Linga and Shakti's Yoni are the representations of fertility and the pleasure of creation—life as joy. And why does Satan have horns—indeed why a Horned God throughout Western European Pagan and Wiccan history? Because this is the depiction of Shiva as Lord of the Beasts (Shiva Pasupati), known for 30,000 years, and carried into the Near East and the European continent as the image of the God of Animals and Nature.

People who call themselves Bible historians (which I generally consider to be a contradiction of terms) claim that the Israelites settled in Egypt to escape a famine circa 1500 B.C.E., at a time when Israelites did not exist. Indeed, the Vedic Aryans were initiating their destruction of the lower Indus Valley Civilization, continuing their assault against Mohenjo-daro until its fall in 1200 B.C.E., and it was during this time frame, with the fall of the Mycenean civilization, that the Canaanites abandoned their valley cities to move into the hills. If escaping Dravidians came into Canaan, this would have contributed to the difficulties experienced by the Levite priesthood in controlling their Hebrew flock. The Dravidic presence could aggravate the tenuous grip the Levites had on the Hebrews, and result in a number of resurgent Dravidic practices among the people they interacted with. Over time this would create a need for a codified form of Jewish law, based on Babylonian and Aryan codes, in the form of the Pentateuch around 621 B.C.E.

The early excavations in the Indus produced astonishing discoveries, but this occurred at a time when the British Empire was entertaining notions about the superiority of the white European Christian in a barbarous world—when people like Rudyard Kipling were writing about the "white man's burden" in caring for what was seen as the inferior, subhuman, non-European peoples of the world, be they Chinese, Japanese, Polynesian, African, or Indian, the latter of whom were called "colored." Nineteenth-century theories of Social Darwinism supported the idea of a human social evolution producing a superior, white, European people who had the obligation of dominating the less evolved for their own good. Anything that upset the perspective of a Eurocentric greatness would not receive very much credence or support for popular dissemination. Thus the writings and studies concerning the value of the ancient culture of India were kept in the realm of the educated elite, while the Indian temples and art were vandalized by the prudishly civilized west.

I wonder if the reasoning behind the partition of the subcontinent by the British prior to their departure was not a deliberate effort to bury the new discoveries by placing this important region containing Sind under the control of fundamentalist Moslems. It is interesting to note that on some historical timelines, the tenuous dating for Mohenjo-daro is 2500 B.C.E. and the Aryan invasion as beginning in 2150 B.C.E., yet the fact is that there has never been a time that people know of today when the region was not inhabited and when Shiva was not worshipped. It takes historians of courage to admit that the Indus civilization actually dates back further than 5000 B.C.E. (when the Dravidians created a mythology about the Creation taking place in seven days), but they also know that the region has been actively occupied since 470,000 B.C.E., and evidence shows its people worshipping Shiva since at least 28,000 B.C.E. With persistence, perhaps one day the censorship of historical reality will be eliminated from the education materials used in public schools.

Despite Aryan alterations, Shiva is seen today in India as a God of love (both sexual and selfless), grace, and beauty. He is the God of asceticism, and is called "unperturbed." He does not require any religious observances or sacrifices, but simply *is*, making no demands on people and requiring no priesthood. He is the King of the Dance—Cosmic Energy in Cosmic Time. Devi, or Shakti, or Parvati, or Uma, is the Mother Goddess, the Great Goddess, the Earth Mother, and the Queen of the Universe respectively. Together, as Ardhanari, Isha and Uma, the Lord and the Lady are One and All. This constituted the earliest form of religious veneration in Sind, Mesopotamia, and the European Continent until the advent of the new Aryan male deities invented to support a new power structure of rulers and warriors through an elite clergy.

During the Aryan expansions, the religion of the Goddess and the God, lacking the addition of the political gods, was considered a threat to the new rulers of the conquered lands. Ultimately, a new religion was developed that would eliminate the lower portion of the Teutonic pyramid and declare as supreme the upper deity of the ruler. This then is the source of Judaism, and male dominance was established by the eradication of the powerful female and gentle male deities of natural religion.

When the Vedic invaders attacked the Indus Valley, they brought a patriarchal religion with them that upset the balance of nature in the Indus culture by eliminating any real equality between the sexes. This aspect first became softened by contact with the Dravidians, which resulted in a backlash of strictness that would include the required suicide of the widow in her husband's funeral pyre. Historians are divided on whether the original Indus people buried or cremated their dead, but the various writings and archaeological finds indicate that burials occured in the earlier history of the Valley civilization, and at a later date (when the influence of the Vedics would have been felt) cremation came to displace the burial system. Among the Shivaite sects of India today, however, the traditional Dravidic burial is used. It was due to Vedic influence that Shiva was scornfully called an inhabitor of burning places, and this is the source of Satan's fiery hell for Christians, yet even in Vedic myths, still the Earth Goddess (Parvati) loved him.

The Aryans brought with them their male mountain god, who came to be viewed also as a volcano deity. The Judaic name for God, *Yahweh*, can be traced to the Sanskrit for "Everflowing," as a reference to volcanic lava. The Hebrew tradition places God on his mountain just like the God of the northern European Aryans. The Levites were cautioned not to intermarry with any other Jewish tribe, and were authorized the best of everything the tribes had to offer. They were the priests of Yahweh, but they were also the Aryan conquerors perpetuating a caste system, just as had been done in India under the Brahmins. The same religious command that prevented the Brahmins from intermarrying with the conquered people applied to the Levites, and the wealth of the land and its people went directly to the Levites, just as it did to the Brahmins. This was only natural since they are both the same people, the Levites proudly descended from a Brahmin—Abrahm, Abraham.

The need to wipe out any trace of Shiva/Devi worship by whatever form or name became an Aryan imperative and can be traced back to their inability to do so in India. Dravidic Indians fled the region and prospered in the southern part of the Indian subcontinent and Sri-Lanka (Ceylon), where Shiva remains very prominent among the Tamil populace. The modern warfare between the Tamil Hindus and Buddhists comes from the Buddhist backlash to the gentler aspects of a Shiva-dominant Hinduism. India, prior to its division by Britain into India, West Pakistan, and East Pakistan (now Bangledesh), extended from Sind eastward, and in India, Shiva could not be obliterated, but became incorporated into the pantheon along with all the aspects of his female form.

There are today different denominations of Hinduism that stress Vedic gods (Indra, Vishnu, and his incarnation as Krishna) as well as sects of Shiva and Devi in all her names and forms. The merging of deities as it occured in India was not tolerated by the Levite Aryans in the Middle East, and was continuously being stamped out whenever it resurfaced. Today this remains a challenge in Judaism: how does the religion address the needs of women in a time when women are seeking reaffirmation of their rights and value as individuals equal with their male counterparts? Fundamentalist Christians rely on the Aryan Bible as the reason for male domination of women and actively teach women to be submissive and ruled by men—fathers, brothers, uncles, or husbands (as occurred in the Victorian age), and thus constitute a reactionary element equivalent to that of Orthodox Judaism when compared to modern, progressive Judaism (Reformed).

This lack of status for women was not the natural state of life in pre-Christian Europe, and after the Christianization of Europe, the holdouts were labeled Pagans, Witches, Wise Ones (in the arcane, occult arts), or Wiccan (Wise Ones/Full of Life, hence spiritually powerful). Northern European Pagans had female deities whom they honored in the older, lower level of their religion, particularly in terms of fertility and the phases of the Moon, but the male deities of the upper stratum dominated.

The modern Wiccan tradition evolved from the earlier tradition of Green Witchcraft merged with the religion of the displaced Dravidians who fled from the Indus Valley in all directions, taking their God and the Goddess with them. Devi was worshipped as Danu at the time of the initial merging of the Dravidic and Aryan cultures, but subsequent waves of Aryan attackers in India saw the popular denomination as serpent demons. By this time, the Goddess was worshipped with her Son/Consort (the Shakti aspect dominant over the Shiva aspect); and the Fertility God impregnated the Earth Goddess with himself and was born as her Son, indicating the seasons of the year in relation to solstices and equinoxes, and planting/harvesting times. This tradition was carried over into Judaic literature and considered as *prophecy* for a promise of renewed life, appearing later in the Christian tradition as God begetting his only Son (himself) in the Virgin Mary (the Mother Goddess made subordinate to the Father God), as a perfect sacrifice to himself (Odinist Paganism).

Shiva is often represented in art and sculpture with serpents (the Pagan symbols of wisdom and rebirth) in his hair and about his neck, arms, and waist. The sacred serpent and sacred cow were symbols of Danu at the time of the later Aryan invasions (1500–1200 B.C.E.) when the Dravidic religion was being suppressed. As derived from the Judaic mythology, the image of Satan is that of a beautiful serpent who offers knowledge and wisdom to humankind through Eve. When she takes the fruit of knowledge and gives it to Adam, she upsets the Aryan patriarchal deity. The priesthood could not allow people to see that immortality was a given fact of existence (energy cannot be destroyed) because this was the source of their power as intermediaries between the people and the God. In myth, they denied Adam and Eve the fruit of the Tree of Life and the Tree of Knowledge, which was the gist of the Mother Goddess religion. Humanity was banished from the Garden of Eden (lying to the East—the location of Sind and the Indus Valley), and Shiva's bull was declared an appropriate sacrifice for the Aryan god. The two trees: God of Life and Goddess of Knowledge, with their serpent of immortality, were obscured with a garden myth that confused two trees as one forbidden tree, yet referred to them each separately. The imagery was retained, however, and may be seen in most tarot decks as the pillars flanking The High Priestess.

The Indus followers of Danu fled to Europe and eventually to Ireland, where they were known as the Tuatha de Danu (*The People of Danu*), and formed part of the roots of modern Witchcraft. The

Witch's heritage is a mixture of Celtic Pagans, Gaulic Pagans, and Mediterranean Pagans combined with the Dravidic religion of Shiva and Shakti. The duality of the God and the Goddess is shown by the division of the modern Wiccan Altar into three sections dedicated to female, both, and male (U-M-A demonstrated, hence Wicca is often seen as a "Goddess" religion). The people of Sind, Dravidic and proto-Australoid, also fled in other directions and made settlements in Japan, where they were despised by the later-arriving ethnic Japanese (who originated in China) as the aboriginal "Hairy" Ainu (non-Oriental), and called a white race (which would no doubt have annoyed the Vedic Aryans). Further migrations may have taken the people of Danu across the Pacific to touch and leave their mark upon South Pacific Islands, Central and South America, and perhaps even North America, where they may have been the Anasazi Cliff Dwellers.

Modern Wiccans evolved from migrating peoples, Indo-Europeans, whose belief systems incorporated some aspects of Hinduism and found expression through the European Green Craft as well as Hindu Tantric practice and worship of the Great Goddess. When the Celtic Indo-European people, who were themselves a Dravidic derivation, met up with the earlier Tuatha de Danu, their traditions combined and the emphasis for this disenfranchised people fell on the deity of Power rather than on the deity of Grace. But the God was not ignored. Instead he became revered as Pan, Herne the Hunter, Lord of the Greenwood, and as the Green Man in his role as tree god. He was honored as Cernunnos (*The Horned One*), Lord of Beasts and Lord of Fertility, and these forms easily cojoined with the local prehistoric fertility religions of Europe.

As the Indo-Europeans became more settled, the God's own form of power became recognized. Shiva possesses a Third Eye, which opens in the face of danger or enemies, flashes a powerful and destructive light that reduces the foe to ashes, and thus he is likened to the Sun. Here is another form of the Sun God of the eastern Europeans. Now both God and Goddess were beings of power and grace, and their equality was a return to the Dravidic tradition of AUM/ UMA. The God and the Goddess continued to be interchangeable in their aspects, which is sometimes confusing to newcomers to Wicca. Some people prefer to address the Goddess—others, the God—but both are the same deity, and it is wrong to suggest that only males may attune to the God and only females to the Goddess. They are both highly accessible to either sex.

Just as Atum of Egyptian tradition was the Great He/She that produced Shu (Air) and Tefnut (Moisture) who then produced Nut (Goddess of the Sky) and Geb (God of the Earth), the precedent for the Hindu Atman (*Self*, and Adam of the Bible) dividing into male and female, comes from the Dravidic source. That depiction was the recognition by those early people that everything comes from the interaction of the principles of male and female, spirit and matter, passivity and activity. Reversal of roles is not seen as a problem, but as a means of depicting various combinations. Thus, the Earth God can be seen to interact with the earth goddess; the sky god with the sky goddess; the earth god with the sky goddess; the earth goddess with the sky god. The focus can be either male or female, as with Ishtar, Queen of Heaven and her consort Tammuz, God of Earth; or Shiva the Sky God and Parvati the Earth Goddess, and so forth.

Herein lies the basis for the differences between the Teutonic and Wiccan traditions. The northern source can emphasize the dominance of male deities without reference to female deities of power— a male mountain (volcano) God whose worship developed as a support for the rise of power in the chiefs and a warrior class. The Wiccan source is derived from the southern Sind tradition which allows for an emphasis of either a female deity—a Goddess of Power and Fertility—or a male deity—a God of Grace and Fertility—but neither is whole without the other. The two Pagan traditions in Europe existed side by side until being overwhelmed by the political might of Christianity after the Roman Emperor Constantine used the religion to hold together and control his empire. The names used in worship at the lower level of the Teutonic religious structure may differ by regions, but the symbology is the same as in Sind and could well date back to the Indus, as signs of religious awareness showed up in the Valley thousands of years before appearing in Europe.

When modern African-centric professors speak of the warlike Northern Ice People and the peaceful Southern Sun People, the words are descriptive in general terms but the locations are in error. It was not Africa that brought forth the Sun People, but India. This Ice and Sun dialog represents the Aryan and Dravidic confrontation from which sprang the modern Indo-European and Near Eastern cultures. It was this blending and how it was incorporated in geographic locations that led to modern Europe and the rise of the Near Eastern states.

The Indus Valley culture was perhaps the most advanced and peaceful civilization in the early history of humankind. Like Shiva the Unperturbed, the people seem to be have been extremely tolerant of differing beliefs and ideas, and did not live under the power of any organized clergy or priesthood with attendant temples and religious bureaucracy. As a racially integrated people before the time of the pyramids, they were civic-minded and communal, or were well-organized farmers, herders, and builders, and had the first-known urban planned cities with running water, sewers, baths, indoor restrooms, courtyards, shops, and warehouses dispensing food. They had no temples, but followed religious practices in the privacy of their homes—they were the original solitary practitioners (making this, then, a significantly earlier tradition than covens). They were incredibly wealthy. When the Aryans arrived and plundered this Bronze Age people with their stronger weapons and horse-drawn chariots, the Dravidians could only give way to them a bit at a time, first the outlaying borders of Sind, then the perimeter farmsteads, then the rural villages, until at last, the Aryans took it all.

It is from this remembered and drawn-out encounter (it took 950 years for the Aryans to finally subdue the Indus civilization) that so many of the legends of the Sidhe, or Fairy Folk, have endured. The

Dravidians are the Sidhe, the Tuatha de Danu; and there can be no doubt that the tales of the fall of fabulously rich Faerie cities, the forced withdrawal of the Sidhe, the Sidhe aversion to iron, and the power of their females and Sidhe Goddess (the Queen of Faerie), can all be traced to the impact of the invading Aryans on a gentle nation. So far only three major cities have been discovered in the Indus Valley, but more are likely as yet undiscovered. The vast quantity of riches in this land as described in the Vedas and other historical sources make the wealth of Egypt pale in comparison.

When the Moslems arrived in the Indus centuries later, they were amazed at the wealth of the Hindu Brahmins. For although there was now a wretched caste system and harsh religious strictures, the nation was still rich and bountiful. The Dravidic aborigines, however, were no longer a party to the grandeur that now belonged to the Aryan conquerors, the Brahmins. The Moslems saw everything about Hinduism as an abomination to Al-Lah (*The God*—having suppressed worship of Al-Lat, *The Goddess,* early on in Moslem history) just as the Christian legislators of the Roman Empire reviled the Pagan images of Europe. Moslems and Christians in both regions responded in the same manner, destroying uncountable numbers of beautiful shrines, temples, public works, and art. The Moslems massacred hundreds of thousands of Indians and established their mosques on the sites of ancient Hindu temples and Dravidic holy places, just as Christians killed their rivals and built their churches over the temples of pagan Europe. And yet the Moslems could not destroy the Hindu religion, any more than the Church could totally eliminate the Old Religion. Instead, their actions may have encouraged the rise of Shiva worship and the subsequent Golden Age of Shiva in the twelfth through fifteenth centuries C.E., and in Europe, the rise of occult societies and Neo-Pagan revival in the nineteenth and twentieth centuries C.E.

The Moslem rulers confiscated land and wealth, melted down the golden statues and art works, and destroyed the economy in a ruthless rampage that lasted until the British conquest of India.

They were a raiding force that far outstripped the Aryans in ferocity and devastation, and inspired the hatred that still underscores Hindu-Moslem relations today. Even so, when the British arrived in the seventeenth century to begin their attempted conquest of this land, the wealth of India was still a marvel. Between Aryan, Moslem, and Christian domination over India, the historical roots of religion were swept aside and often deliberately erased. Only faint clues remained as guideposts to the truth. Europeans hated to admit that the cradle of civilization was not in the Judeo-Christian-Islamic stronghold of the Near East, but on the banks of the Indus River and in the hearts of the worshippers of Shiva and Shakti.

The British bias against Indian history was typified by their practice of defacing the erotic statues of the gods to make them less offensive to Victorian sensibilities. But perhaps it was also alarming to them to discover a similarity between the deities of the conquered Hindus and those of Britain's own Pagan past; to see that some of the classical gods of Greece and Rome may be traced back to ancient India, and to realize that prying too deeply might negate their attitude of cultural superiority. Today, you can still buy timeline maps that do not even show the country of India until 1500 C.E., as though the subcontinent were vacant while a "superior" western civilization was developing and flourishing. Such maps are still displayed in some public school rooms and many show a reference line depicting human history as beginning around 4000 B.C.E., with Adam and Eve.

The late twentieth century C.E. in America has seen the resurgence of White Supremicists, the Aryan Nation, the Ku Klux Klan, Skinheads, Neo-Nazis, and a movement to segregate the Pacific Northwest states of Washington, Idaho, Oregon, and Montana as a White Homeland. The people involved in these groups tend to claim a rigid adherence to their interpretation of *Christian values*, particularly interpreting them to advocate the subjugation of women, the extermination of homosexuals and independent women, the dominance of the Aryan god of wrath, and the separation of the races. The alignment of these extremist groups with high-profile Christian Fundamentalists has encouraged them to see their own objectives promoted as a pseudo-Christian agenda.

People who support the prejudice and bigotry of the most rabid evangelists are in effect supporting the Neo-Nazis and the White Supremicists today just as people of 1930s Germany and other parts of Europe did the Nazis. The first target is always the least acceptable to the majority—the mentally ill, the homeless, the homosexuals, and the nonwhites (Native Americans, Blacks, Vietnamese, Chinese, Indians, Pakistanis, Mexicans, and so forth), and then come the Jews, and finally the rest of the population is subjected to racial scrutiny for impure blood to be removed through sterilization of those considered to be (or targeted as) undesirable members of the population, and imposition of miscegenation laws. There are still laws on the books of some U.S. states making it a crime for a white person to marry a Native American. Where certain groups are dominant there exists a lack of enforcement of the Constitutional separation of church and state in America; the result is a continuation of the same distortions of history taught in schools today as were taught in the days of Christian persecutions of non-Christians in Europe.

Religious control and domination of people begins with small matters like "dry" counties in states (wherein one set of people deny another group the right to buy an alcoholic beverage), to the countywide cancellation of cable television stations such as MTV (Music Television) that are considered too progressive, to such mundane things as interfering in a Halloween Parade, taking children out of school for wearing a "Penguin" character t-shirt (merchandise from the "Batman Returns" movie, but this is an arbitrary scapegoat, with new icons of "evil" found daily to replace the previous one; thus one week it is the penguin shirt, another week it is a Marilyn Manson shirt, and on it goes), black clothes, or black trenchcoats, and creating high business fees for tarot card readers because a highly vocal minority claim all these things are Satanic. These highly vocal zealots intimidate others into agreeing, lest they be called immoral. People can wear necklaces with a crucifix or a star of David in public with impunity, yet anyone wearing a pentacle runs the risk of being accosted, challenged, and even attacked. An atmosphere of fear and tension exists for the nonconformist, and therefore many Wiccans remain "in the broom closet." It is not the witch who is a threat to public safety, but the Neo-Christian fanatic, who is a threat to the constitutional right of freedom of religion.

There is an application of the same arrogance left over from the British and European (and even American) Imperial Age seen in modern standards of what constitutes spirituality or religion. Some states or counties make the reading of tarot cards illegal or require the reader to have an "entertainment" license. Yet who does not understand that people who freely choose to consult a reader are seeking spiritual guidance, not entertainment? Such a license is not required for fundamentalist preachers who work up a sweat for their congregation to outcries of "Amen!" then pass the collection plate around.

One school district nearly had to rescind an already financed reading program in the elementary schools because of misleading propaganda from local fundamentalist ministers accusing the program of being Satanic, promoting demonism and occultism. The school board, faced with a bankrupting situation, invited concerned parents to examine the controversial books. Highly publicized denouncements by the ministers and their congregation members led many to look over the materials. Instead of the Devil and occultism, people saw funny stories and fantasy—just the sort of thing to get children interested in reading. The matter was put on the ballot of the local election and the reading program overwhelmingly accepted, but for a few weeks, the community had been stirred up into a frenzy over "Satanism in the schools," local ministers received a lot of publicity, and many people decried the books authoritatively, with absolutely no idea of what they were talking about. It was only one notch shy of hysteria, and the desire to actively persecute Wiccans was no doubt waiting just beneath the surface. One day the target is the Devil, the next, any-one wearing black, and after that any fantasy writing or gaming. The lists of little infringements would be another book, but the message here is that these things add up and have been adding up all over the nation.

These events would be laughable except that they have an impact on people who have had no representation in the matter, and who usually have no recourse except through the individual expense of long-term court fights. Uniforms for public school students, no pentacles, no jewelry or t-shirts that hint at Wicca, allowing Christ-ian prayer in the classroom and at school events, posting of some version of the Biblical Ten Commandments in classrooms and pub-lic places, the inclusion of "under God" in the Pledge of Allegiance, Christian prayer days around the flagpole in front of schools—all are demagoguery intended to impress the mind with the notion that somehow "if it ain't Christian, it ain't American." The Founding Fathers were not Christian Fundamentalists, but Deitists and, yes, Masons. But as late as 1999 Republican Bob Barr, Congressman from Georgia, demanded that the Army rescind its policy of free-dom of religion and stop all practice of Wicca on military bases. He was quoted as writing to the base commander to "stop this non-sense now." Wicca is called "nonsense" by a person in a position of political power, but Christianity, with its checkered past, is sensible? Episodes like these are highly offensive to Wiccans, and should be of concern to everyone.

I am always astonished that historians can talk about the anti-female stance of the Greeks of our Western heritage, but fail to rec-oncile this alleged attitude with the high standing of female deities such as Athena (an entire city and culture was named after her!), Artemis (so popular that the Christian fathers found it necessary to attack her followers and close down her temples with laws), Hera whose power was a given even in mythology, Demeter who was honored everywhere in harvest rites, and Persephone, whose realm with Hades was the object of pilgrimages (there is actually a deep, wide cavern entrance in Greece that is still revered as the entry to Hades—but it is blocked off), just to name a few.

Could it be that the anti-female writings we are familiar with were actually those of a minority opinion? That these were the exception rather than the rule? That anything which contradicted this misogynistic view has been hidden away in the Vatican Archives (where a supposedly lost treatise of Aristotle turned up recently) or destroyed? A true historian would not simply look at what is in hand, but at what is missing, and what forms an incongruity.

It's time for tea.

Frustration Tea

I try to put a little information into the atmosphere with the hope that it will pass into the general understanding by osmosis, but sometimes the bizarre situations we are faced with daily can lead to aggravation. Then it is time for a relaxing, tension-relieving tea. Sometimes I like to use an automatic drip teapot for non-divination tea where I don't require tea leaves. The nice thing about the automatic pot (like Mrs. Tea) is that it has a good-sized filter basket. I place a filter in it just as for an automatic drip coffee pot), and put in my selection of loose herbs. Generally, a black tea such as an English Breakfast style gives extra body, and you can open a couple of tea bags and dump the contents into the filter along with the herbs. Here is my recipe for easing stress:

> 2 tea bags of English Breakfast tea
> 1 teaspoon chamomile
> 1 teaspoon hyssop
> 1 teaspoon raspberry leaf

The resulting tea is fruity, smooth, and has a reddish tint to it. Add sugar and milk (not cream) to taste. If stress is leading to headaches, add a teaspoon of wood betony or rosemary to the tea. Enjoy your soothing drink, then you are ready to face the chaotic energies of life with a smile.

As long as any group of people is able to dominate others through the codification of their religious beliefs into civil law, the human species will remain in the Dark Ages of ignorance and superstition.

Today, as in the past, there is a great deal of both ethnic prejudice and nationalistic pride to overcome in rationally discussing history. Because history is a social matter, and relates to the differences as well as the similarities between peoples and cultures, it remains the battleground for those who wish to justify their biases or force their particular ideologies onto others. Unfortunately, the evidence that ties together the religions of the human family is under threat because the cradle of civilization and of religion is in the midst of Pakistan, now a Fundamentalist Islamic State. How long the artifacts of Mohenjo-daro will survive under this atmosphere is now a matter of speculation, but the region of Sind is an important site for Neo-Pagans and Wiccans, as well as for open-minded mainstream religionists, seeking to find their theological taproot.

The history of the migrations of the Dravidians has entered into the mythic roots of European culture in the form of legends of the Minoans, the Etruscans, the Celts, the Fairies, the Tuatha de Danu, and the ignored heritage of the Eastern European Gypsies of Romania and Hungary, while the mythology of Levitic Aryans involving numerous elements, from Adam and Eve to Jesus, has been accepted as historical truth to the present time. Finally, however, professional archaeologists and historians are digging out and reporting significant new discoveries untainted by ecclesiastical domination. It is up to historians, scholars, and the writers of school textbooks to set history and mythology in their proper context, and it is up to educators to no longer bow to the pressure of those people who persist in perpetuating myth as history and history as myth.

Perhaps a meditation on two tarot cards is a good way to persevere in the current situation. We need to draw upon our inner strengths to overcome obstacles, and we still need to live in harmony with others through patience and moderation.

Strength–Temperance Meditation

Take the Strength and Temperance cards from your favorite tarot deck, cast your Circle, light a white candle, and a pleasant, cleansing incense such as frankincense, sandalwood, or rain. You may want to play some soothing music softly.

Set the two cards between the incense and candle so you can gaze at them. Get into a comfortable position, either siting on the floor or perhaps at a table, and breathe in to the count of two, hold for two, the slowly release your breath to the count of two. Repeat. Let the tensions of the day gather in your shoulders, then release the tension to cascade down your arms and out your fingertips like dripping water. Inhale, hold, release. Let your muscles relax. Let your mind relax. Focus on breathing, and looking at the cards. These two cards may at first seem incongruous together, yet they compliment each other. Soon you are calm, grounded and centered.

Look at the card of Strength. This is normally depicted as a woman with a lion whose mouth she holds shut, or whom she rides, or holds on a flowery leash. What does this mean to you? Is this a woman controlling her violent emotions? Reining in, controlling her power? These are not answers, merely suggestions you may consider. Strength is usually a woman with a wild beast that she has

Strength   Temperance

some power over. Is that what strength is? Nurturing woman with the power of the wild beast within? My mother used to say that she was a tigress when it came to protecting her children (and she meant it!). Can the meaning be maternal power used in defense of the weak—power you should not arouse carelessly?

With Temperance, there is usually an angel-form with one foot in the water, one on land, and pouring liquid from one goblet into another. What can this mean? Meekness, balance, inaction? Or is it a connection between earth and water, between form and spirit? What does the motion of the fluid in the cups mean? Wine is poured to make it breathe—is the water or wine of life poured from one cup to another in a sensation of balance for life to breathe?

Now look at the cards. Both imply restraint, self-control, energy, and power; and both indicate a harmony between forces. With Strength, the harmony lies in self-confidence and self-mastery. There is the willpower and the energy of the lion, who is the emblem of the Sun (Leo). With Temperance, the harmony lies in the motion, the bridging of elements and redistribution of energies. There is fire in the shimmering aura of the personage with the cups, air in the passage of the water or dark wine between the cups, water and earth in the stance of the radiant being with one foot in the river and the other on land. Meditate on the images of the tarot, and as our journey concludes, lift your own Hermit's lamp to the future:

Balance and Strength are part of my life,
Willpower and patience curbing all strife.
Courage and energy flow in my soul,
Harmony and peace I always will know.

Time Line

470,000–200,000 B.C.E.—Soan stone-age cultures in North and South Sind with Proto-Australoids and Negritos

30,000 B.C.E.—Cave paintings in Sind showing people with scimitars, swords at their waists, bows and arrows, double-headed drum, and both wild and domesticated animals

28,000 B.C.E.—Shiva, Lord of Animals cave painting

20,000 B.C.E.—European cave paintings

5000 B.C.E.—Indus myth of Creation in seven days; names for the seven days of the week; Indus city-states extend from Himalayas to Arabian Sea

4000 B.C.E.—Neolithic culture in Mysore

3600 B.C.E.—Civilization begins in Sumeria

3500–2631 B.C.E.—Egypt's Old Kingdom

3100–2965 B.C.E.—First Egyptian dynasty

2980 B.C.E.—Egyptian accounts of famine and plenty

2900 B.C.E.—Mohenjo-daro, a thriving urban city, already very old

2872–2817 B.C.E.—Sargon I unites Sumeria and Akkad

2780 B.C.E.—First pyramid built

2700–1700 B.C.E.—Suggested as 1,000 year height of Indus

2474–2398 B.C.E.—Golden Age of Sumerian City of Ur; first Code of Laws

2375–1800 B.C.E.—Egypt's Middle Kingdom

2357 B.C.E.—Sumerian Empire destroyed by Elamites

2169–1926 B.C.E.—Babylonian Empire

2150 B.C.E.—Aryans invade outlaying area of Indus Valley (Sind), using chariots and hardened bronze weapons

2123–2081 B.C.E.—Hammurabi rules Babylon; Code of Laws

1925 B.C.E.—Aryan Hittites, armed with iron weapons, conquer Babylon

1860 B.C.E.—Stonehenge started

1800 B.C.E.—Civilization in Palestine (Canaanite)

1600 B.C.E.—Indus region falling into decline

1500 B.C.E.—Syrian poem prototype for Hebrew Daniel

1580–1100 B.C.E.—Egypt's Empire (until Dynasty of Libyan Kings); Egyptian literature prototypes for Hebrew Solomon, Lazarus, feeding the multitude

1500–1200 B.C.E.—Aryans invade Indus cities in Sind

1400 B.C.E.—Iron Age begins in India & Western Asia

1276 B.C.E.—Assyria unified

1250 B.C.E.—Mycenea falls; Canaanite cities abandoned

1232 B.C.E.—Hebrew pastorialists begin new Canaanite communities on hilltops

1200 B.C.E.—Mohenjo-daro falls

1200–700 B.C.E.—Etruscans settle in Italy (named Etruria); highly civilized city-states; influenced later arriving Romans who conquered them

1193 B.C.E.—Troy destroyed by Greeks

1000–600 B.C.E.—Phoenicia and Syria Golden Age

1000–500 B.C.E.—Hindu Vedas (hymns)

900–500 B.C.E.—Hindu Upanishads and Brahmanas, Vedas completed

509 B.C.E.—Roman Republic founded

884 B.C.E.—Assyria centralized

732–609 B.C.E.—Assyrian Empire

624–544 B.C.E.—Life of Gautama Buddha

621 B.C.E.—Writing of the Pentateuch (five books of Old Testament Bible) begun

    1600–1220 B.C.E.—Alleged Egyptian Captivity

    1025–1010 B.C.E.—Saul allegedly rules Jerusalem

    1010–974 B.C.E.—David allegedly rules Jerusalem

    974–937 B.C.E.—Solomon allegedly rules Jerusalem

    937 B.C.E.—Jewish schism allegedly creates Judah and Israel

615 B.C.E.—Jewish colonists in Egypt

609 B.C.E.—Assyrian Empire ends

605 B.C.E.—Egypt under Greek influence of Niku (Necho)

599–527 B.C.E.—Jainism in India

586–538 B.C.E.—Babylonian Captivity of Jews

559 B.C.E.—Persian Empire under Cyrus I

539 B.C.E.—Persian conquest of Babylon

525 B.C.E.—Persian conquest of Egypt

520 B.C.E.—Temple of Jerusalem built (called the second temple)

518 B.C.E.—Persian invasion of India by Skylax, under Darius I

500 B.C.E.—Beginnings of Hindu orthodox system (lasts through 500 C.E.)

329 B.C.E.—Greek invasion of India by Alexander

325 B.C.E.—Alexander leaves India

200 B.C.E.—Roman conquest of Etruscan city-states

138 B.C.E.—Jewish written history starts with the Maccabees; prior to this Jerusalem was under the control of the Babylonians, the Assyrians, and the Persians; Israel consisted of the city and outlying lands

100 B.C.E.—Images of deities in Hindu temples

—Cybele and Attis processions popular in Rome with Attis' death on a tree, burial in a tomb, and resurrection three days later with devotees running through the streets of Rome shouting, "He is risen!"

50 C.E.—Images of Hindu deities with multiple arms

170 C.E.—First attempt at creating a Christian Gospel states that Jesus sprang from the head of God (like Athena from Zeus)

250–300 C.E.—Christian Church becomes wealthiest religious organization in Roman Empire

300–400 C.E.—Krishna worship spreading in India and Near East by Hindu missionaries

—Twelve Christian Gospels and contents reviewed with four being selected to be "official," and three-quarters of the Gospel of Luke being discarded

323 C.E.—Roman Emperor Constantine declares support for Christianity and establishes the power of the Christian priesthood

400 C.E.—Great Goddess elevated into Vedic Hindu orthodoxy; beginnings of officially accepted Tantricism

—Shiva worship flourishing in South India and Kashmir

476 C.E.—General date for "Fall of Roman Empire"

455–500 C.E.—India invaded by Huns

712 C.E.—Arab conquest of Sind (then rest of India)

900–1100 C.E.—Shiva worship spreads to Indonesia; formal Vedic scriptures for Shiva written (the Puranas)

999–1026 C.E.—Series of Moslem invasions and widespread looting and destruction

1100 C.E.—Buddhism nearly extinct in India

1100–1400 C.E.—Rise of "Heroic" Shiva

1186 C.E.—Turkish invasion of India

1211–1236 C.E.—Extensive Moslem control of India; massive looting/destruction

1288–1293 C.E.—Marco Polo in India

1300 C.E.—European Renaissance just getting started

1350–1610 C.E.—"Heroic" Shiva state religion in Mysore

1498 C.E.—Vasco de Gama reaches India

1500–1800 C.E.—Height of Mother Goddess worship in Bengal

1510 C.E.—Portuguese occupy Goa, India

1525 C.E. (generally)—Kabbalah tradition of Agrippa (1486–1535) and Paracelsus (1493–1541)

1527–1608 C.E.—Dr. John Dee, astrologer to England's Queen Elizabeth I (1558–1603)

1570–80 C.E.—Dr. Dee develops Enochian System of Ceremonial Magic

1600 C.E.—(British) East India Company founded

1756–1763 C.E.—French-English War in India

1765 C.E.—Robert Clive made Governor of Bengal

1858 C.E.—British Crown takes over India

1884–1964 C.E.—Gerald Gardner, founder Gardnerian Wicca

1877 C.E.—Hermetic Order of the Golden Dawn established by three Masons

1875–1947 C.E.—Aleister Crowley, ceremonial magician

1897 C.E.—Charles Leland wrote *Aradia*, about Italian Witchcraft

1924 C.E.—Mohenjo-daro discovered in Sind

1939 C.E.—Gerald Gardner initiated into Witchcraft

1947 C.E.—Britain divides India into Hindu India and Moslem Pakistan (which includes the Indus Valley and the archaeological sites of pre-Vedic Shiva/Shakti worship)

—India and Pakistan gain independence from Great Britain

Glossary

Adept: The state acquired by an initiate into a group, particularly Ceremonial Magic, when material gain is no longer desired, and spiritual growth has come to such a degree that nature is at one's command

Aesir: The Gods and Goddesses of the Warrior and Ruler levels of the Teutonic pantheon

Anathema: Damned, detested, cursed

Androgyne: Both male and female, a hermaphrodite; symbol of Shiva

Ardhanari: Half Male and Half Female; a name of Shiva

Aryan: Iron-using invaders of Bronze Age India and the Near East from the North

Asatru: Loyal to the Aesir Gods; a name for Odinists of the Teutonic tradition

Asgard: Realm of the Teutonic Gods

AUM: The sound of the name of God, with the letters meaning male, female, and both; with male emphasized, Aum namah Shivaye: a mantra to Shiva

B.C.E.: Before Common Era or Before Current Era; used instead of B.C.: Before Christ

Bible: Compilation of religious books of Judaism and Christianity; Old Testament began with fifty-two versions circa 621 B.C.E. and orthodox version developed in which books were deleted and/or revised; New Testament began with twelve Gospels and assorted writings, with the first Book of Luke describing Jesus as having sprung from the head of God; by 400 C.E. orthodox versions edited and deleted numerous books, and deleted three-quarters of the Book of Luke

Black Mass: Perverted celebration of Catholic Mass in which the rites were a parody of Christianity (or even of the Roman Empire since the Mass evolved from the Emperor's audience ceremonies from the time of Diocletian); often erroneously labeled by Christians as the same as a Witches' Sabbat

Brahma: God of Hindu Trinity—The Creator

Brahmin: Upper Caste of Hindu society descended from the Aryan warrior-priests

Buddhism: Reformation of Hinduism to reclaim the exclusive powers of the Brahmin caste

Caste: Hindu hereditary class distinctions in four levels; Brahmins at the top, Dravidians at the bottom, and below them the Untouchables; derived from combination of ethnic, racial, and occupational background

C.E.: Common Era or Current Era; used instead of A.D. Anno Domino: Year of Our Lord

Celts: Indo-Europeans of Dravidic derivation who arrived in Ireland from the Near East by way of Spain

Ceremonial Magic: Magic system based on the kabbalah

Coven: Group of Wiccans, usually twelve in number with one Priest or Priestess to make a total of thirteen members, although there may be two leaders, male and female

Craft: Practice of Wicca

Deva: Shining Ones of Hinduism; Divine Beings

Devi: The Goddess, name for Shakti

Dhumavati: "Crone" aspect of Shakti without Shiva

Digambara: Sky-Clad, or Clothed in Space; a name for Shiva

Dravidian: Commonly used name for the early inhabitants of Mohenjo-daro and the Sind region in the Indus Valley

Elohim: Male aspect of Judaic God, Yahweh

Frey: Lord; Vanir God of lower level of Teutonic system, God of the World, land, animals, fertility, eroticism, peace and well-being, twin of Freya

Freya: Lady; Vanir Goddess of lower level of Teutonic system who is able to travel to the highest level; Goddess of magic, cycles of nature, taught Odin magic, twin of Frey

Galster: Practice of Teutonic runic magic system

Green Sabbats: The four Nature Sabbats of Equinoxes and Solstices: Yule, Ostara, Litha, and Mabon

Green Wicca: Lower level of Teutonic system, centered around the Lord and the Lady (Frey and Freya) of Nature; witchcraft of Natural magics

Hari: Yellowish-green; a name of Vishnu and reference to Krishna

Hara: The one who takes away; a name of Shiva

Heroic Shiva: Hindu reform movement seeking to re-establish equal rights for castes and women in religion and society

Hinduism: derivation of religious beliefs of the Dravidians of Sind and the conquering Vedic Aryans

Indra: Vedic warrior God displaced in Hindu Trinity by Shiva

Jaganmatri: Divine Mother; name for Shakti

Jehovah: Female aspect of Judaic God, Yahweh

Kabbalah: Supposed Jewish magical system of correspondences for all aspects of the universe, popularized in the sixteenth century C.E. and used in Ceremonial Magic

Kali: Black; a "terrible" aspect of Shakti, but really the passage from life to death and rebirth; Kali, called the Black Mother, is highly revered in Hinduism

Karma: Law of retribution by which one's actions in this life dictate the nature of one's reincarnation

Krishna: Incarnation of Vishnu, whose devotees were active missionaries in Asia Minor during time of birth of Christianity; history of Jesus matches the mythological history of Krishna

Linga: Phallic symbol of creation; emblem of Shiva

Mahadevi: Great Goddess; name of Shakti

Mantra: A chant designed to raise energy during worship of Shiva and Shakti

Nataraja: Lord (or King) of the Dance; aspect of Shiva as the Cosmic Dancer

Parvati: Earth Mother aspect of Shakti; wife of Shiva in Vedic Hinduism

Pasupati: Lord of the Animals; aspect of Shiva

Pentateuch: First five books of the Bible; the books of the Torah

Sabbat: Wiccan celebration ritual, of which there are eight: solstices; equinoxes; and four harvest/deity celebrations

Seidh: Teutonic concept of the power of magic

Seidhr: The Practitioner of the Green level in the Teutonic system; the Green Witch

Siddha: Charged with energy; occurs in Hinduism with chanting of mantras

Sidhe: Fairie people of Ireland; the Tuatha de Danu

Sutee: Self-immolation of widows upon the funeral pyre of their husbands

Tantra: Complex Hindu system of practices likened to the weaving on a loom; generally emphasizes Shakti

Tat: That; name for the Supreme Being in Hinduism

Tryambaka: Wed to the Triple Goddess; name for Shiva

Tuatha de Danu: People of the Goddess Danu; name of Dravidians in Sind during 1500–1200 B.C.E. final push of Aryans into Mohenjo-daro and name of the Sidhe, or Fairies of Ireland

UMA: Sound of the name of God with the female aspect emphasized; name for Shakti, and for primal Goddess of Sumeria and Babylon

Vanir: Lower level deities of Teutonic system, include worship of Frey and Freya, and the practice of natural magic

Vishnu: Second deity in Hindu Trinity; called the Preserver

Vitki: Wise One; Teutonic name that became Wiccan, Witch

White Sabbats: The four Agricultural/Deity Life Myth Sabbats of Imbolc, Beltane, Lughnassadh, and Samhain

Wicca: Old name for Witch; used popularly to avoid the negative imagery

Wiccan Rede: "An' it harm none, do as thou wilt"; Witches' Law

Witchcraft: "Craft of the Wise," based generally on natural magic

Yggdrasill: Teutonic World-Tree upon which Odin sacrificed himself by crucifixion to gain Runic magic and become King of the Gods; Aryan basis for story of Jesus' crucifixion

Yoga: Hindu practice involving meditation and self-mortification to gain wisdom and union with the All (from which early Christians derived system of asceticism)

Yogi: One who practices Yoga

Yoni: Vagina, or womb; symbol of Shakti as One who gives birth to all life

Selected Bibliography and Recommended Reading List

Adler, Margot. *Drawing Down the Moon: Witches, Druids, Goddess-Worshippers, and Other Pagans in America Today*. Boston: Beacon Press, 1986.

Ashe, Geoffrey. *The Dawn Behind the Dawn: A Search for the Earthly Paradise*. New York: Henry Holt and Company, 1992.

Baring, Anne, and Jules Cashford. *The Myth of the Goddess*. London: Arkana Penguin Books, 1993.

Basham, A. L. *The Wonder That Was India*. New York: Hawthorne Books, Inc., 1963.

Briggs, Katherine. *An Encyclopedia of Fairies, Hobgoblins, Brownies, Bogies, and Other Supernatural Creatures*. New York: Pantheon Books, 1976.

Burns, Edward McNall, Phillip Lee Ralph, et al. *World Civilizations*. Vol. C. New York: W. W. Norton & Company, Inc., 1986.

Campbell, Joseph. *The Masks of God: Primitive Mythology*. New York: Penguin Books, 1976.

_____. *The Masks of God: Oriental Mythology*. New York: Penguin Books, 1976.

_____. *Transformations of Myth Through Time*. New York: Harper & Row, Publishers, 1990.

Coomaraswamy, Ananda K., and Sister Nivedita. *Myths of the Hindus & Buddhists.* New York: Dover Publications, Inc., 1967.

Cunliffe, Barry. *The Celtic World.* New York: Greenwich House, Crown Publishers, Inc., 1986.

Danielou, Alain. *Gods of Love and Ecstasy: The Traditions of Shiva and Dionysus.* Rochester, Vermont: Inner Traditions, 1992.

Durant, Will. *The Story of Civilization: Part I, Our Oriental Heritage.* New York: Simon and Schuster, 1954.

_____. *The Story of Civilization: Part II, The Life of Greece.* New York: Simon and Schuster, 1966.

Eisler, Riane. *The Chalice & The Blade: Our History, Our Future.* San Francisco: HarperCollins Publishers, 1988.

Eliot, Alexander. *The Universal Myths: Heroes, Gods, Tricksters and Others.* New York: Meridian Books, 1990.

Evans-Wentz, W. Y. *The Fairy Faith in Celtic Countries.* New York: Citadel Press, Carol Publishing Group, 1994.

Frazer, Sir James George. *The Golden Bough.* New York: Simon & Schuster, 1996.

Gibbon, Edward. *The Decline and Fall of the Roman Empire,* Vols. I & II. New York: Bennett A. Cerf, and Donald S. Klopper, The Modern Library, N.d.

Gilbert, Martin. *The Holocaust: A History of the Jews of Europe During the Second World War.* New York: Henry Holt & Company, 1985.

Gimbutas, Marija. *The Civilization of the Goddess: The World of Old Europe.* Edited by Joan Marler. San Francisco: HarperCollins Publishers, 1991.

Goetz, Herman. *India: Five Thousand Years of Indian Art.* New York: McGraw-Hill Book Company, Inc., 1959.

González-Wippler, Migene. *The Complete Book of Spells, Ceremonies & Magic.* St. Paul: Llewellyn Publications, 1988.

Goodrich, Norma Lorre. *Priestesses*. New York: Harper Perennial, 1989.

Gottner-Abendroth, Heide. *The Dancing Goddess: Principles of a Matriarchal Aesthetic*. Translated by Maureen T. Krause. Boston: Beacon Press, 1991.

Graves, Robert. *The White Goddess*. New York: Farrar, Straus and Giroux, 1996 edition.

Green, Marion. *A Witch Alone*. London: The Aquarian Press, 1991.

Guenon, Rene. *The Crisis of the Modern World*. Ghent: Sophia Perrennis, 1996.

_____. *Fundamental Symbols: The Universal Language of Sacred Science*. Cambridge: Quinta Essentia, 1995.

Hawkes, Jacquetta. *The First Great Civilizations: Life in Mesopotamia, the Indus Valley, and Egypt*. New York: Alfred A. Knopf, 1977.

Heyerdahl, Thor. *Aku-Aku*. New York: Rand McNally, 1958.

_____. *Kon-Tiki*. New York: Rand McNally, 1950.

Highwater, Jamake. *Myth and Sexuality*. Ontario: New American Library, 1990.

Hoffman, Michael A. *Egypt Before the Pharoahs*. New York: Dorset Press, 1990.

Holzer, Hans (Introduction). *Encyclopedia of Witchcraft and Demonology*. London: BPC Publications Ltd., Octopus Books, Ltd., 1970–71.

Johari, Harish. *Tools for Tantra*. Rochester, Vermont: Inner Traditions International, Ltd., 1986.

Kersten, Holger. *Jesus Lived in India: His Unknown Life Before and After the Crucifixion*. Dorset, England: Element Book Ltd., 1986.

Klostermaier, Klaus K. *A Survey of Hinduism*. Albany: State University of New York Press, 1989.

Kramer, S. N. *The Sumerians: Their History, Culture, and Character.* Chicago: University of Chicago Press, 1963.

Kramrisch, Stella. *The Presence of Siva.* Princeton: Princeton University Press, 1981.

Legg, Stuart. *The Barbarians of Asia.* New York: Dorset Press, 1990.

Marshall, John. *Mohenjo-daro and the Indus Civilization.* 3 vols. London: University of Oxford Press, 1931.

Massa, Aldo. *The World of the Etruscans.* Translated by John Christmas. Geneve, Italy: Minerva, 1989.

Neumayer, E. *Prehistoric India Rock Paintings.* Delhi: Oxford University Press, 1983.

O'Flaherty, Wendy Doniger. *Other People's Myths: The Cave Of Echoes.* New York: Macmillan Publishing Company, 1988.

———. *Siva, The Erotic Ascetic.* New York: Oxford University Press, 1973.

Robertson, J. M. *Pagan Christs.* New York: Barnes & Noble Books 1993.

Ross, Nancy Wilson. *Three Ways of Asian Wisdom.* New York: Simon & Schuster, 1966.

Scholem, Gershom. *Origins of the Kabbalah.* Princeton: The Jewish Publication Society, Princeton University Press: 1987.

Scott, Michael. *Irish Folk & Fairytale Omnibus.* New York: Barnes & Noble Books, 1983.

Silberman, Neil Asher. "Who Were the Israelites?" *Archaeology,* March/April (1992).

Sjoo, Monica, and Barbara Mor. *The Great Cosmic Mother.* San Francisco: HarperCollins Publishers, 1991.

Squire, Charles. *Celtic Myth and Legend.* Newcastle: Newcastle Publishing Co., Inc., 1975.

Starhawk. *The Spiral Dance: A Rebirth of the Ancient Religion of the Great Goddess*. New York: HarperCollins Publishers, 1989.

Stone, Merlin. *When God Was a Woman*. New York: Dorset Press, 1976.

Subramuniya, Swami Satguru Sivaya. *Dancing with Shiva: Hinduism's Contemporary Catechism*. India: Himalayan Academy, 1993.

Tacitus. *The Annals. Book XV 36–43*. Translated by Alfred John Church & William Jackson Brodribb. New York: Modern Library, 1942.

Taylour, Lord William. *The Mycenaeans*. London: Thames and Hudson Ltd., 1994.

Thorsson, Edred. *Northern Magic: Mysteries of the Norse, Germans & English*. St. Paul, Minnesota: Llewellyn Publications, 1992.

Vaughan, Agnes Carr. *The Etruscans*. New York: Barnes & Noble Books, 1993.

Wilson, A. N. *Jesus: A Life*. New York: Norton, 1992.

Woolley, C. Leonard. *The Sumerians*. New York: W. W. Norton & Company, 1965.

Index

☽ REACH FOR THE MOON

Llewellyn publishes hundreds of books on your favorite subjects! To get these exciting books, including the ones on the following pages, check your local bookstore or order them directly from Llewellyn.

ORDER BY PHONE

- Call toll-free within the U.S. and Canada, 1-800-THE MOON
- In Minnesota, call (651) 291-1970
- We accept VISA, MasterCard, and American Express

ORDER BY MAIL

- Send the full price of your order (MN residents add 7% sales tax) in U.S. funds, plus postage & handling to:

    Llewellyn Worldwide
    P.O. Box 64383, Dept. K648-3
    St. Paul, MN 55164–0383, U.S.A.

POSTAGE & HANDLING

(For the U.S., Canada, and Mexico)

- $4.00 for orders $15.00 and under
- $5.00 for orders over $15.00
- No charge for orders over $100.00

We ship UPS in the continental United States. We ship standard mail to P.O. boxes. Orders shipped to Alaska, Hawaii, The Virgin Islands, and Puerto Rico are sent first-class mail. Orders shipped to Canada and Mexico are sent surface mail.

International orders: Airmail—add freight equal to price of each book to the total price of order, plus $5.00 for each non-book item (audio tapes, etc.).

Surface mail—Add $1.00 per item.

Allow 2 weeks for delivery on all orders.
Postage and handling rates subject to change.

DISCOUNTS

We offer a 20% discount to group leaders or agents. You must order a minimum of five copies of the same book to get our special quantity price.

FREE CATALOG

Get a free copy of our color catalog, *New Worlds of Mind and Spirit.* Subscribe for just $10.00 in the United States and Canada ($30.00 overseas, airmail). Many bookstores carry *New Worlds*—ask for it!

Visit our website at www.llewellyn.com for more information.

GREEN WITCHCRAFT
Folk Magic, Fairy Lore & Herb Craft

Ann Moura

Very little has been written about traditional family practices of the Old Religion simply because such information has not been offered for popular consumption. If you have no contacts with these traditions, *Green Witchcraft* will meet your need for a practice based in family and natural Witchcraft traditions. *Green Witchcraft* describes the worship of nature and the use of herbs that have been part of human culture from the earliest times. It relates to the Lord & Lady of Greenwood, the Primal Father and Mother, and to the Earth Spirits called Faeries.

Green Witchcraft traces the historic and folk background of this path and teaches its practical techniques. Learn the basics of Witchcraft from a third-generation, traditional family Green Witch who openly shares from her own experiences. Through a how-to format you'll learn rites of passage, activities for Sabbats and Esbats, Fairy lore, self-dedication, self-initiation, spellwork, herbcraft, and divination.

This practical handbook is an invitation to explore, identify and adapt the Green elements of Witchcraft that work for you, today.

1-56718-690-4, 288 pp., 6 x 9, illus.   **$14.95**

GREEN WITCHCRAFT II
Balancing Light & Shadow

Ann Moura

The Green Witch is a natural witch, a cottage witch, and a solitary witch. This witch does not fear nature and the woods, but finds a sense of belonging and connection with the earth and the universe. Now, in this sequel to *Green Witchcraft*, hereditary witch Ann Moura dispels the common misunderstandings and prejudices against the "shadow side" of nature, the self, and the Divine. She presents a practical guide on how to access and utilize the dark powers in conjunction with the light to achieve a balanced magical practice and move toward spiritual wholeness.

Guided meditations, step-by-step rituals, and spells enable you to connect with the dark powers, invoke their energies, and achieve your goals through magical workings. Face your greatest fears so you can release them, create an elemental bottle to attract faery life, burn herbs to open your subconscious awareness, learn to use the ogham for travel to other worlds, recognize and name a familiar, and much more.

1-56718-689-0, 288 pp., 6 x 9, illus.   **$12.95**

GREEN WITCHCRAFT III
The Manual
Ann Moura

An eight-class course of instruction for the Green Craft.

Green Witchcraft is a core practice of the traditions of earth magics, the Witchcraft of the Natural Witch, the Kitchen Witch, and the Cottage Witch. It is herbal, attuned to nature, and the foundation upon which any Craft tradition may be built. This book presents the Craft as a course of instruction, based on classes taught by the author. It utilizes Green Witchcraft as a textbook. Students will participate in assignments and practice activities as they learn techniques for circle casting, altars, divination, and spell working. Sample rituals and additional information is introduced to round out the student's instruction.

- Class One: Introduction to the Craft, Basic Equipment, Altars/Working Area
- Class Two: Green Rules of Conduct, Circle Casting
- Class Three: Casting a Learning Circle, Meditation, and Technique
- Class Four: Divinations—Crystal Ball Skrying, Black Mirror Gazing, Pendulum, Tea Leaves, Tarot, and Runes
- Class Five: Divination with the Celtic Ogham
- Class Six: Stones & Crystals, Elixir Preparations, Obsidian Skrying
- Class Seven: Consecration of a Statue, Divine Couples, Holy Days and Creating Your Own Calendar of Observances, Palmistry
- Class Eight: Spell Creating and Casting, Types of Magical Spells, Herb Craft, Oils, Candle Magics

1-56718-688-2, 264 pp., 6 x 9, illus.   **$12.95**

HEREDITARY WITCHCRAFT
Secrets of the Old Religion
Raven Grimassi

This book is about the Old Religion of Italy, and contains material that is at least 100 years old, much of which has never before been seen in print. This overview of the history and lore of the Hereditary Craft will show you how the Italian witches viewed nature, magick, and the occult forces. Nothing in this book is mixed with, or drawn from, any other Wiccan traditions.

The Italian witches would gather beneath the full moon to worship a goddess (Diana) and a god (Dianus). The roots of Italian Witchcraft extend back into the prehistory of Italy, in the indigenous Mediterranean/Aegean neolithic cult of the Great Goddess. Follow its development to the time of the Inquisition, when it had to go into hiding to survive, and to the present day. Uncover surprising discoveries of how expressions of Italian Witchcraft have been taught and used in this century.

1-56718-256-9, 288 pp., 7½ x 9⅛, 31 illus. $14.95

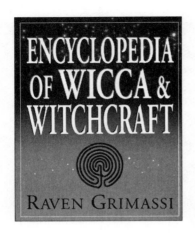

ENCYCLOPEDIA OF WICCA & WITCHCRAFT

Raven Grimassi

This indispensable reference work provides both a historical and cultural foundation for modern Wicca and Witchcraft, and it is the first to be written by an actual practitioner of the Craft.

Other encyclopedias present a series of surface topics such as tools, sabbats, Witchcraft trials, and various mundane elements. Unique to this encyclopedia is its presentation of Wicca/Witchcraft as a spiritual path, connecting religious concepts and spirituality to a historical background and a modern system of practice. It avoids the inclusion of peripheral entries typically included, and deals only with Wicca/Witchcraft topics, old and new, traditional and eclectic. It also features modern Wiccan expressions, sayings, and terminology. Finally, you will find a storehouse of information on European folklore and Western Occultism as related to modern Wicca/Witchcraft.

1-56718-257-7, 496 pp., 8 x 10, 300+ illus. & photos   **$24.95**

BUCKLAND'S COMPLETE BOOK OF WITCHCRAFT

Raymond Buckland

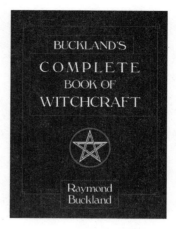

Here is the most complete resource to the study and practice of modern, nondenominational Wicca. This is a lavishly illustrated, self-study course for the solitary or group. Included are rituals; exercises for developing psychic talents; information on all major "sects" of the Craft; sections on tools, beliefs, dreams, meditations, divination, herbal lore, healing, ritual clothing, and much, much more. This book unites theory and practice into a comprehensive course designed to help you develop into a practicing Witch, one of the "Wise Ones." It is written by Ray Buckland, a very famous and respected authority on Witchcraft who first came public with the Old Religion in the United States. Large format with workbook-type exercises, profusely illustrated and full of music and chants. Takes you from A to Z in the study of Witchcraft.

Never before has so much information on the Craft of the Wise been collected in one place. Traditionally, there are three degrees of advancement in most Wiccan traditions. When you have completed studying this book, you will be the equivalent of a Third-Degree Witch. Even those who have practiced Wicca for years find useful information in this book, and many covens are using this for their textbook. If you want to become a Witch, or if you merely want to find out what Witchcraft is really about, you will find no better book than this.

0-87542-050-8, 272 pp., 8½ x 11, illus.   **$16.95**

Llewellyn's Modern Witchcraft Series

The Witches Tarot

Created by
Ellen Cannon Reed
Illustrated by
Martin Cannon

THE WITCHES TAROT KIT

Ellen Cannon Reed
Illustrated by Martin Cannon

The Witches Tarot deck has become a favorite among paganfolk who enjoy the presentation of the mystical Qabalistic symbolism from a clear and distinctly Pagan point of view. Creator Ellen Cannon Reed has replaced the traditional Devil with The Horned One, the Hierophant with the High Priest, and the Hermit with the Seeker. Each of the Magical Spheres is included, in striking color, on the corresponding cards. Even nonpagans have reported excellent results with the cards and appreciate their colorful and timeless beauty.

In the book, Reed defines the complex, inner workings of the Qabala. She includes is a complete section on divination, with several layout patterns. In addition, she provides instruction on using the cards for Pathworking, or astral journeys through the Tree of Life. An appendix gives a list of correspondences for each of the Paths including the associated Tarot card, Hebrew letter, colors, astrological attribution, animal, gem, and suggested meditation.

1-56718-558-4, Boxed set:
Book: 320 pp., 5¼ x 8, Deck: 78 full-color cards,
Layout sheet: 21 x 24   **$34.95**

WICCA
A Guide for the Solitary Practitioner
Scott Cunningham

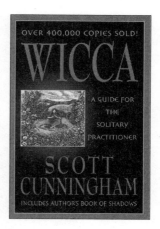

Wicca is a book of life, and how to live magically, spiritually, and wholly attuned with Nature. It is a book of sense and common sense, not only about Magick, but about religion and one of the most critical issues of today: how to achieve the much needed and wholesome relationship with our Earth. Cunningham presents Wicca as it is today: a gentle, Earth-oriented religion dedicated to the Goddess and God. This book fulfills a need for a practical guide to solitary Wicca—a need which no previous book has fulfilled.

Here is a positive, practical introduction to the religion of Wicca, designed so that any interested person can learn to practice the religion alone, anywhere in the world. It presents Wicca honestly and clearly, without the pseudo-history that permeates other books. It shows that Wicca is a vital, satisfying part of twentieth- century life.

This book presents the theory and practice of Wicca from an individual's perspective. The section on the Standing Stones Book of Shadows contains solitary rituals for the Esbats and Sabbats. This book, based on the author's nearly two decades of Wiccan practice, presents an eclectic picture of various aspects of this religion. Exercises designed to develop magical proficiency, a self-dedication ritual, herb, crystal and rune magic, as well as recipes for Sabbat feasts, are included in this excellent book.

0-87542-118-0, 240 pp., 6 x 9, illus.   **$9.95**

TO RIDE A SILVER BROOMSTICK
New Generation Witchcraft
Silver RavenWolf

Throughout the world there is a new generation of Witches —people practicing or wishing to practice the craft on their own, without an in-the-flesh magickal support group. *To Ride a Silver Broomstick* speaks to those people, presenting them with both the science and religion of Witchcraft, allowing them to become active participants while growing at their own pace. It is ideal for anyone: male or female, young or old, those familiar with Witchcraft, and those totally new to the subject and unsure of how to get started.

Full of the author's warmth, humor, and personal anecdotes, *To Ride a Silver Broomstick* leads you step-by-step through the various lessons with exercises and journal writing assignments. This is the complete Witchcraft 101, teaching you to celebrate the Sabbats, deal with coming out of the broom closet, choose a magickal name, visualize the Goddess and God, meditate, design a sacred space, acquire magickal tools, design and perform rituals, network, spell cast, perform color and candle magick, divination, healing, telepathy, psychometry, astral projection, and much, much more.

0-87542-791-X, 320 pp., 7 x 10, illus. $14.95